America's Right Turn

How Conservatives Used New and Alternative Media to Take Power

RICHARD A. VIGUERIE
and DAVID FRANKE

Foreword by Tim LaHaye

BONUS BOOKS
Chicago and Los Angeles

08   07   06   05   04   5   4   3   2   1

Library of Congress Cataloging-in-Publication Data

Viguerie, Richard A.
   America's right turn : how Conservatives used new and alternative media to take power / Richard A. Viguerie and David Franke.
   p. cm.
Includes bibliographical references and index.
ISBN 1-56625-252-0 (alk. paper)
   1. Conservatism—United States—History. 2. Mass media—Political aspects—United States. I. Franke, David. II. Title.

JC573.2.U6V53   2004
324.7'3'0973—dc22

2004009609

Bonus Books
875 North Michigan Avenue
Suite 1416
Chicago, Illinois 60611

Printed in the United States of America

M y dedication is to the hundreds of men and women who have worked with me at my various companies for almost 40 years. Of course I cannot begin to name them for fear of leaving some out and also boring you, the reader. However, without the encouragement, dedication, loyalty, leadership, intelligence, and incredibly hard work of my world-class team, I would have achieved very little.

In fact, a good number have gone on to run their own companies. I sometimes say that I don't run a direct mail agency so much as I run a university. Many if not most of my competitors are former executives at my companies, but this has been good for the conservative movement since with few exceptions they have continued to work for right-of-center causes.

The A-team men and women of the Viguerie companies came together at a point in time and helped change the course of history. You made a difference—thank you. May God bless you and your families.

Richard A. Viguerie

F ew 21-year-olds have the opportunity to participate in the very beginning of a new political movement that ends up as the dominant ideological force in the nation. I had that opportunity, with my college roommate Doug Caddy, in 1959, as we started the first nationwide conservative activist organization. How ironic that both of us now disagree with so much of what the movement has become—but that's life.

Even when you have grown apart ideologically, you remember the friendships, the idealism, the fun that made life anything but boring. So I dedicate this book to six people who contributed so much to me in those early years: to Doug; to my Greenwich Village roommate in the early '60s, present coauthor Richard Viguerie; to Louis K. Timolat, whose underwriting of my scholarship to the first *Human Events* journalism class made it possible for me to move from Texas to Washington, D.C., and begin my lifelong career in alternative media; and to the three greatest editors I've had in my lifetime—M. Stanton Evans at *Human Events*, Bill Buckley at *National Review*, and Neil McCaffrey at the Conservative Book Club and Arlington House Publishers. With their red pens (this obviously was before the computer era) those three made mince-meat of my copy, but from them I learned. They are not to be faulted if I didn't learn enough. Thank you, one and all.

David Franke

CONTENTS

CHARTS

FOREWORD

Tim LaHaye

The Christophers, who come from a different religious tradition than my own, have a wise saying that "it's better to light a candle than to curse the darkness." Conservatives have been following that advice for almost half a century, with the result that conservatism has risen from obscurity to a position of power despite all the powerful forces aligned against it.

Now Richard A. Viguerie and David Franke have lit another candle with this book, revealing how conservatives used new and alternative media to rise to power. Indeed, this is the first book to show the direct correlation between two revolutions that have transformed America in the past half century—the conservative political revolution and the alternative media revolution. That alone makes this an immensely valuable book to conservatives and liberals alike.

In case you are wondering what, exactly, are the "alternative media," Viguerie and Franke first explain that until the late 1980s the vast majority of Americans got their news primarily from the three broadcast television networks—NBC, ABC, and CBS—plus major newspapers like the *New York Times* and the *Washington Post*, their syndication services, and the Associated Press. All of these media were dependably liberal and hostile to conservative causes and candidates. They decided what was and what wasn't news. Anything conservative was not news—unless it could be portrayed as a threat.

Because of this hostility, conservatives had no choice but to develop their own means of communications as a way of bypassing the gatekeepers at the liberal establishment media. These are the "new media" or "alternative media," starting with direct mail in the 1960s and '70s, followed by talk radio, cable television, and the Internet in the decades since then. These alternative media have given conservatives a way to communicate their message to each other and directly to the American people, without distortion by the gatekeepers at the liberal establishment media. Today, the authors say, 50 percent of Americans get most of their news from the alternative media, and the situation is only going to get worse for the liberals in the future.

Part of this story, covered so well in this book, is the role of religious conservatives utilizing direct mail, talk radio, cable television, and the Internet to spread *their* message. I know from personal experience, for example, that the people at the *New York Times* don't have much use for the message of the Left Behind series of books written by myself and Jerry Jenkins. Well, I have to admit that I don't have much use for many of the messages promoted by the *New York Times* as well. Now that both sides—liberal and conservative, secular and religious—have their own preferred media, we can each promote our views but will have to learn to live civilly with each other in this pluralistic nation. Pluralism doesn't mean giving voice only to myriad types of secularists, as so many liberals assume, but to religious viewpoints as well.

This is not a religious book as such, but a notable work of politics and history. Liberals need to read it to understand how they lost the power they once wielded. And conservatives need to read it and understand its message if they hope to achieve the goals of returning this nation to moral sanity and true freedom of the media.

Power to the People

DEMOCRATIC NATIONAL COMMITTEE WANT ADS, 2003–2004

WANTED: A liberal (correction: progressive) Rush Limbaugh. Must have engaging personality and riveting ideas/positions/crusades (we do not supply) that will motivate millions of radio listeners. Mario Cuomo, Jim Hightower, Jerry Brown, Alan Dershowitz, Lowell Weicker, Gary Hart, and Doug Wilder need not apply.

WANTED: A liberal (correction: progressive) Bill O'Reilly. Must have engaging personality and riveting ideas/positions/crusades (we do not supply) that will motivate millions of TV viewers. Phil Donahue need not apply.

WANTED: A liberal (correction: progressive) Rupert Murdoch. Must have big bucks, pervasive guilt feelings about how he got his money, and a Don Quixote complex, willing to spend hundreds of millions to create a liberal TV news network to counter Fox News Channel. <u>Anyone</u> with big bucks may apply.

Granted, the Democratic National Committee never placed these ads in the classified sections of the *Washington Post* or the *New York Times*. It

1

didn't have to. The most prominent Democrats of our day—Bill Clinton, Al Gore, and Tom Daschle—did the job for them. Each of them had to explain in late 2002 and early 2003 why the Republicans, now a conservative party, had won the Grand Slam—the White House, Senate, and House of Representatives. And in doing so, the Three Whiners updated Hillary's 1996 enumeration of a "vast right-wing conspiracy." *They* weren't at fault for the Democrats' failure, they agreed: It's all the fault of the right-wing media.

This book is the story of how the conservative movement got to be such a thorn in the behinds of Bill Clinton, Al Gore, and Tom Daschle. It is not a history of the conservative movement (that's been done before), but rather a look at how conservatives defied the liberal media monopoly of the 1950s, '60s, and '70s by creating their own alternative media channels. Conservatives of a certain age know what *real* media bias is like. In the Golden Age of Liberal Media the general public didn't hear about our candidates, issues, causes, books, or magazines (except as hysterical warnings about the "Far Right threat") because the liberal establishment truly controlled America's media forums—as we'll show in these pages. Of necessity, not by choice, conservatives learned to communicate with each other below the radar of the liberal establishment, first through direct mail, then later through talk radio and cable TV and other forms of media.

Indeed, all liberals and Democrats could read our book to their profit, as a how-to manual. We're not worried about giving away intelligence secrets to the enemy, because they will learn in these pages that whining about the media won't do them any good, just as it never did the conservatives any good. And they will discover that what they need most are ideas that resonate with the American public. In effect that means they have to stop being liberals—and hiding behind a fig-leaf term like "progressives" won't do the job.

Now look again at those made-up want ads at the beginning of this introduction. Look especially at the names of prominent liberals who "need not apply." Those are all previous hosts of *failed* liberal radio and TV programs. Not a good start.

Now supporters of the liberal taxpayer-subsidized National Public Radio are trying to thwart the inroads of Christian radio stations with a new national nonprofit entity called Public Radio Capital, which seeks funding through tax-exempt bonds and tax-deductible contributions. But money isn't the liberals' root problem. Polls show that even National Pinko Radio, as NPR is affectionately known on the Right, has more conservative listeners than liberal listeners. As Mickey Kaus said (relayed by Ann Coulter), "No wonder conservatives are so pissed off."

More prominently, a group of Democratic fundraisers have raised enough venture capital to launch a liberal answer to conservative talk radio called Air America Radio, with comedian Al Franken as its major star. We tell you more about Air America Radio in Chapter 10, and we explain why we think the odds are against it in our Conclusion.

And that's the way it was . . .

We'll leave the details of the conservative media revolution to the text that follows, but in this introduction we would like to note that there is no conservative media monopoly today, the way that there truly was a liberal media monopoly in the 1950s and '60s. What we have today is just more of a level playing field. Most of the mass media are still liberal, so what Bill Clinton, Al Gore, and Tom Daschle are really complaining about is that they now have competition.

What they really long for are the good old days when Americans had little choice but to get their political news through the gatekeepers at the three liberal networks—NBC, ABC, and CBS. Indeed, it would be a wonderful world for liberal Democrats if cable news TV and talk radio could be banished for polluting the political environment, because the three networks' news departments remain as staunchly liberal as before.

We don't have to rely on the conservative Media Research Center to make our case that the broadcast television networks are hopelessly liberal. We need only glance at the archives of the independent and nonpartisan Center for Media & Public Affairs, which conducts its own scientific (measurable) studies of the news and entertainment media. Here is what they say about network coverage of the glorious Clinton era.

1992: Clinton vs. Bush I vs. Perot

ABC, CBS, and NBC broadcast 730 election stories from Labor Day (September 7) through election eve (November 2). Conclusions:

> "Throughout the fall, Clinton's campaign prospects were portrayed as favorable, while Bush's were seen as bleak. . . . At its closest point, 75 percent of Clinton's horse race evaluations were positive, compared to 37 percent positive for Bush. . . ."

> "Partisan Republican criticism of Clinton was balanced by praise from voters and pundits, while partisan Democratic criticism of Bush was echoed by non-partisan sources all year."

> "Overall . . . George Bush was the big loser in election coverage throughout Campaign '92. During the primaries, the summer, and the general election, Bush received more negative evaluations than his rivals. . . . Even during his *best* period (the general election), more than 70 percent of non-partisan news sources criticized Bush, a figure no other candidate matched even during their *worst* periods." (Emphasis added.)

1996: Clinton vs. Dole

> "Incumbent presidents typically endure highly negative media coverage when they run for a second term. Studies have documented the aggressive press scrutiny faced by George Bush, Ronald Reagan, and Jimmy Carter on the road to re-election. This year, however, Bill Clinton has enjoyed the best press of his presidency."

"The president was treated more favorably than his
GOP rival on all three network newscasts . . . "

The Clinton Scandals

But surely, you say, the networks skewered Bill Clinton about his vast
accumulation of scandals. Well, no, actually. As the press release for a
study from the Center for Media & Public Affairs headlined it:

SCANDAL NEWS NOT SO BAD FOR BILL
Network News Treats President Better than Accusers

And as the press release explained, "The big three network evening
news shows have provided relatively balanced coverage of the latest al-
legations regarding President Clinton. . . . The study also found that
the president's top accusers—Monica Lewinsky, Linda Tripp and Kenneth Starr—all received mostly bad press."

It is easy to see why Bill Clinton, Al Gore, and Tom Daschle would prefer that you get all your political news from the three big networks.
Those days are over, however, and no establishment genie can put direct mail, talk radio, and cable news TV back in the bottle—or, more
accurately, the bottle*neck* where your political news is filtered by the
likes of Peter Jennings and Dan Rather and Tom Brokaw. Moreover, as
we demonstrate in this book, the Internet is only making things *worse*
for the liberals.

Liberal "gatekeepers" take heed. There's a word for this new news
environment. It's called *democracy.*

Give Us *Your* Views

Access our questionnaire at www.rightturn.us and let the national
media know your thoughts about the November 2004 election. See
our box on page 348 for more details.

PART I

Two Media Revolutions Transform the World

1

The Media Revolution
of 1517

Lutheranism was from the first the child of the printed book,
and through this vehicle Luther was able to make exact,
standardized, and ineradicable impressions on the mind of
Europe. For the first time in human history a great reading
public judged the validity of revolutionary ideas through a
mass-medium which used the vernacular languages together
with the arts of the journalist and the cartoonist . . .

Arthur Geoffrey Dickens, *Reformation and
Society in Sixteenth Century Europe*

Traditional imagery of the Reformation period shows Lutherans holding books (usually the Bible) in their hands, contrasted with Catholics
holding rosaries. For an era in which the printing press was transforming the world, that symbolism alone tells us which side had the upper
hand technologically.

9

The revolution of 1517 did not begin on October 31, when Martin Luther posted his controversial 95 theses on the door of the Castle Church in Wittenberg (if, indeed, he ever really did that). Clerical debates over indulgences and other practices were common, and church doors were a customary place to announce a theological debate. The revolution came in the weeks following Luther's posting of his 95 theses, as his arguments spread across Europe with a rapidity never before seen, and reached the lay public—beyond the clerical community—that until this point had been precluded from involvement in theological issues. Luther's theses spread across Germany within a couple of weeks, and throughout Europe in a month. *That* was the revolution, and it was a revolution wrought by the printing press.

Six months later, Luther would insist, in a letter to Pope Leo X, that he had no idea how and why this happened. "It is a mystery to me," he said, "how my theses, more so than my other writings, indeed, those of other professors were spread to so many places. They were meant exclusively for our academic circle here . . . They were written in such a language that the common people could hardly understand them."

Was the rebellious monk being just a little disingenuous here? In a March 1518 letter he tells another correspondent that he "had no wish nor plan to publicize these theses"—but left it to his friends to decide whether they were to be "suppressed or spread outside." Did he have any doubt how his friends would choose? He was already experienced at editing texts in Latin and German for printers, and he was quite sophisticated in appealing to specific book markets. He noted in a pre-Reformation letter, for example, that he was aiming his German translation of the penitential psalms at "rude Saxons," not cultivated Nurembergers. Those aren't the reflections of an inexperienced novice.

Whatever Luther's private intentions and desires, he would soon be the West's first media star, and in print he dominated the mass movement that he spearheaded—the Lutheran Reformation—to an extent rarely again equaled in history. Only Lenin and Mao Zedong, with their monopolies of force, could dominate their media to the extent Luther dominated his.

Luther's achievement is chronicled by Mark U. Edwards, Jr., former president of St. Olaf College in Minnesota, in his groundbreaking book, *Printing, Propaganda, and Martin Luther.* Edwards relates how, and why, the pamphlet was the medium of choice in Luther's day. Since it was short, a pamphlet was relatively cheap to print, and a printer could sandwich it in between larger print jobs. It could be printed quickly, responding rapidly to changing events. And it was handy—you could even hide it under your clothing when the authorities were around. In short, it was an excellent tool of subversion.

From 1517 to 1518, the first year of the Reformation, the number of pamphlets printed in German-speaking lands increased more than fivefold. Between 1520 and 1526, these presses turned out something like 7,500 printings of pamphlets, most of them on Reformation topics. Martin Luther alone was the author of more than 20 percent of those publications.

Indeed, Luther had more works printed in German (between 1518 and 1525) than did the 17 other major Evangelical publicists combined. And during Luther's lifetime, Edwards tells us, "These presses produced nearly five times as many German works by Luther as by all the Catholic controversialists put together."

Small wonder, then, that later on Luther wouldn't be so bashful about his alliance with the printing press. He would describe printing as "God's highest and extemest act of grace, whereby the business of the Gospel is driven forward." And he would praise printing for emancipating the Germans from Rome: "As if to offer proof that God has chosen us to accomplish a special mission, there was invented in our land a marvelous new and subtle art, the art of printing. This opened German eyes even as it is now bringing enlightenment to other countries."

A "subtle art"? That's a curiously modest depiction considering that the printing press had been invented around 1450, less than 70 years before the outbreak of the Reformation, and it was already having a revolutionary impact on society.

The Lutheran advantage, the Catholic dilemma

As the world's first media war, the Lutheran-Catholic battles of the early Reformation teach us some enduring lessons about using the media. First and foremost, they teach us how important it is to be *first*.

Martin Luther and his followers embraced the new printing technology without hesitation. The Catholic Church approached it with suspicion and used it cautiously, and then only in reaction to the Lutherans. It wasn't until the Catholic Counter-Reformation in the second half of the sixteenth century that the Roman church began to use printing as a tool for proselytizing, just as the Protestant churches had been doing for at least 40 years. Catholic entrepreneurs proved equally as adept as Protestants in publishing and promoting devotional works, tracts, and polemics, and their skill helped save southern Europe for Catholicism. But by then it was decades too late to stem the Protestant tide in northern Europe.

Why did the Catholic Church hesitate? In answering this question, we observe some of the dynamics underpinning how new media technology provides rebels and underdogs with a slingshot of the sort that David used to slay Goliath.

The Catholic Church was *the* establishment of Europe in 1517. It saw itself as the only legitimate religious institution, and since it possessed juridical power it was accustomed to relying on intervention by secular authorities to suppress rebellions—what Mark Edwards calls the Church's "law-and-order" conception of affairs. This time, however, German princes found it convenient to utilize the swelling anti-Roman religious sentiment to bolster their anti-Roman *political* ambitions. And the printing press, as we've seen, spread the rebellion with a speed never before encountered, catching the Catholic Church off guard and unable to respond fast enough.

The Catholic Church found it distasteful, at the least, to use the printing press to fight the rebels on their own turf. Doing so acknowledged not only the legitimacy of the debate but also the propriety of involving the laity in ecclesiastical matters, which ostensibly undermined the Catholic Church's claim to be the only legitimate religious institution. Even on those occasions when Catholics *did* reply in print to the Protestants, they were inadvertently helping their opponents. In these early years of the Reformation, Luther above all needed to get his message out, and the Catholic tracts—no matter how slanted they were against Luther's positions—nevertheless spread word of his movement and its general complaints.

"Not to reply," says Edwards, "was to surrender much of the vernacular reading public to Luther and his friends. To reply was to further by both message and medium the position of the Evangelicals. This was the Catholic dilemma."

The few Catholic printers and polemicists who entered the fray had virtually no support—financial or otherwise—from their church. The duke of Saxony provided some limited support to Catholic printers, but when he died his successor became a Lutheran. One of the few Catholic polemicists writing to the laity was Georg Witzel, himself a former Lutheran. Witzel complained about the difficulty of getting into print as a Catholic. A printer had held his manuscript for a whole year with unfulfilled promises of publication. "If I were a Lutheran there would be no difficulty," Witzel said, "but as a Catholic I am writing in vain." (How modern this sounds to conservative authors trying to get their manuscripts accepted by liberal publishers!) So it went that the Catholic Church pretty much conceded the media battle to the Lutherans.

The impact of the Protestant head start far outlasted the early Reformation. From 1550 to 1800, in fact, typesetting, printing, publishing, and bookselling were essentially Protestant preserves in Europe.

Aiming for a "mass" audience

Forget any images you have of angry hordes of Germans rising *en masse* against their perceived enemies. That would come later (unfortunately). The Reformation was more like a bitter fight between academics and their college trustees, where the students do not get involved.

Magnifying the power of Luther's theological arguments was the inherent advantage of the new over the old: All the flaws of the new are not yet obvious. The Catholic Church had been around for centuries, allowing plenty of time for its shortcomings to be obvious to even its staunchest supporters. The Evangelicals were touting a new order, full of promise, with no track record of failure to detract from that promise.

The Lutherans did aim their message at a mass audience, but a "mass audience" in 1517 was not that big. Only about 5 percent of the total German population was literate, and even in the largest cities that number didn't rise above 30 percent. That's counting literacy in the vernacular language, German. Literacy in Latin was found in a mere fraction of that 5 percent.

In this environment, two significant factors came to the fore. One, the Lutherans by and large aimed their message at those who were literate in German (which included those who were literate in Latin), while the Catholics by and large aimed their message only at the much smaller population literate in Latin. Two, the Lutherans pursued their objectives with a sophisticated two-step approach: One, reach the literate population—the "opinion leaders"—by print, and, two, get them to reach the general population with oral persuasion, primarily through sermons.

As we've already seen, the presses in German-speaking lands produced nearly five times as many works *in German* by Luther as by all the Catholic polemicists combined. Here are some more revealing statistics: In the first full year of the Reformation, 1518, a little less than half of Luther's writings were printed in German. In 1519, 60 percent of his works appeared in German, and this rose to 80 percent in 1520 and 1521, then 90 percent over the rest of the decade. Overall, counting all authors, the proportion of German to Latin pamphlets completely reversed itself between 1519 and 1521, going from three Latin pamphlets for each German one, to three German pamphlets for each Latin one. Thereafter, German pamphlets constituted 90 percent of all pamphlets published.

And the pamphlets were just the beginning of this lopsided preponderance of Evangelical works in German. Luther worked ceaselessly to translate the New Testament into German, and then to teach the Germans how to interpret it through his large and small catechisms. Eventually the Catholics would produce their own catechism in the vernacular for the laity, but—as with the polemical pamphlets—that came much too late to have an effect in the early Reformation.

It wasn't as if Catholics were technologically illiterate, and could only copy the Bible and other works by hand, using scribes. Between the invention of the printing press and 1520, 156 Latin editions of the Bible were published, as well as 17 German translations under the auspices of the Catholic Church. They had the ability to use the printing press, they just didn't have the *will* to use it as a weapon in the new type of warfare.

Luther's German New Testament was the sixteenth century's best seller, with some 43 editions appearing between 1522 and 1525. Edwards says an average of 2,000 copies per printing would be a conservative estimate, meaning that at least 86,000 copies were sold in 40 months. This is especially amazing given the low literacy rate and the relatively high cost of a full-fledged New Testament. A cheap unbound, undecorated edition cost the equivalent of two weeks' wages for a baker. Reaching an audience as large as Luther's was a revolution indeed.

Spreading the capitalist gospel, too

This chapter is primarily concerned with the Reformation, but the impact of the printing press certainly didn't stop there. We must take a moment to honor our conservative and libertarian heritage by noting the often-overlooked impact of early printers on the development of capitalism.

Elizabeth Eisenstein, author of *The Printing Press as an Agent of Change*, notes that the early printer was a "natural" capitalist, for he had to be both an entrepreneur and an innovator. This was long before today's specialized job functions, and the sixteenth-century printer was an intellectual trend watcher, typesetter, publisher, publicist, and advertiser all in one.

Other urban entrepreneurs shared many of his attitudes and perspectives, but the printer was in an especially strategic position: He dealt directly with the ideas being promulgated in print, in this new print era. He was a gatekeeper of the new communications industry, and as such was able to *influence* the intellectual and political currents of his day. We've already noted a Catholic writer's (Witzel's) complaint about that influence.

As a hands-on capitalist, the printer had to recoup large investments, which meant he had to become adept at time-motion analysis, if only informally. He faced stiff competition from rival printers. And he could not afford an idle press and idle workers, so he was constantly searching for ways to expand his markets, and he would arrange print jobs to keep the presses flowing evenly. This also explains two of his pet peeves—labor strikes and religious or political censors. Both caused work stoppages.

Being of necessity a practical man, the sixteenth-century printer wasn't running a leisurely coffee house for monkish scribes—and he had little use in general for the very unbusinesslike begging orders. The high priest of the new merchant order, Adam Smith, put it quite succinctly: "Penance, mortification . . . and the whole train of monkish virtues are everywhere rejected by men of sense." Little surprise, then, that these early printers took naturally to the Reformation.

Eisenstein writes:

> As self-serving publicists, early printers issued book lists, circulars and broadsides. They put the firm's name, emblem and shop address on the front page of their books. Indeed, this use of title pages entailed a significant reversal of scribal procedures; they put themselves first. Scribal colophons had come last. They also extended their new promotional techniques to the authors and artists whose work they published, thus

contributing to the celebration of lay culture-heroes
and to their achievement of personal celebrity and
eponymous fame.

The new hard-sell business tactics didn't stop with the printer. We have
a letter from one Beatus Rhenanus to Reformation leader Huldrych
Zwingli, recommending that a particular book peddler go from town to
town, village to village, and house to house selling nothing but Luther's
writings. "This will virtually force the people to buy them," notes
Rhenanus, "which would not be the case if there were a wide
selection."

Once the original enthusiasm of the Reformation wound down,
printers were quick to exploit the growing market for practical information. Almanacs were a staple, and by the seventeenth century the almanac was outselling the Bible in England. Printers also turned to
other kinds of practical manuals—directories, maps, globes, road
guides, and business books of all types. Even books on bookkeeping.
Eisenstein suggests that "the slow spread of scientific bookkeeping before the sixteenth century and its more rapid spread thereafter is probably related to the shift from script to print." "Reckon masters"—early
bookkeepers—wrote manuals featuring the advantages of double-entry
bookkeeping, still a mystery to most merchants. The bookkeeper's goal
was not so much to educate the merchants as to encourage the merchants to hire the bookkeeper's firm to do the merchant's books.

The modern age had most definitely arrived!

2

The Media Revolution of 1776

The American Revolution was the first event of its kind in which the media played a salient role—almost a determining one—from first to last. Americans were already a media-conscious people. They had a lot of newspapers and publications, and were getting more every month. There were plenty of cheap printing presses. They now found that they had scores—indeed hundreds—of inflammatory writers, matching the fiery orators in the assemblies with every polysyllabic word of condemnation they uttered. There was no longer any possibility of putting down the media barrage in the courts by successful prosecutions for seditious libel. That pass had been sold long ago. So the media war, which preceded and then accompanied the fighting war, was one the colonists were bound to win and the British crown equally certain to lose.

Paul Johnson, *A History of the American People*

With its use in the Protestant Reformation, the printing press made a shambles of Europe's church and court establishments. But it was a war between establishments, with the masses generally accepting the dictates and shifting allegiances of the kings and princes and priesthoods that wielded local power over them. Now, with its use in the American colonies, the printing press would take the revolution a giant step farther. Now the masses would have their turn, and the world would never again be the same. It would indeed be "the world turned upside down," the tune played in defeat by the British military band at Yorktown.

It didn't start out that way. In the beginning America was just an extension of the Old World idea that the establishments—whether Puritan, Anglican, or agents of the British crown—set the rules, usually under the pretense of divine right. It was up to the rest of society to work and live within those rules. Boston printer Benjamin Harris learned that lesson the hard way when he decided in 1690 to publish a newspaper. Without asking anyone's permission or guidance, he printed his first issue of *Publick Occurrences Both Foreign and Domestick*, promising to publish all the information he received. That didn't sit well with the oligarchs of the Massachusetts Bay government. The public was entitled only to the news *they* deemed suitable, and so the authorities made sure Harris's paper never had a second issue.

This Old World system stayed intact for a while—as long as there were only a few printing presses around, and the market for printed goods remained small and consisted mostly of members of the ruling establishment. For the time being, printers made their profit off of government contracts to publish official documents. In a situation like that, you don't cross the people paying your bills. Most early newspapers also found it practical to concentrate on foreign news, which everyone was anxious to get, and give a pass to local issues that might ruffle official feathers.

For a number of reasons, though, this system did not last long in the New World. It was hard to maintain authority when so much raw land was available, and dissidents could just pack up and leave for a

more congenial locale. Being rid of your dissidents that way might preserve the peace for the short term, but in the longer run it meant that
Americans in general were learning that they didn't need government
to tell them what to do. They knew perfectly well how to survive and
prosper on their own. Soon this growing self-reliance manifested itself
in political and ecclesiastical affairs as well.

The colonies' rapid growth also undermined the Old World order.
It's easier to control a small group of people than a large group, especially when the sources of your authority are thousands of miles away
across an ocean. Also, population and economic growth provide a hos-
pitable environment for innovation—new ways of doing everything, including organizing society. The American colonies were the population
growth engine of the Western world. Their population in 1700 was
257,060. Sixty years later it was 1,593,625, and it would continue dou-
bling every 20 years. Americans were moving into new territories "like
the goths and Vandals of old," said William Byrd. And even in the established cities, new immigrants had limited respect for the reigning
establishments—Boston's new Anglican population didn't exactly cotton to Puritan rules, for example.

Then there was the impact of current events on the demand for
news and the growth of outlets to provide that news. The authorities
would find it more difficult to control a multitude of news outlets, especially since they were now serving the public rather than government
officials. In our day we have seen how the Gulf War propelled the
Cable News Network into the media establishment, because CNN was
able to use the new satellite technology to provide around-the-clock,
on-the-scene coverage of the war. So, too, with the French and Indian
War, which lasted from 1754 to 1763. Americans wanted to know what
was happening, and newspapers started popping up everywhere to provide them with answers. Enter the war correspondent (called a "weekly
news writer") to American journalism—quite an innovation when
newspapers previously were content to crib their news from foreign
newspapers.

At the beginning of the French and Indian War, only 11

newspapers existed in all of the colonies. By the end of the war there were 19. Further crises, such as the Stamp Act controversy, kept the hunger for news on a roll, and by the time of the American Revolution the colonies had 38 newspapers—at least one in every colony except Vermont. Their circulation was increasing dramatically, too. In 1750 they had an average circulation of some 600 copies per week. By the Revolution some circulations had grown to 1,500 or even more than 3,500. Since newspapers were commonly read aloud in taverns, their ultimate audience was far larger than their circulation numbers.

From the beginning, Americans had demonstrated a hunger for information that surpassed anything seen in Europe. Living on the edge of the known world, about as far from the madding crowds as you could get, it's quite natural that the pioneers ached for news from the world they left behind. By 1750, the middle of the eighteenth century, this hunger for information was much too great and demanding to be satisfied with official government handouts.

Another reason for this news hunger: Americans—white male Americans, that is—were more literate than any European peoples with the possible exception of the Scots. Literacy was stronger in the North than in the South, but the best guess is that half of the white male population was literate, and often even the poor were literate. There was a large male-female literacy gap in 1700, but this gap all but disappeared during the course of the eighteenth century.

Word-of-mouth, face-to-face news

As America entered the Revolutionary Era, many *types* of media competed to deliver the news, and they all played a role in making the Revolution possible. These media forms included face-to-face news dissemination, broadsides and couriers, newspapers, and, above all, political pamphlets. These media outlets also made possible the explosive growth of America's first political action committee (PAC), the Sons of Liberty, which led directly to the Committees of Correspondence, the

Continental Congress, and the Declaration of Independence on July 4, 1776.

Newspapers were not necessarily the most important media outlet. During this era they were all weeklies, and by the time an issue was printed a newspaper's really important news had been spreading for days, on a face-to-face, word-of-mouth basis. Virtually all of the colonies' external trade was carried by ocean-going ships, and in the colonies' ports, incoming ships brought news along with the cargo. This made port cities the point of contact with the outside world, and almost without exception they were the largest cities in the colonies. Philadelphia, Boston, and New York led the way, with Charleston and Savannah serving the smaller populations of the South.

Three types of individuals were the chief disseminators of news— ship captains, postmasters, and merchants. In our era of instant news, it's difficult to remember that news from London or the Continent could take as long as six months to reach the colonies—and usually took at least a couple of months. Then it would take another three weeks for news to spread from one end of the colonies to the other. But it was still *news*—that is, something the colonists had not known until the ship arrived in port.

The very first news, quite naturally, would come from the ship's captain, and he would be wined and dined while he told all. But he was only one man, and his connections on the other side of the Atlantic, while quite good, were not necessarily the best sources for the types of news the Americans craved. The more detailed "inside" accounts of what was going on came with the letters merchants received from their business associates. They shared these accounts widely— deleting sensitive business intelligence, we presume.

Not that privacy was guaranteed with the packets of letters. It is somewhat surprising how "public" the contents of letters were considered. An amusing account has General Gage sending for the postmaster because, as he put it, he wished "to see a letter [he] received from Thomas Griffith." Apparently word of the letter's contents reached him before the letter itself!

Once the merchants received their treasured letters, they began sharing the contents verbally in every possible venue—and in the busy port cities this included coffee houses, taverns, markets, and shops. Even a barbershop could be described as the "Fountain Head of Politics for the most grand Disputations."

A word about the preachers: Yes, they were important sources of guidance in public matters, first and foremost within their congregations, and the New England ministers in particular magnified their audience and influence by printing and disseminating their sermons. They were also disseminators of news, particularly in rural towns, but they were as dependent as others on the real sources of that news, chiefly the merchants in the port cities.

From the revolutionary perspective, it is significant that while all segments of American society showed support for independence by July 1776, that support was strongest among the merchant class. That means that the primary news filters in these critical years had a decidedly pro-American bias.

Broadsides, couriers, and the midnight ride of Paul Revere

As we have seen, a piece of hot news from England or one of the other colonies would start spreading in the port city as soon as the vessel carrying that news docked. But what about people in outlying and interior communities? With no telephones and no daily newspapers, the task of getting hot news to them quickly was assumed mostly by couriers of various sorts.

Broadsides—single sheets of paper—were a favorite way of presenting the news. Broadsides could be printed quickly, given to couriers on horseback, and in the outlying communities they would be nailed to trees in the village green, placed in taverns and other strategic locations, and simply passed from hand to hand. These weren't just notices of a meeting, the kind we find today on community bulletin boards in libraries or supermarkets. They could be essays or polemics of several thousand words, crammed onto the broadside in tiny type and arranged into three or four columns.

If the broadside had news of political importance from, say, the Sons of Liberty, members or friends of that organization might deliver a packet of these broadsides to a group of communities. Then there were the postriders carrying government ("public") mail and private postriders, many of whom presumably could be prevailed upon to carry some extra cargo, either for patriotic motives or with some compensation involved.

Governing authorities from the days of Persia and the Roman Empire set up postal systems for carrying sovereign dispatches. By the time of the American colonies, the idea had taken root that making these postal deliveries available for a fee to private citizens could raise money for the crown. By the time of the Revolution, around 65 government post offices were in operation, or about one for every 25,000 people. Merchants used the system, but otherwise private use was limited.

Not surprising to anyone using today's U.S. Postal Service, there were two problems with using colonial postriders—high cost and low reliability. Ordinary people would rather ask a friend or acquaintance to deliver a letter if they were headed in the right direction. If you had the money, but your letter was important and you needed to be sure it would get to its destination on time, you would probably give the job to a private postrider—the colonial equivalent of today's Federal Express or UPS. Some things never change.

Newspapers and magazines did not go by government post at all, instead using private postriders. In time of war or peril, some private messengers advertised that they would take letters into the war zone for a shilling or more each. At that time it cost a shilling to get a letter (under one ounce) across the Atlantic, so the messenger assured that he would be adequately compensated for putting his life in danger.

Back to the patriotic messengers. None stands out more in American history than Paul Revere, and deservedly so. The true story of Paul Revere's ride is actually far different from the myths we learned in school (back when schools still taught American history, at least), but the truth only adds to his luster and accomplishment.

The mythical Paul Revere was a lone rider—itself one of the most popular, recurring images in American folklore. The real Paul Revere did indeed make that ride, was captured and escaped. He put his life in danger as he rescued Hancock and Adams (twice), saved the secret papers of the Revolution, and warned the patriots that the British troops were advancing on Lexington and Concord. He did all that, but he also was the organizer of an efficient network of more than 60 riders who spread the word in all directions from Boston that night of April 19, 1775. And he was able to accomplish this because he was, in today's parlance, the patriot networker without equal.

We can thank historian David Hackett Fischer for piecing together this amazing story in *Paul Revere's Ride* (Oxford University Press, 1994), not only the first scholarly look at the subject but also a model of riveting taletelling that everyone can enjoy. Fischer deserves special thanks for rescuing Revere from "multiculturalism and political correctness" as well as the "broad prejudice in American universities against patriotic events of every kind." As Fischer notes, "The only creature less fashionable in academe than the stereotypical 'dead white male,' is a dead white male on horseback."

As America headed for open revolution, Boston was the center of patriot activity. British troops had been stationed there since 1768, and after the Boston Massacre (1770) and the Boston Tea Party (1773) there was about as much chance of reconciliation as you'll find today in the Middle East. Now, in April 1775, passions were coming to a head again.

We have lists of the members of seven key groups of Boston Whigs (patriots): the St. Andrews Masonic Lodge, which met at the Green Dragon Tavern; the Loyal Nine, out of which developed the Sons of Liberty; the North Caucus that met at the Salutation Tavern; the Long Room Club in Dassett Alley; the Boston Committee of Correspondence; the known participants in the Boston Tea Party; and the Whig leaders on a Tory enemies list.

John Hancock and James Otis were each on only one of those lists. John Adams was on two. His activist cousin Sam Adams was on four. But only two men were in five of those groups: Paul Revere and his friend Joseph Warren. (Yes, our hero was on the Tory enemies list!) Revere was the perfect person to organize a courier network because he knew everyone of importance, and they knew (and trusted) him. He also knew who the best riders were for his network of messengers, and who could be trusted to get the job done.

Not only that, he knew the leaders of the outlying towns as well, so they, too, trusted him when he arrived with his news that night of April 19. After all, Paul Revere had made his first revolutionary ride on December 17, 1773, spreading the news of the Boston Tea Party. Between 1773 and 1775, he made at least five journeys as far as New York and Philadelphia. On eighteenth-century highways these weren't pleasure trips—they were major expeditions. We have records of at least 18 trips by Paul Revere in the patriot cause. This man got around like no one else.

On the night of April 19, one member of Paul Revere's network of couriers galloped north at such speed that he had traveled 30 miles, almost to the New Hampshire border, by two o'clock in the morning—normally a long day's ride. The speed and efficiency of Revere's couriers was essential to the extraordinary success of the colonial militia the next day. Fischer writes,

> Had they acted otherwise, the outcome might well have been different. A few hours' delay in the alarm—perhaps less than that—might have been enough for General Gage's troops to have completed their mission and returned safely to Boston before an effective force could muster against them. The result would have been a small success for British arms, and an encouragement to the Imperial cause at a critical moment. On the other side, the revolutionary movement would have lost a moral advantage that had a major impact on events to come.

We can only imagine what the members of the British Regular Infantry thought as they precision marched in their bright red (and hot) coats through the Massachusetts countryside. This was *terra incognita,* far from the Boston Commons that was their usual home. And as they marched in the dead of the night, the silence would be shattered—from all directions—by the pealing of village church bells, the beating of drums, the boom of cannons, and muskets repeatedly firing in the distance. These were all signals to the colonists that the British were on the march, signals sent out as Paul Revere and his network of riders made their rounds spreading the word. It was one of the most successful examples of war communications in American history, and for that we can thank patriot Paul Revere above all.

Colonial newspapers

The first newspaper to take a determined antiestablishment stance, and to write about local affairs as much as foreign affairs, was Boston's *New England Courant.* Its publisher was London-trained James Franklin, and he employed his younger brother Benjamin as apprentice. In London James had noticed that a combination of entertainment and political controversy seemed popular with readers, and he sought to bring that winning combination to America.

In Boston the reigning establishment was Puritan, but the Franklin brothers published several Episcopalians and others of no discernible religious orientation as contributors—a group that became known as the "Hell-Fire Club." The Puritan clergy didn't take kindly to satire, *especially* when it was aimed at them, and in 1722 the local authorities ordered the Franklins to clear all issues with them in advance. The Franklins refused and instead added the civil authorities to their list of targets. This double-barreled assault on both the religious and political authorities was too much for the Boston of that day, and the Franklin brothers moved on to the freer press climates of Newport, Rhode Island, and Philadelphia.

It wasn't until the 1730s that another seriously antiestablishment newspaper appeared in the colonies. A faction of New York politicians founded the *New-York Weekly Journal*, printed by John Peter Zenger, to oppose the administration of the royal governor. The printer was always the easiest target for the establishment—put him out of business and the writers and other neer-do-wells have no forum for attacking you. When Zenger was inevitably tried for seditious libel, Alexander Hamilton, Zenger's lawyer, pleaded truth as his defense. Unfortunately, British and American courts (strange as this sounds today) held that telling the truth against authorities constituted the greatest libel—"the greater the truth, the greater the libel." The judge predictably ruled against Zenger, but the jury acquitted him despite the judge, thereby guaranteeing Zenger's place in American history.

Contrary to legend, Zenger's trial didn't assure freedom of the press in America. There were no appellate and Supreme Court systems at that time, of course, so the Zenger case wasn't binding anywhere outside of New York. Other colonial governments continued to prosecute for seditious libel. But political events would soon establish freedom of the press in America, in effect if not legal theory, while prosecutions for criminal libel continued in England well into the nineteenth century.

The political event that demolished the crown's control over American newspapers was the Stamp Act passed by Parliament in 1765. This legislation placed a tax "upon every paper, commonly called a pamphlet, and upon every newspaper," as well as almanacs and "upon every advertisement to be contained in any gazette, newspaper, or other paper." While this tax would be passed on to the consumers of those printed items, as all corporate taxes ultimately are, the direct burden of the tax was placed on printers.

And that was a mistake that London would soon regret. Printers and the media they printed had proliferated and grown far beyond the days of a few "court" printers who got their money from the political authorities and meekly obeyed their masters. London didn't seem to understand this. It had declared war on American printers, and in response, American printers, newspapers, and other publications formed a *unified* opposition to the Stamp Act. Not only that, but they also changed the language by which they referred to themselves. Most printers now called themselves *Americans*, not British citizens living in America.

The press had no difficulty convincing the American public that the Stamp Act was British perfidy. And it wasn't the first time—nor would it be the last—that the Brits found themselves confused by their American cousins. A letter writer in a London newspaper found the outrage over the Stamp Act "surprising" and "remarkable." After all, this wasn't something important. Parliament had not affected "the necessaries of life" by taxing, say, Americans' "small beer an half penny a quart." *That* would have been "most severely felt," while "the tax on News-papers concerns only a very few—the common people don't purchase news-papers."

The Brits obviously were due for a consciousness-raising session. And they'd get a lot more in the coming years, because the broad-based opposition to the Stamp Act had repercussions far beyond forcing Parliament to repeal it. The Sons of Liberty began organizing throughout the colonies, pretty much spontaneously and without centralized direction, to oppose the Stamp Act. This gave the Americans their first taste of what they could do politically, and it became addictive. The press, too, had found its voice. Whatever the issue from here on out, publishers would not hesitate to speak out forcefully and fervently.

While it was true that there were other ways to spread the news more quickly, newspapers had one big advantage for news-hungry colonials: They could provide the entire text of proclamations, acts, and other documents that affected the Americans. As these multiplied in the pre-revolutionary years, newspapers became the major forum for colonials to see and judge for themselves what the Brits and patriots were up to. It is also noteworthy that two of the most influential pamphlets of the Revolutionary era, John Dickinson's *Letters from a Farmer in Pennsylvania* and Tom Paine's *The American Crisis*, first appeared in print in newspapers, as a series of letters or essays.

Few Tory printers remained in America by the time revolution came in 1776, and those remaining few fled with the outbreak of war

or experienced the joy of instant conversion. This was no time for
fence-straddling objectivity, either, as *Rivington's New-York Gazetteer*
discovered. When Rivington printed both American and British versions of the battles of Lexington and Concord, furious patriots de-
stroyed his printer's press and type.

Obviously freedom of the press had not yet come to America. But
the prevailing side, in the battle for public opinion, had most emphati-
cally changed from pro-British to pro-revolution.

The pamphleteers:
Tom Paine and the others

The political pamphlet—virtually a forgotten art form today—reached
the zenith of its importance in the American Revolution. George Orwell, himself no slouch at political propaganda, explains why the pamphlet was an ideal form for this historical period:

> The pamphlet is a one-man show. One has complete
> freedom of expression, including, if one chooses, the
> freedom to be scurrilous, abusive, and seditious; or, on
> the other hand, to be more detailed, serious, and "high-
> brow" than is ever possible in a newspaper or in most
> kinds of periodicals. At the same time, since the pam-
> phlet is always short and unbound, it can be produced
> much more quickly than a book, and in principle, at
> any rate, can reach a bigger public. Above all, the pam-
> phlet does not have to follow any prescribed pattern. It
> can be in prose or in verse, it can consist largely of
> maps or statistics or quotations, it can take the form of
> a story, a fable, a letter, an essay, a dialogue, or a piece
> of "reportage." All that is required of it is that it shall
> be topical, polemical, and short.

The flexibility in size noted by Orwell was particularly important in
colonial and revolutionary days. American pamphlets usually ranged
from 5,000 to 25,000 words, arranged on 10 to 50 pages. This was long

enough to develop the writer's polemical points, and short enough to avoid the time and expense of producing a full-fledged book. Thus pamphlets were a quick-response medium of the day, perfect for a polemic on the Stamp Act, or the Boston Massacre or the Boston Tea Party—or the Continental Congress and independence.

When the editor in chief of the John Harvard Library asked noted scholar Bernard Bailyn to prepare a collection of pamphlets of the American Revolution, Bailyn readily agreed—it couldn't be that hard to bring together a dozen or so pamphlets. Then he "discovered the magnitude of the project [he] had embarked on. The full bibliography of pamphlets relating to the Anglo-American struggle published in the colonies through the year 1776 contains not a dozen or so items but over four hundred. . . ."

These pamphlets "include all sorts of writings—treatises on political theory, essays on history, political arguments, sermons, correspondence, poems," says Bailyn, who discovered that he was "studying not simply a particular medium of publication but, through these documents, nothing less than the ideological origins of the American Revolution."

The first star among these hundreds of pamphleteers was the Reverend Jonathan Mayhew. His widely printed and distributed sermon, *A Discourse Concerning Unlimited Submission and Nonresistance to the Higher Powers* (1750), became—says Bailyn—"the most famous sermon preached in pre-Revolutionary America," and "quickly became regarded as a classic formulation of the necessity and virtue of resistance to oppression." John Adams remarked that Mayhew's *Discourse* was "read by everybody, celebrated by friends, and abused by enemies."

In 1767 John Dickinson published his *Letters from a Farmer in Pennsylvania*. These letters were printed in most of the colonial newspapers, then brought together in what became the most influential pamphlet published in America before 1776. *Letters from a Farmer in Pennsylvania* was published as a pamphlet not only in New York, Boston, and Williamsburg, but abroad in London and Amsterdam.

Dickinson denied the legality of not only Parliament's internal taxes on Americans but also the port duties levied on the colonials. He went far beyond the position of Benjamin Franklin, who was currently representing America in London, and Dickinson's popularity revealed that Franklin had perhaps been abroad too long and wasn't keeping up with the thrust of American opinion. This wouldn't be the last time that the pamphleteer was more attuned to the will of the people than the politician.

Enter Tom Paine, pamphleteering superstar of 1776—and all time. Mayhew, Dickinson, and hundreds of other writers prepared the way, but Tom Paine's *Common Sense*—published on January 9, 1776—lit the fuse that became the American Revolution. In slightly less than six months, the Continental Congress that was assembled in Philadelphia took Paine's advice and declared America's independence of Britain. Few would have predicted such a radical course on January 8, 1776, but once again a fiery pamphleteer was far ahead of the cautious politicians.

Are we overstating the case? Consider that up to January 1776 John Dickinson was still the most influential pamphleteer in America, and he wanted to stay within the British Empire. At his persuasion, in fact, the Pennsylvania delegation to the Second Continental Congress was instructed to vote against independence if the issue were raised. Four other colonies did the same, and not one colony was instructed to vote *for* independence. "The best estimates," says Paine editor Isaac Kramnick, "are that no more than a third of the members of the Congress assembled at Philadelphia through the winter of late 1775 and early 1776 were in favor of independence."

It was Tom Paine who weaned Americans off their royalty fetish— at least until the time of Princess Di. Only a year before revolution, Americans were still more respectful of King George III than the Brits themselves. They excoriated Parliament and members of the king's court, but most Americans remained enamored of the idea of a "patriot king." British philosopher David Hume wryly suggested that because the colonials were so far away, they never knew what a king was really like. The situation also reminds us of today's excuse makers, who, conservative and liberal alike, will proclaim that President So-and-So "is *really* conservative [or liberal]. It's his staff that is messing up everything."

Tom Paine had no patience or sympathy for such nonsense. He took aim with a cannonball at the "Royal Brute of Great Britain." For a condensed version of his complaints about the Brute you need look no further than the enumeration in the Declaration of Independence. "No scholar, no graduate of Harvard, or Yale, or the College of New Jersey at Princeton, however radical his politics, could have written *Common Sense*," says historian Page Smith. "Their class, their backgrounds, their education had made them too conventional in their language, too academic, too logical, to speak with such power or touch such common chords. To say that it was the most successful political pamphlet in history is to do it insufficient credit. *Common Sense* belongs in a category all its own."

Within three months, *Common Sense* had sold 120,000 copies; before all was said and done, it's likely that more than 500,000 copies were printed and sold. Since they were passed hand to hand, says Smith, "a conservative estimate would be that a million Americans read it, or almost half the population of the colonies." Today a book would have to sell on the order of 70 million copies and be read by 140 million to reach that level of audience penetration. Not even Oprah gets results like that.

Edmund Randolph of Virginia said *Common Sense* "put the torch to combustibles which had been deposited by the different gusts of fury." George Washington himself added that "*Common Sense* is working a powerful change in the minds of men"—and he thereafter stopped toasting the king at official meals.

Nearly two centuries later, British socialist Harold Laski would write that *with the exception of Karl Marx*, Paine was "the most influential pamphleteer of all time." Okay, we'll cut Laski, the old socialist, some slack. He was writing in the 1950s, when all the politically correct intellectuals were prating about the inevitability of Marxism. In that statist fog, Laski could hardly guess that three inconsequential economists of that day—Ludwig von Mises, Friedrich A. Hayek, and Milton Friedman—were already building the intellectual base for a movement that would eventually topple the Soviet Union and world communism. And with the demise of socialism as a world force, Tom Paine no longer has any competition for the title of the "most influential pamphleteer of all time."

Having lit the fuse that exploded as the American Revolution, Tom Paine soon found that his talents were needed once again. And he came through once again with his golden pen.

In the harsh winter of 1776, the brash optimism with which the war had started now faced the chilling reality. George Washington's ragged troops at Valley Forge were a poor match in numbers and equipment and training for the Hessians employed by the British crown and camped just across the Delaware River in Trenton, New Jersey. Patriot morale had hit bottom, and only George Washington's character and leadership kept the war going. Then Washington got some help.

On December 23, 1776, Tom Paine published the first essay in what would eventually be known as *The American Crisis*, or *The Crisis*. It opened with what may be the most memorable words ever written on behalf of the American cause:

> These are the times that try men's souls. The summer soldier and the sunshine patriot will, in this crisis, shrink from the service of their country; but he that stands it now, deserves the love and thanks of man and woman. Tyranny, like hell, is not easily conquered; yet we have this consolation with us, that the harder the conflict, the more glorious the triumph. What we obtain too cheap, we esteem too lightly: it is dearness only that gives everything its value. Heaven knows how to put a proper price upon its goods; and it would be strange indeed if so celestial an article as Freedom should not be highly rated. Britain, with an army to enforce its tyranny, has declared that she has a right [not

only to tax] but "to bind us in all cases whatsoever,"
and if being bound in that manner is not slavery, then
is there not such a thing as slavery upon earth. Even
the expression is impious; for so unlimited a power can
only belong to God.

General Washington read those words aloud to his troops before they
attacked the Hessians in Trenton, successfully. It was said that Paine's
words were then read aloud in every American military encampment.
"Militiamen who, already tired of the war, were straggling from the
army, returned," wrote contemporary James Cheetham. "Hope succeeded to despair, cheerfulness to gloom, and firmness to irresolution."

Paine continued his writings for *The American Crisis* for the duration of the war, and George Washington, for one, never forgot the unfathomable debt America owed to its oracle. Well into the future, Tom
Paine also gave the new nation a motto that would epitomize America's
can-do spirit to this day: "We have it in our power to begin the world
over again."

Timeline of the Media Revolution of 1776

1638 Arrival of first printing press in America (Cambridge, Mass.)

1690 Publication in England of John Locke's *Two Treatises on Government*

1690 America's first newspaper, *Publick Occurances Both Foreign and Domestick* (Boston), closed by government after first issue

1704 *Boston News-Letter* becomes America's first newspaper to publish for an extended period of time

1720 The book *Cato's Letters*, by John Trenchard and Thomas Gordon, is published in England

1735 Trial of John Peter Zenger for seditious libel, in New York City

1750 Rev. Jonathan Mayhew (Boston) delivers the sermon "A Discourse Concerning Unlimited Submission and Nonresistance to the Higher Powers"

1754–1763 French and Indian War

May 9, 1754 America's first editorial cartoon (the disjointed "JOIN, or DIE" snake) appears in Benjamin Franklin's *Pennsylvania Gazette*

Mar. 22, 1765 Stamp Act enacted by Parliament

May 29 (?), 1765 Patrick Henry's Virginia Resolutions against the Stamp Act ("Sir, if this be treason, make the most of it")

Nov. 1, 1765 Stamp Act scheduled to become law in America

1765–1766 Sons of Liberty, America's first PAC, organize throughout colonies to resist the Stamp Act

1767 Townshend Acts add new taxes on colonies

Dec. 2, 1767– Publication of John Dickinson's *Letters from a*
Feb. 15, 1768 *Farmer in Pennsylvania* in the *Pennsylvania Chronicle and Universal Advertiser*

1768 British troops stationed in Boston

1770 Parliament repeals all taxes in Townshend Acts—except for the tax on tea

Mar. 5, 1770 Boston Massacre

Nov. 2, 1772 Creation of Committees of Correspondence

1773 Parliament passes Tea Act of 1773, creating monopoly for the British East India Company

Dec. 16, 1773 Boston Tea Party

Sept. 5– First Continental Congress meets in Philadelphia
Oct. 26, 1774

Apr. 18–19, 1775 Paul Revere's ride

Apr. 19, 1775 Battles of Lexington and Concord ("The Shot Heard around the World")

May 10, 1775– Second Continental Congress meets in Philadelphia
Dec. 12, 1776

Jan. 9, 1776 Publication of Tom Paine's *Common Sense*

Jul. 4, 1776 Declaration of Independence

Dec. 19, Publication of Tom Paine's *The American Crisis*
1776–1783

3

The Recipe for Creating a New Mass Movement

The media revolutions of 1517 and 1776 were the precursors of our modern world of mass communications and ever-faster communications. And this ongoing revolution in media technology has made possible mass political and social movements on the scale we take for granted today.

No man or woman has ever been less of an island than they are today. Our political ideas, our social practices, our religious beliefs—all are shaped and influenced by information and misinformation we get from around the nation and across the globe.

Not that mass movements didn't exist before 1517. Military movements have always been with us, it seems, spreading change through physical violence. The Christian revolution that overtook the Roman Empire spread almost entirely on a person-to-person basis. What has changed since 1517 and 1776 are the multiplying forms of communication, their growing geographical scope, and their increasing speed in spreading news and views. Those factors are the result of the revolution in media technology.

At the same time, this means there is ever-increasing competition for your attention among *potential* mass movements. If you were a cobbler in Altenburg, Germany, in 1520, chances were that the Lutheran Reformation was pretty much the only exciting new trend you and your friends talked about. Today a thousand movements and causes—political, social, religious—vie for your attention.

How, then, does a potential new political movement emerge and succeed in this media-dominated world? That's what will concern us in this chapter. Obviously many factors contribute to the formation of something as complex as a mass political movement, so we will attempt to identify the major factors and concoct a "recipe" of how they work together. We will use the revolutions of 1517 and 1776 as laboratory examples of this recipe. Then, in succeeding chapters, we will show how this recipe resulted in the emergence, growth, and success of the conservative movement in the middle of the 20th century—the era of our personal political experience.

Issues that motivate

Any cause that hopes to become a mass movement must have at its core burning issues that motivate people into action. Lukewarm issues—"my copyright reform bill is better than yours"—won't do. Political inertia is the normal state for most people, and it takes a sledgehammer of an issue to distract them from their ball games, shopping sprees, and daily work preoccupations.

What kinds of issues have this power?

- A perceived crisis that is not being managed by the ruling establishment—for example, a national security threat that politicians are ignoring.
- Threats to a way of life, or to the economic security of a large number of people, such as onerous taxation or regulations that are grinding the economy to a halt. An economic threat to a few people isn't likely to motivate you into action

unless you're one of those few people, and even then, we're no longer talking about a "mass" movement.

• Idealistic revulsion against corruption or power grabs by people in a position of power.

• Idealistic projections of a better life once the "bad guys" have been overthrown.

The Lutheran Reformation had two red-hot issues—doctrinal disputes and church corruption—that motivated the German clergy into rebellion, the merchant class into supporting them (partly out of revulsion against the begging orders), and parishioners to "support their local monk." Another hot issue aiding the revolution was political and ecclesiastical control from far beyond Germany's borders, in this case, Rome. Sending money to Rome and getting a pittance back was about as popular as sending money to Washington (and getting a pittance back) is today with the American people.

The American Revolution, as we've seen, had a much broader litany of burning issues—political and economic control from abroad, taxation without representation, the Stamp Act, royal corruption and arrogance, the quartering of soldiers in Boston. See the Declaration of Independence for a more complete list of grievances.

A dedicated vanguard

A mass movement doesn't start out as such. It begins with the soapbox gripes of a small group of people, most often composed primarily of intellectuals, young people, and those we today call "the chattering class"—people whose business or profession is talk and advice (whether you want their advice or not). Disaffected economic groups are often another part of the early mix of combustibles.

The intellectuals are always there because they, above all others, understand that "ideas have consequences," to appropriate the title of Richard Weaver's seminal 1959 book. Ideas are intellectuals' path to power and influence, whether their motivations are idealistic or pecuniary—or both. Youth always seem to be more idealistic, in general, than their world-weary elders, who know all the reasons why something *can't* be done. Young people also have the energy (and time) to devote long hours to nitty-gritty organizational tasks. The chattering class thrives on talk, of course, if not always action. And there's nothing like the feeling that you're being robbed to motivate you into action, and to seek redress in a new movement.

In the Lutheran Reformation, the clergy were both the intellectual class (running the monasteries, seminaries, and universities) and the chattering class—just think of the pulpit as their forum. "Youth" were not a distinct constituency. Life was short back then, compared to now, so there was no time for a prolonged adolescence—you went directly to adulthood from childhood in short order. And among the economically motivated there was the emerging merchant class, chafing at medieval social and religious restrictions.

The American Revolution was largely a product of the finest assemblage of *practical* intellectuals (as opposed to ivory-towered intellectuals) in the history of our civilization. They were aided significantly by a fully emerged merchant class, with a particular role for the printers of the new continent. The chatterers—think of the hundreds of pamphleteers— were not a separate group, but were drawn from the ranks of the practical intellectuals and merchant/businessmen. Youth still had not emerged as a distinct class—that's a modern phenomenon—but it certainly helped to be relatively young in order to have the energy to pursue revolution in this tough new land (think of Paul Revere and his arduous rides).

Self-identification as a movement

The world is always full of people who are angry at something that's going on, or stirred deeply by some current issue. They don't become part of a *movement*, however, until and unless they become aware that other people—organized people—share their concerns, that they can join these people, and that by doing so they can make a difference.

For this to happen, we must first add to our recipe: *self-identification* by some people that they constitute a movement with a mission. It doesn't matter, at the beginning, that the group is small and that its ultimate goal seems visionary and unrealistic. What is required is a clear sense of mission and commitment. Look at what tiny original groups of people with commitment and a mission can do—for good or evil—having, ultimately, a phenomenal impact on the world: Think of Christ's disciples and the first Bolsheviks.

As American philosopher William James noted: "A small force if it never lets up will accumulate effects more considerable than those of much greater forces if these work inconsistently."

Luther started out as one monk sharing his concerns with fellow clerics in his community. It was only when they started thinking of themselves as a *movement* to reform the church—sharing that mission with others through the printing press—that the Reformation actually *became* a movement. Without that mission and self-identification by Luther and his circle, they might have ended up as only a bunch of dissatisfied monks in a small town in Germany that history would soon forget.

Colonial Brits in the New World were unhappy over certain actions by the mother country almost from the get-go. That's the common plight of an expatriate. A revolutionary movement didn't exist, however, until the Stamp Act caused a small but influential group—printers—to start thinking of themselves as *Americans*, not as British citizens living in America, with a mission to separate from Britain.

Communication networks
(sometimes including a secret weapon)

Once you have some burning issues to motivate people, and a mix of core constituencies in your vanguard, you need *communication networks* to bring that movement and that mission to the attention of others. Person-to-person communication is fine for bucolic times, but a revolution needs speed—to catch the ruling establishment off guard before that establishment can marshal its full powers against the insurgents.

Nothing has expanded as dramatically in the past 500 years as these pulpits of dissemination. Luther depended pretty much on just two communication networks, the first being the church pulpit. He didn't need much more, though, because his second network was a secret weapon—the printing press—and he used that secret weapon to produce an arsenal of Bibles, Bible studies, catechisms, and pamphlets.

The printing press wasn't *literally* a secret weapon, of course, not on the line of the development of an atomic bomb during World War II. It had the *impact* of a secret weapon, though, because Luther understood the potential of this new technology and he had the will to use it, unlike his opposition in the Catholic Church. We will see this same phenomenon at work when we turn to the conservative revolution in the pages ahead.

By the time of the American Revolution, there was no secret weapon in the form of a distinctly new technology but rather the harnessing of the current technology on a more massive scale than had ever been attempted before. The colonials' communication networks included the church pulpit and the courier, but even more prominent were the products of the printing press—books, newspapers, and pamphlets. And the pamphlets, as we've seen, were a phenomenal success in reaching virtually the entire free population.

Money to fund the revolution

Everyone complains about the role of money in politics, but nobody's figured out how to run a political movement or party without money.

In the case of the Lutheran Reformation, most of the money came in the form of church members' tithes, and the big change came when the collection plates stayed in Germany rather than following the path to Rome. Merchant entrepreneurs put up the funds for presses, but they did that for profit, not charity, which no doubt explains why the new printing industry grew so fast—it wasn't a government printing office run by bureaucrats. It was a free-market venture propelled by capitalism and competition. The German princes were Luther's third source of funding (as we've seen, the Catholic Church got even less financial support than verbal support from these German princes).

By the time of the American Revolution, we had a fully developed merchant class, unlike anything the world had seen before. Merchants now had real financial power, and they were committed to independence ahead of the rest of the population. As a result of the Stamp Act, the printers above all were united for independence and took a lead in supporting the cause with their presses. Of course, actually fighting a war takes a lot more money than agitating for one, and George Washington had great difficulty getting that funding—until Tom Paine came to the rescue.

And then there's the establishment . . .

On the surface, the establishment holds all the important cards—power, prestige, and the big bucks, obtained through taxation and generous donations from special interests that want access to power. That can work very well, for long periods of time, as long as most people are generally contented—or too powerless to pose a threat.

Under the surface, however, the establishment may be vulnerable in ways that are not readily apparent. Support may appear to be widespread, when in reality it is very thin—a veneer of support without substance. Most important, power corrupts—as Lord Acton reminded us—and that corruption isn't limited to pecuniary concerns or arbitrary police powers. Often most fatal is the conceit to which power holders fall victim that they *deserve* to be in power—perhaps even by divine will—and therefore *will* remain in power, tomorrow as today.

You get that conceit when you only talk and listen to people just like you—the other members of your establishment. Court intrigues abound, but the peasants—who cares or worries about them! And so, when some incipient protest first surfaces, your first reaction is to ignore it. If that doesn't work, you ridicule it. And if *that* doesn't work, you take steps to try and suppress it. You rely on your *authority*, not persuasion, to maintain the status quo.

Both the Catholic Church (in Luther's day) and the British king and his court (in the 18th century) were so impressed by their own claims to authority—and so isolated from the reality of the world about them—that they failed to take action in time to forestall revolution. The Catholic Church saw no need to employ the printing press in the way those "rude Germans" were using it. The Church relied, instead, on its centuries of authority by decree. King George was just as removed from reality, and 3,000 miles of ocean between his throne and the colonies exacerbated his plight. How was he to know that the colonists had become a different breed of people from his subjects at home?

As the new revolutionary movement grows, of course, some elements of the establishment opt to join the new order. In Luther's case, this brings us once again to those German princes, who needed little persuading to stop the money flow to Rome. And in the case of the Americans, they had considerable support among the Whigs in England, while in the colonies there was a steady stream of conversions to the revolutionary cause, especially when the alternative became banishment to Canada.

Fast-forward to the year 1955

It is now time to advance to the main object of this book—to show how the conservative movement rose from obscurity to attain power in the second half of the 20th century. What was the "recipe" that brought this new mass movement into power? We'll look at the motivating issues, the dedicated vanguard, the communication networks, and especially the conservatives' new media weapon, which also served as their main source of funding.

Most intriguing, as we'll see, history once again repeated itself in the actions of the ruling liberal establishment, which sought first to ignore the conservatives, then to ridicule them, then to suppress them, while refusing to utilize the new media weapon until it was too late.

Now, push that fast-forward button in your mind . . .

PART II

The Conservative
Revolution Begins

4

1955
A Liberal Hegemony
over America

In 1955, liberalism reigned supreme over the politics of the United States. But the natives were grumbling—a lot.

Why pick this particular year? Look again at the ingredients in our recipe for creating a new mass movement (Chapter 3). In 1955, as we will now see, plenty of issues motivated "the Right"—forerunners of those who soon became better known as conservatives and libertarians. A dedicated vanguard was developing, but not yet fully formed. Missing was the self-identification as a movement. A lot of grumbling does not a movement make. At the end of 1955, however, a new development would go a long way toward changing that, and in the following five years the new movement would be born.

In the pages that follow you'll read about a lot of intellectuals, writers, politicians, organizations, magazines, and books—all grumblers or the work of grumblers. This may lead you to believe that an organized insurgent army was already in the field. Do not be deceived. Grass-roots anarchy would be a better description of the state of the conservative non-movement in 1955. Probably 90 percent of all Americans didn't know that these grumblers existed, even if they shared many of their gripes. The grumblers were so under the radar, they could be called stealth grumblers. Polite (liberal) society didn't discuss them, except to exorcise them as "McCarthyites."

We do not exaggerate when we say that in 1955 liberalism reigned supreme over the politics of the United States. Both political parties were under the control of their liberal wings. The Democrats were the party of Harry Truman and Adlai Stevenson, while the GOP came under the control of its liberal Eastern wing once Ike decided he was a Republican and became their front man. In Congress, conservatives had their champions even if they didn't control the agenda or direction of the two parties. In the national media, however, conservatives were nearly shut out. And the national media decided what issues would be discussed, as well as the "correct" positions on those issues.

Where did Americans get their news in 1955? Almost entirely from the three television networks and their local newspapers. The slant of TV news and commentary was solidly liberal, without exception, as the names Edward R. Murrow and Walter Cronkite make all too evident. As for local newspapers, many of them were nominally Republican, but any Republican perspective was found only on the editorial page— the least-read section of a newspaper. Then, as now, most reporters were Democrats and liberals, consciously or unconsciously, and they followed the lead of the TV commentators and the major "respectable" papers in terms of what they reported, and how they reported it.

The most influential newspapers were virtually all liberal, too. Leading the way in national influence were the *New York Times* and the *Washington Post*. Just a year earlier the *Post* had bought out the Republican *Washington Times-Herald*, killing its voice through merger and creating a morning newspaper monopoly in the nation's capital. This was an incredible coup for the liberal establishment. Each morning, lawmakers would get their news and opinion from the liberal *Washington Post* and in the evening from the liberal television networks, which hardly created an atmosphere for placing conservative or Republican ideas on the agenda.

Radio, in 1955, was mostly an entertainment medium rather than a news medium. There were conservative grumblers on the radio—John T. Flynn, Clarence Manion, and Fulton Lewis Jr. come to mind—but they had to pay for their commentary time by obtaining sponsors, usually small businesses. They didn't enjoy the federally granted monopoly of the TV networks, and they had nowhere near the same sized audience.

Where was public policy formed? Those ideas were formed primarily in the universities and the foundations, which played the role later assumed by think tanks. Liberals controlled the academy as tightly as they controlled the TV networks, especially in the more prominent "respectable" universities, and liberal academics were just as merciless toward conservative dissenters—this *was* the heyday of Arthur Schlesinger, Jr., after all. And the foundation world was dominated by liberal giants like the Rockefeller and Ford foundations. They led the way in funding academic and public policy research, and no conservative need apply.

All the major book publishers were liberal, and the two most prominent and influential ideological periodicals were *The Nation* and *The New Republic*—both leftist.

The three most prominent conservative voices were the *Chicago Tribune, Reader's Digest*, and David Lawrence's *U.S. News*. The *Digest* was never that influential politically, however, as its main thrust was to provide middlebrow audiences with easy-to-read articles and books on mostly nonpolitical topics. The *Tribune*, while owner Colonel McCormick was alive, *was* influential, but only in the midwestern heartland. Elsewhere it was routinely disparaged by the liberal establishment, and it held little influence on Washington as compared to the *New York Times* and the *Washington Post*. David Lawrence brought a businessman's common sense to matters of public policy, both in his weekly *U.S. News* and in his widely distributed newspaper column, but his influence was nowhere on the order of that of *Time* or *Newsweek*.

Put together all the influential media and you get a score of something like liberals 95, conservatives 5. Or perhaps it was more like 97/3. That's the sort of monopoly enjoyed by Pravda in its Soviet heyday.

Bear in mind that this liberal media monopoly existed even while the country, then as now, was overwhelmingly conservative (little "c") in its social character, and probably somewhat evenly divided politically between liberals and conservatives. (There were more liberals then than now because we were closer to the Great Depression. There were also more Democrats than Republicans, because the conservatives in the South were Democrats.) When you have that sort of imbalance between the nation's people and the nation's opinion leaders, a considerable amount of dissident grumbling is likely to be going on, even if underground. And it was.

The grumblers' motivating issues

When we look at the people, in 1955, who were about to be incorporated into the conservative movement, it is clear that their overriding concern was with communism and socialism. Conservatives and libertarians were united on this, even when they disagreed on what to do about the leftist ideologies and how to fight them. More conservatives than libertarians liked Senator Joseph McCarthy, but even an esteemed libertarian like the political economist Murray Rothbard came to the defense of "Fighting Joe."

This was an era, after all, when communism was thought to be in almost inevitable ascendancy—by the Right as well as the Left. Communist armies had taken over much of the world; their political operatives had created an international propaganda and proselytizing apparatus unlike anything that had existed before in history; and at home in the United States, more Soviet spies and fellow-travelers were busy transferring secrets to the Soviet Union than even Joe McCarthy could have imagined (as we later learned from Soviet archives and defectors). This was the era of "who lost China?" and "who promoted Peress?" The era of our nonvictory in Korea, President Truman's dismissal of General MacArthur, the Alger Hiss and Julius and Ethel Rosenberg trials, and the soon-to-come Hungarian revolution (and our betrayal of it). Through it all, nearly all of the Left defended the two biggest butchers of our time—Stalin and Mao—and most liberals at the least felt we had to be accommodating toward them, making concession after concession.

Communism, in short, was *the* most important issue in 1955 for the people who would become the conservative movement. Which is not to say that it was the only issue. Labor unions were at the height of their power, pursuing a leftist agenda. Foreign aid was a hot topic. National sovereignty (the United Nations, the Bricker Amendment) was another. Conservatives and libertarians were united on all these issues—their split over "social" issues would come in the future.

Not that it was all peace and harmony on the Right. Libertarians and many conservatives were believers in the noninterventionist approach to foreign policy so prominently advocated by America First in the years before World War II, while most conservatives thought the United States must stand up militarily to communism even if war was the result. Their complaint wasn't that we went to war in Korea, for example, but rather that the Democratic administration had not let our troops win, and had us fighting under the United Nations flag.

Libertarians also tended to be more interested in economic issues than conservatives were and more adept at theoretical arguments than specific policy positions. (There was nothing like the Cato Institute at that time, to develop libertarian legislative policy based on free-market principles.)

Eventually these divergences on foreign policy and economic emphasis would lead to a split between the conservatives and libertarians. The conservatives would become primarily enmeshed in political activism, while the libertarians mostly followed more academic pursuits. Both would be successful, with the conservatives taking over the Republican Party and then the presidency, and with the libertarians providing the intellectual and economic foundation for the worldwide triumph of free markets over collectivism. But for now, in 1955, all of that was just a pipedream for the most ambitious and optimistic members of both camps.

The grumblers' networks of communication

So, the grumblers of the Right—the dissidents from liberalism—had their motivating issues. They were starting to recruit and convert people who could become a dedicated vanguard for a movement. But as of now, there was no encompassing *movement* for these people to attach themselves to. First there was a period of gestation—decentralized and somewhat anarchic, but highly creative, as only the future would show. Individual, grassroots conservatives honed their concerns through books, newspapers, and magazines, and then began to find an outlet in activist organizations.

Books. Ideas have consequences, as Richard Weaver reminded us in his 1959 book by that title, and a surge of politically themed books almost always precedes political action. Many libertarian classics had appeared in the '40s, among them Rose Wilder Lane's *Discovery of Freedom* (1943), Henry Grady Weaver's *The Mainspring of Human Progress* (1947), Friedrich Hayek's enormously influential *The Road to Serfdom* (1944), and John T. Flynn's *The Roosevelt Myth* (1948, with over 100,000 copies sold) and *The Road Ahead* (1949). More popular, with a far wider audience, were the acerbic writings of the *Baltimore Sun's* H. L. Mencken. But the best-selling libertarian author, by far, was Ayn Rand, of *The Fountainhead* (1943) and *Atlas Shrugged* (soon to be published in 1957). Most conservatives consider Ayn Rand's philosophical ideas to be, well, nutty, but her political novels have undoubtedly jolted more people out of their complacency, or converted them from some left-of-center ideology, than any other books—and many of those people ended up in the libertarian and conservative movements. Indeed, in a 1991 survey conducted by the Library of Congress and the Book of the Month Club, *Atlas Shrugged* was named the "second most influential book for Americans today" after the Bible.

The problem, if you were a conservative or libertarian author who didn't have the mass appeal of a Mencken or Rand, was that you had to settle for being published by an obscure house. The big Manhattan publishers had liberal attack dogs that sniffed deviant ideas and would tear up your manuscript the moment it arrived in the mailroom, lest it contaminate the place. Worthy libertarian titles were published by the likes of Caxton Press (Caldwell, Idaho), Devin-Adair (Manhattan, and later New Rochelle, New York), and The Bookmailer (operating from a post office box in Manhattan).

Conservatives had a more vigorous, if unprofitable, publishing house with Henry Regnery's firm in Chicago. The Great Books classics were a staple of the Regnery line, and Regnery himself introduced top contemporary European authors and politicians to an American audience. In the 1950s he became the main hope for conservative American authors, just as the firm bearing his name fills that role again today.

Right up to our year of 1955, Regnery and other firms were publishing books now deemed to be conservative classics. These included William F. Buckley Jr.'s *God and Man at Yale* (1951), Whittaker Chambers's *Witness* (1952), Russell Kirk's *The Conservative Mind* (1953), James Burnham's *The Web of Subversion* (1954), and *McCarthy and His Enemies* (1954) by William F. Buckley Jr. and L. Brent Bozell.

Henry Regnery, in his *Memoirs of a Dissident Publisher*, wrote: "It would be too much to say that the postwar conservative movement began with the publication of Russell Kirk's *The Conservative Mind*, but it was this book that gave it its name, and, more important, coherence."

Yes, a lot of book grumbling was going on.

Magazines. Right-of-center periodicals, in 1955, were small and barely surviving. Yet they filled a necessary, even heroic role in creating underground networks of communication. The two most important periodicals were *Human Events* and *The Freeman*.

Human Events at this time was a Washington newsletter, not the tabloid it is today, and advertised itself as "A Weekly Analysis for the American Citizen." In 1955 its 13,500 subscribers paid $10 a year,

$11.50 for first-class delivery. Its editor was a crusty veteran reporter, Frank C. Hanighen, who had gained fame earlier as coauthor of *Merchants of Death*, the exposé of the role played by arms merchants in the World War I era. Hanighen was well connected with Republican senators and congressmen on Capitol Hill, as well as with other reporters. *Human Events'* publisher was a small-town newspaper owner, James L. Wick, who ironically had been a member of Governor Tom Dewey's research staff in 1944. Wick kept the small-circulation letter afloat (barely) with fundraising appeals by the likes of actor Adolph Menjou.

For the flavor of this feisty newsletter, here's the very first line in its first issue for 1955: "Behind the Thought Control Curtain: Congress begins the new year under the usual smoke-barrage of New Deal Republican and Democratic propaganda." *Human Events* (and conservatives in general) did *not* like Ike. Noted writer Freda Utley vowed that "there was never any ground for the supposition that Eisenhower, if elected as President by Republican votes, would prove more capable of understanding and more courageous in combating communism than the Truman-Marshall-Acheson combination." Also, she said in the same article, "Today it is much clearer than three years ago that Eisenhower received certain powerful financial and press support, not because he could defeat Truman or Stevenson, but because he could eliminate Taft and the truly American policies for which the late, great Senator from Ohio stood."

As opposed to *Human Events,* which was an inside-Washington newsletter, *The Freeman* was a lively opinion journal. It was also somewhat more libertarian than *Human Events*, though there was a lot of inbreeding between the two periodicals. Frank Chodorov, editor of *The Freeman*, was also a contributing editor at *Human Events*, and Frank Hanighen, editor of *Human Events*, also wrote a Washington column for *The Freeman*.

The Freeman began 1955 with a continuation of its previous year's debate on fighting the Soviet Union, pitting William F. Buckley against Frank Chodorov. This was the issue that, more than anything, split the libertarians from the conservatives. An entire March issue was devoted to "One Worldism and the United Nations"—something both sides could agree on. Then there's an ironic cover ad advising potential advertisers (very scarce for a periodical this outspoken): "Don't feel bad because all advertising space in the *Reader's Digest* is sold out for more than a year ahead. Space in *The Freeman* is available right now."

Elsewhere, there were grass-roots publications like Kent and Phoebe Courtney's *Free Men Speak* that were not as intellectually coherent as *Human Events* and *The Freeman*, but nevertheless important in building a following that could later be incorporated into the conservative movement. *The American Mercury* gave right-wing authors like Ralph de Toledano another venue; it was no longer Mencken's revered journal, but it had not yet been bought and turned into an anti-Semitic voice. The libertarians had two religiously oriented publications, *Faith and Freedom* and *Christian Economics*, demonstrating that there is no necessary antagonism between libertarianism and religion, despite Ayn Rand.

As we've noted, *Reader's Digest* was the Big Bertha of conservative publications, even though it was mostly nonpolitical in content. It may have performed its most valuable service, however, by introducing Friedrich Hayek and a condensed version of his *Road to Serfdom* to an American audience. Elsewhere, *U.S. News* editor David Lawrence wrote a conservative business-oriented column on its last page, Whittaker Chambers was an editor at *Time*, and *Newsweek* had two conservative/libertarian columnists—Raymond Moley and Henry Hazlitt.

Newspapers. We've mentioned that the big, influential, "respectable" newspapers were all liberal. The *Chicago Tribune* was the only conservative (at that time) paper with any real clout, and that only in its midwestern heartland. (The *Tribune*'s iconoclastic publisher, Colonel Robert McCormick, died in our year of 1955. After his death, the great paper declined in influence, then in its conservatism.) The *Philadelphia Evening Bulletin*, the *Houston Chronicle*, and other out-of-Washington-and-New-York papers had conservative editorial pages but little clout nationally.

Some of the most interesting writings were found in smaller papers such as William Loeb's *Manchester* (New Hampshire) *Union-Leader*, a bane to pro-tax liberal politicians in election years; the *Richmond News-Leader*, with James Jackson Kilpatrick writing its highly literate editorials; and the nobody's-more-libertarian-than-us Freedom Newspapers, published by R. C. Hoiles. Robert LeFevre, editor of that chain's *Colorado Springs Gazette-Telegraph*, was also a colorful and articulate libertarian activist who ran the anarchist/libertarian Rampart College and Freedom School in the foothills of the Rockies.

Organizations. At the grass-roots level, a number of conservative and anti-communist organizations would flourish for a while, then wither away when their overworked founders were no longer able to keep them afloat. They never turned into a coherent *movement*. Some of the groups making news in conservative and libertarian periodicals in 1955 were For America, Pro-America, the Committee for Constitutional Government, the American Good Government Society, We the People!, and grassroots actvisits Kent and Phoebe Courtney's New Party, which in the end didn't become a new party.

Educational groups also abounded, among them the Manion Forum, Facts Forum, and John T. Flynn's America's Future. Operations such as these produced a steady torrent of literature. The American Legion was powerful at this time, and took hard anti-communist positions, as you would expect. There was even a conservative-oriented professional organization, the American Bar Association—no longer! In 1955 its past president, Frank E. Holman, was an ardent supporter of the Bricker Amendment, which was designed to protect U.S. sovereignty against UN and other treaties. Also, the January 29, 1955, issue of *Human Events* noted the formation of a future giant in the conservative movement, the National Right-to-Work Committee.

Libertarian organizations tended to be more educational or academic than activist. The Mont Pelerin Society, founded in 1947, brought together the top free-market economists and political scientists from around the world. The Foundation for Economic Education (FEE), in Irvington-on-Hudson, New York, produced a steady stream of pamphlets and articles, and later assumed publication of *The Freeman*. FEE's publications and debate kits were valuable resources for students of this era seeking an alternative to the prevalent statist fare served them at school.

The educational organization that probably had the greatest influence on the conservative movement was the Intercollegiate Society of Individualists (ISI), founded by Frank Chodorov following an article he wrote in *Human Events*, proposing such an effort. ISI, run by E. Victor Milione for decades, was educational, not activist, but it gave hundreds of future activists a firm grounding in conservative and libertarian philosophy.

The grumblers' political spokesmen

Robert A. Taft, the Republican senator from Ohio, had been the favorite of both conservatives and libertarians of this era, but he died in 1953. Wisconsin's Senator Joe McCarthy was still alive, but after his censure in December 1954 his influence (and sobriety) waned significantly.

The removal of these two men left a void, and a new political movement needs at least *one* elected spokesman to give it visibility and recognition. Two Utah politicians were outspoken conservatives: Governor J. Bracken Lee and Eisenhower's secretary of agriculture Ezra Taft Benson. Neither managed to become a national *movement* spokesman, however.

Former president Herbert Hoover was a regular on some dinner circuits. Some conservatives adored him, others considered him an ineffectual has-been, and the libertarians considered him the first New Dealer. At any rate, he wasn't of the age or temperament to lead a new movement.

The U.S. Senate held some powerful and articulate Southern Democrats—Harry S. Byrd of Virginia, Walter F. George and Richard B. Russell of Georgia, and South Carolina's Strom Thurmond, who had been the Dixiecrat candidate for president in 1948 and who in 1954 became the first person in U.S. history to be elected to a major office by write-in ballot. None of them had any hope of national leadership in the liberal Democratic Party, though, and it was hard to imagine them leading a national movement, most of whose members outside the South were Republican. Some conservatives in the pages of *Human Events* were advocating a political realignment of the parties, but that's an even more difficult change than starting an effective new party.

That left a band of powerful conservative Republicans in the U.S. Senate—Minority Leader William Knowland of California (also known as "the senator from Formosa," for his ardent support of the Republic of China); Styles Bridges of New Hampshire, chairman of the Republican Policy Committee; and Ohio's John W. Bricker of Bricker Amendment fame, chairman of the Committee of Committees. They performed valuable services for conservatives on Capitol Hill, but they were not willing to speak out publicly against the liberal leader of their party, Dwight David Eisenhower, except in the most modulated tones (and usually behind closed doors). That's not the way to become a movement leader, even assuming you want to become one.

Oh yes, there was one young fellow, new to town—one Barry Goldwater of Arizona, who had defeated the Democratic majority leader of the Senate, Ernest W. McFarland, in 1952. Unusually blunt and honest for a politician, he would soon be blasting Eisenhower's programs—publicly!—as a "dime store New Deal." The rest, as they say, would be history.

For now, though, there was no overriding need for a national political spokesman because there was no movement for him to lead. Before our assortment of conservatives and libertarians could think of themselves as a distinct political movement, they had to have a center of gravity, some focal point, that addressed them as members of a movement and taught them, in Lenin's words, what is to be done. That giant step was taken in November of our year of 1955 with the founding of *National Review* magazine, edited by the charismatic young William F. Buckley Jr.

5

The Birth of a Movement

If you ask 10 conservatives today to name their favorite journalist, their favorite author, their favorite intellectual, and their favorite TV talk show combatant, you'd probably get close to 10 different answers in each category—there are so many to choose from. If you had asked the same questions of conservatives in the era from 1955 to 1960, one name would have dominated all those categories—William F. Buckley Jr.

Given the multitude of prominent conservative spokesmen available today, it is sometimes difficult to explain to younger conservatives the impact of "WFB Jr." and his magazine, *National Review*, way back then. For those of us who experienced the late '50s and early '60s as the formative period of our youth, there are two explanations for WFB Jr.'s dominance.

First, there's the marketing explanation. In their epochal bestseller, *The 22 Immutable Laws of Marketing*, Al Ries and Jack Trout present as the #1 marketing law: "The Law of Leadership: It's better to be first than it is to be better." They give many examples, one of the most famous being the marketing contest between Coke and Pepsi. Blind taste test after taste test shows Pepsi winning out over Coke, yet Coke is the giant among giants in sales. Why? It was there first. The same principle applies to the political market.

Second, while "it's better to be first than it is to be better," if you can be first *and* better than your opposition you've got a grand slam. Bill Buckley did just that.

The key to the Buckley phenomenon of this period is that he was, first and foremost, *a debater*. The nascent movement had more profound intellectuals, but no one could verbally best the young Bill Buckley on the debate podium or printed page. He took no prisoners, and that sort of aggressive stance was exactly what was needed to jumpstart a new movement. Conservative kids were sick of being humiliated and branded as yahoos by their liberal professors. Older conservatives were just as sick of being marginalized in politics by the pundits of TV and the "respectable" print journals. In Bill Buckley they found someone who not only could make mincemeat of liberal totems, like Arthur Schlesinger Jr. and John Kenneth Galbraith, but who could do it with a theatrical flair and quick response not seen in political forums until our modern era of *The McLaughlin Group*, *Crossfire*, and other television talk shows.

The magazine Bill Buckley created, *National Review*, was similar in scope to and included many of the same contributors as *The Freeman*, but it was how the *National Review* was *different* that mattered in jumpstarting the conservative movement and helping the struggling young movement survive. "The new journal would be militantly *engagé*," wrote William A. Rusher, who became publisher in 1957, "dedicated to waging political war against the liberals, rather than merely restating conservative principles in some safely abstract form." Or, in the words of Lee Edwards, a historian of the conservative movement, "*National Review* was not a journal of opinion but a political act."

Also, Buckley controlled all of the voting stock. While *National Review* couldn't avoid the factional fighting that rocked *The Freeman*, by giving Buckley undivided control, *National Review*—unlike *The Freeman*—was able to survive the infighting.

Another way in which *National Review* was different from *The*

Freeman was in the overall emphasis of its contributors. *The Freeman* had an ideologically wide range of contributors, but their general thrust was undeniably libertarian. *National Review* had articles from libertarians, including Frank Chodorov, Karl Hess, and Murray Rothbard, but they were libertarian adornments. The power was with editors and contributors, many of them former communists and socialists, whose thrust was anti-communism with an interventionist bent. Whittaker Chambers and Frank Meyer formerly were communists of the orthodox sort; James Burnham and Willmoore Kendall were former Trotskyites. *National Review* sought to combine elements of traditional conservatism, libertarian market economics, and anti-communism, but anti-communism was dominant among these three thrusts.

No matter where you personally stand on the ideological panorama, an objective look at the political landscape of the era shows why this change in emphasis was crucial to the molding of the conservative movement in several ways.

First, anti-communism was the "glue" that held together the broadest array of prospective members of a new movement. In putting together our "recipe" for creating a new mass movement in Chapter 3, we gave priority to "issues that motivate"—and the communist threat was the foremost motivating issue of this era. The communist issue— more precisely, how to fight the threat of communism—divided and demoralized the libertarians, but it was the glue bringing conservatives together into a *movement.*

Second, most intellectuals and writers who were communists or socialists in their youth were *activist* intellectuals and writers, and that predisposition remained strong even after they changed sides. At *National Review* one editor, above all others, had the ear of owner/editor Buckley. He was James Burnham, formerly one of the world's leading Trotskyites and author of such seminal books as *The Struggle for the World, The Managerial Revolution,* and *The Machiavellians.* Intellectually he was in the league of George Orwell and Sidney Hook, and he was the commanding presence at *National Review* editorial meetings, enjoying the full confidence—if not *always* the agreement—of Buckley. With

Buckley as captain and Burnham at the intellectual helm, *National Review* saw itself, and acted, as the house organ of a movement to take over the nation and defeat communism.

This communist/socialist strategic and tactical mindset—encompassing the whole world, not just the nation, though now utilized for a different ideology, of course—also explains the emphasis on keeping the movement on the straight path to power, expelling "right" or "left" deviationists who were seen as obstacles to taking power. In the context of the new conservative movement, Objectivists—followers of the anti-religious Ayn Rand—were "left" deviationists, and in its early years *National Review* turned all its big guns on the Randians with a fury usually reserved for liberal targets. A couple of years later, it was the "right" deviationists of the John Birch Society who were accused of overly conspiratorial thinking and expelled from the movement by *National Review*. The purpose of these purges was to keep the new movement on the path to power, without giving liberals handy targets for scaring the American people about a threat from the Right. They also served to keep the *National Review* type of anti-communist conservatives in firm control of the growing movement.

Down from the ivory tower, into the streets

We said at the end of Chapter 4 that *National Review* gave conservatives "a center of gravity, some focal point, that addressed them as members of a movement and taught them, in Lenin's words, what is to be done." This didn't happen all at once. When reviewing the first few years of *National Review,* we find very little emphasis on activism—the thrust was on getting the message straight. Having made some progress in that direction, *National Review* began to turn more and more attention to the *movement* as the 1960s approached.

In the beginning, the main coverage of activism came from the pen of Revilo Oliver. "Reflections on a Right-Wing Protest" (Sept. 29, 1956), for example, covered the National States' Rights Conference in Memphis, with Dean Clarence Manion as keynote speaker. Oliver describes the dominant elements there as Southern Dixiecrats, activists of the Constitution Party (formed in 1950), pro-segregationist members of the Citizens Councils, and "a chaos of impressive but shadowy names. The North evidently contains a bewildering number of small conservative or pseudo-conservative organizations."

In what was the first actual reference to a "conservative movement" we've been able to find in the pages of *National Review*, Oliver writes: "There were present at Memphis as observers at least three men of means who were prepared to make substantial contributions to a conservative movement that seemed likely to be politically effective. The report is that they left with their checkbooks unopened."

A short while later, activist stirrings took place on the Right that *did* earn the approval of *National Review* and became part of the "respectable" conservative movement. The 1960s were still a few months away when collegiate right-wingers offered a preview of the student activism to come. The first young conservative activist foray was the National Student Committee for the Loyalty Oath, formed by Douglas Caddy and your coauthor David Franke in 1959. Spreading the word of their committee through the pages of *Human Events, National Review,* and *The Individualist* (the publication of the Intercollegiate Society of Individualists), they compiled the names of hundreds of sympathetic college students on three-by-five index cards and successfully pressured Congress to keep the loyalty oath requirement for recipients of National Defense Education Act loans.

Their surprising success in uncovering conservative students soon led to the formation of Youth for Goldwater for Vice President, under the leadership of Robert Croll. This was in 1960, and the students were a major part of the demonstrations for Barry Goldwater at the GOP convention in Chicago. Growing ever larger and stronger, the young activists then founded Young Americans for Freedom (YAF) in September 1960 at the Buckley family estate in Sharon, Connecticut.

YAF would be the major conservative youth organization not affiliated with the Republican Party, and it would be active throughout the Sixties and Seventies. An overflowing YAF rally of more than 18,000 conservatives at Madison Square Garden in New York City, in March 1962, took the liberals completely by surprise. All this young conservative activity—much of it smack in the heart of Rockefeller country—had taken place below their radar, and now they could ignore it no more. Even the *New York Times* gave it play "above the fold"—at the top of the front page. Indeed, if you're looking for a birth date when the conservative movement emerged out of the womb and announced itself to the public, no other event would qualify better than YAF's Madison Square Garden rally.

Prelude to 1964

To backtrack a bit, by 1959 the young people were embarrassing the older Americans for freedom (or OAFs) by their activism, so the grown-ups decided to get organized, too. As with the younger conservatives, their attention was centered on Arizona's Senator Barry Goldwater.

In the period between 1955 and 1960, Goldwater emerged as the leading conservative spokesman pretty much by default—no other politician on the Right was willing to stick out his neck and attack the Eisenhower administration. Goldwater did, accusing the "modern" Republicans of "fiscal irresponsibility" equal to that of the Democrats. People on the Right were looking for a successor to Robert Taft, and they found one in Barry Goldwater.

Facing re-election in 1958, Goldwater succeeded in changing Arizona from a Democratic state to a Republican state (a harbinger of the GOP's Sunbelt strategy to come). His victory stood out against the general GOP carnage that year, which included the defeat of Senate Minority Leader Bill Knowland, who had decided to run for governor of California.

While not the best manipulator of words, Goldwater had other qualities, in addition to political courage, to endear him to the conservatives. He was handsome and personable, important considerations in the coming television age. He was an honest, no-nonsense Westerner in every good sense of the word, offering a full contrast to the regal patricians, like Nelson Rockefeller, who dominated the Republican Party on the East Coast. And coming from a half-Jewish heritage, Goldwater put a lie to the persistent liberal slanders about the Right being anti-Semitic.

As the 1960 GOP convention in Chicago approached, everyone agreed that Vice President Richard Nixon was the heir apparent to Eisenhower. The only question was, which way would he tilt when he took over: toward the party's conservative Taft wing or toward the liberal Rockefeller wing? That question was answered definitively in September when Nixon met secretly with Rockefeller at the New York governor's Fifth Avenue apartment. When word of that meeting of reconciliation leaked out, conservatives were furious. Activist Phyllis Schlafly wrote that this "forbode a turn toward the same 'liberal metooism' which had twice defeated Dewey." And Goldwater called the meeting "an American Munich" and a "surrender."

Rebellion was in the air, but the time was premature for a conservative takeover of the GOP—and the conservatives knew it. A compromise was reached that satisfied most in both Nixon and Goldwater camps. Goldwater's name was placed in nomination for president as a favorite son of the Arizona delegation. A rousing demonstration then took the Nixonites by surprise—hundreds of young conservatives had sneaked onto the convention floor, with the connivance of the Arizona and South Carolina delegations, where they shouted, tooted their horns, and waved their placards backing Goldwater. Then Goldwater took the stand, withdrew his candidacy in favor of Nixon, and issued his memorable challenge to his conservative backers:

> This country, and its majesty, is too great for any man, be he conservative or liberal, to stay home and not work just because he doesn't agree. Let's grow up, conservatives! We want to take this party back, and I think someday we can. Let's get to work!

This dramatic speech brought Goldwater to the attention of the American people over network television for the first time. His demeanor on the podium won the movement countless new recruits, and Goldwater's new book, *Conscience of a Conservative*, won still more recruits. It sold 100,000 copies in the hardcover edition published by Victor Publishing in Shepherdsville, Kentucky—not exactly a mainstream publisher—and has since sold more than 3,500,000 copies in both hardback and paperback. The conservative movement was now operating with a much higher profile than could have been foreseen even a year or two earlier.

Conservatives "get to work"

Taking their cue from their leader, conservatives grudgingly worked to elect Nixon, only to be defeated by Kennedy's theft of the election in Illinois. Then they got to work to take over the GOP.

In that 1960 election year, Americans for Constitutional Action released its "ACA Index," the first scorecard rating members of Congress ever compiled by a conservative organization. Now conservatives had a precise way of knowing which Republicans to support or oppose, based on their voting record, and they used these ratings to help change the face of the GOP.

Outside of the *National Review* orbit, Robert Welch had formed the John Birch Society in 1958. In the following few years it became arguably the largest grass-roots organization in the conservative movement, with some 60,000 active members in hundreds of chapters and operating dozens of bookstores. The society was strongest in California and Texas, two states that became increasingly critical to the fortunes of the new conservative movement.

By the beginning of the Sixties it was obvious that a new movement—conscious of itself as a movement—had indeed emerged. Barry Goldwater was its political spokesman, *National Review* and *Human Events* were its principal organs, and the first major goal had been set: to take control of the Republican Party. Extending *National Review*'s orbit of influence, L. Brent Bozell, Buckley's Yale roommate and brother-in-law and a *National Review* editor, had been the ghostwriter for Barry Goldwater's phenomenally successful *Conscience of a Conservative*. Bill Rusher, *National Review*'s publisher, was a key player in all the politicking to turn the Young Republicans in a conservative direction and, later, to draft Goldwater in 1964. And in 1962, brothers-in-law Dan Mahoney and Kieran O'Doherty—friends of Buckley's and Rusher's—started the New York Conservative Party with *National Review*'s blessing, thereafter changing the dynamics and direction of politics in Rockefeller's back yard.

In Washington, meanwhile, *Human Events* had changed from a newsletter to a tabloid, and in response to *National Review*'s leadership role, *Human Events* itself became more activist. Its pages soon were filled with much broader coverage of conservative activism than you'd find in *National Review*, and in 1961 *Human Events* hosted its first of three conservative political action conferences in Washington, D.C. These were the forerunners to the Conservative Political Action Conferences (CPACs) held annually from 1973 to this day.

In less than a decade, conservative activists had come a long way— from a state of non-existence as a movement, to making a publicity breakthrough in Chicago in 1960, to filling Madison Square Garden in 1962, and creating a veritable grass-roots army of conservatives throughout the United States. But the fun was just beginning.

Addendum: Why was there no *libertarian* movement?

We must always guard against the temptation to view past history as preordained. Most of us don't really believe that—we believe in free will—but the assumption that what happened did so because it had to happen always creeps into our view of the past simply because we know the outcome of what *did* happen.

Before continuing with our story of how the conservative movement came to power, therefore, it may be fruitful to return to 1955 and ask why a *libertarian*, instead of conservative, movement didn't seize the moment. In the process we may uncover some movement-building lessons that transcend this particular example.

In Chapter 3, "The Recipe for Creating a New Mass Movement," we talked about the ever-increasing competition for your attention among *potential* mass movements. Returning to the year 1955, we can find as many seeds for a libertarian or "Old Right" movement as for a conservative movement. Why then, did the conservative seeds result in a robust garden while the libertarian seeds brought forth just a few bushes? Let us offer a few suggestions for your consideration.

Something "new" is almost always more appealing than something "old." Granted there's nothing truly new in the world. We're talking here about marketing, or packaging. Something packaged as "old" invariably has a track record, which invariably includes a record of failures. Something packaged as "new" is unhampered by history and can promise to set everything right. There was a reason FDR promised "a *New* Deal" rather than "an Old Deal," and why John F. Kennedy called for "a *New* Frontier."

Of course, what we now call the "Old Right" was *then* called, simply, the "Right" or the "right wing." Still, the right-wing elements existing in 1955 were hampered by the fact that they had been around since before World War II—and had failed all that time to come to power. Before that, the America First movement—which had sought to keep the United States out of World War II—had *overwhelming* support among the American people, but was undone by the connivance of FDR to get us into war. None of this is to imply that there was anything wrong with the Old Right's positions—merely that in 1955 it needed to reinvent itself to get rid of this baggage. But, thinking in terms of packaging or marketing was anathema to the Old Right.

It is ironic that *conservatives* pulled off this packaging feat, since, after all, "conservatism" by definition is the preservation of what is good from the past. Conservatives succeeded in part because the word "conservative" had long been out of political circulation, and thus could be packaged as something new; and in part because—being something "new"—they could offer solutions without historical baggage of failure.

Conservatives brought together, as the core of their appeal, two of the strongest motivators in America—religion and patriotism. These two motivators were joined against the threat of communism. In this regard, one of the great political accomplishments of the new conservative movement was its use of the communist threat to bring masses of Catholic voters into the Republican fold, and away from their ancestral immigrant home with the Democrats. The election of our first Catholic president, John F. Kennedy, slowed but could not stop this process.

As we've noted, there is no inherent conflict between libertarianism and religion, and in 1955 there were two fine publications combining those elements. Nevertheless, Ayn Rand and her Objectivists were the loudest and shrillest libertarian voices in the 1955–1964 period, and they were vehemently anti-religious. After the American Revolution, most Americans scorned Tom Paine for his skeptical views on religion in _The Age of Reason,_ even though he was probably the man most responsible for the American Revolution. George Washington stayed loyal to the patriot who had done so much for his country, but literally asked him to enter his house by the back door. Clearly, religious skepticism is not a path to power in America.

In addition, America, in 1955, was wracked by doubts and fears on the communist issue. Too many domestic spy rings had been uncovered; too many bloody communist advances had changed the face of the world. The libertarians and Old Rightists never put together a comprehensive _policy_ program for action on this, the gut issue of the day; the conservatives at _National Review_ did. More generally, libertarians always have a problem with "waving the flag" politically, knowing full well the record of our own government in suppressing freedoms under the guise of patriotism; many conservatives had, and have, no such hesitation.

Libertarians were more at home in academic pursuits; conservatives were more at home in political activism. And as we've noted before, both groups were enormously successful—in their own areas of expertise. The conservatives quickly learned how to develop programs that were practical and easily understood by the masses. Libertarians were far more theoretical in their approach to political problems, which meant they had less mass appeal. It took several decades before a libertarian *policy* group, the Cato Institute, was formed to bridge the gap between politics and libertarian academia.

Conservatives mastered the art of compromise; libertarians have a real problem with *any* compromise, which is one reason they fare better as academics than as politicians.

Conservatives also mastered the art of discipline—of being able to purge elements from the movement that might hinder it, yet continuing to forge ahead. Those libertarians who *were* politically motivated could teach the conservatives a thing or two about brutal purges and factional fights, but they never figured out how to bring Humpty Dumpty back together again and continue advancing.

Libertarians had no charismatic leader comparable to the conservatives' William F. Buckley Jr. Ayn Rand had broad charismatic power—in print. In person, she had more of a cult appeal—thankfully not the stuff of which mass movements are made, at least in America. Murray Rothbard had an engaging personality—especially in person—as well as a brilliant mind and nimble wit. That said, he lacked the organizational ability to lead a movement; he was (like other libertarians) better at purging than at coalition building; and he lacked the visual and rhetorical appeal of Bill Buckley in what was fast becoming the age of television.

Among politicians, Robert A. Taft had been the gold standard in terms of appealing both to conservatives and to libertarians. Barry Goldwater called himself a conservative and won the hearts of virtually every conservative in America. With his individualism and frankness, he also appealed to a good many libertarians, especially the less doctrinaire ones. The libertarians could point to a few libertarian-leaning congressmen in this period, but they had no one with the broad appeal of a Goldwater.

While money initially was scarce in both camps, the conservatives quickly outperformed the libertarians in learning how to raise the cash necessary for creating a movement. In these early years, all operations—conservative and libertarian—started out as bootstrap operations, but

National Review always managed to find enough money to survive and grow. Some of the funds came from Bill Buckley himself and other Buckley family members, though the family contributions were undoubtedly far less than the public imagined. While most often compared to the Kennedys, the Buckley family was not nearly as well off as the Kennedys. A good amount of *National Review*'s funding certainly came from WFB Jr.'s annual fund appeals to subscribers, which began in 1958. This was a smart marketing move, as one major lesson in fundraising is to return repeatedly to the people who have already contributed to your cause.

Interestingly enough, though, Buckley said on the PBS program *Talking with David Frost* (June 28, 1996), that *National Review* "lost 19 million dollars" in its early years, adding: "In constant dollars it comes to about 45 or 46 million." If all that red ink was covered by Buckley's annual fund appeals, he missed his calling, for he could have been one of the nation's most successful fundraisers. Whatever the sources of *National Review*'s early funding, it was far greater than that enjoyed by any libertarian enterprise.

In considering why conservatism succeeded as a mass movement, while libertarianism didn't, it is important to remember that all of these elements worked in synergy with each other. Early funding can give one side a head start against the other, but without leadership and broad public appeal the funding will be wasted. And by 1960, the contest was over—it was obvious the new movement would be conservative rather than libertarian.

6

1964
This Is What Happens
When the Other Side
Controls the Mass Media

Warning: This chapter contains excerpts from liberal media that may be offensive to people with a brain.

By the numbers, 1964 was an unmitigated disaster for conservatives. After defeating Nelson Rockefeller at the GOP convention in San Francisco, Barry Goldwater suffered a humiliating defeat himself at the hands of President Lyndon B. Johnson. He got only 27,176,799 votes, or 39 percent of the total. LBJ got 43,126,506 votes—a commanding 61 percent. Goldwater carried only six states—his home state of Arizona and the southern states of Alabama, Georgia, Louisiana, Mississippi, and South Carolina, giving him a pittance of 52 electoral votes.

Furthermore, as Lee Edwards notes, "Johnson's victory was overwhelming in every region (except the Deep South) and every voting bloc (except among Republicans, and even 20 percent of them defected to

LBJ). Republicans lost two seats in the Senate, 37 in the House of Representatives, and 541 in the state legislatures. They added one governor. Of the 54 Republican congressmen who had endorsed Goldwater before the convention and then had run for reelection, 20 were defeated."

Yes, indeed—by the numbers, 1964 was an unmitigated disaster for conservatives.

Yet, as hindsight shows us, the conservative movement not only survived 1964 but went on to establish increasing control over the Republican Party as well as periodic control of Congress and the White House. How could *that* happen?

As Paul Harvey would say, here's the rest of the story.

The "unbiased" and "objective" liberal media

At the beginning, the approach of the establishment media toward the first conservative efforts was to ignore them. When the "rumble on the Right" became too loud to ignore, the tactic was to smear it. Some attacks were pretty bland by the standards of political vitriol—"America needs responsible conservatives, but these guys aren't responsible *or* conservative." The others were increasingly nasty—attaching labels to conservatives ranging from "crackpot" and "ultra-" (*always* "ultra-") "right" to the Big Berthas in the liberal arsenal: "fascist" and "Nazi."

Again, a little historical perspective is in order for today's younger readers. The era we're talking about—1955 to 1964—was obviously much closer to World War II than we are today. And Americans were still assimilating the full extent of Nazi atrocities against the Jews, which FDR had kept hidden during the war. In this environment, to call someone a "Nazi" or a "fascist" was the ultimate exile from respectable and permissible society. And it didn't help American conservatives that the Nazis and fascists in Europe were commonly labeled "the Right" (even though they were national *socialists*, truly placing them on the Left). Sloppy or devious minds would draw up a conspiracy chart for you if you were too dimwitted to make the connection yourself: Nazis in Europe = the "Right." Conservatives in America = the "Right." *Ergo*, "conservatives" = "Nazis."

It didn't matter that the conservative movement was headed by persons representing the two ethnic groups most hated by real American Nazis—Barry Goldwater (half-Jewish in his heritage) and William F. Buckley Jr. (a Catholic). It didn't matter that other Jews played a prominent role in the founding of the conservative movement, people such as the movement's first public relations genius, Marvin Liebman, and the first chairman of Young Americans for Freedom, Robert Schuchman. Heck, it didn't matter that even the head of the most vilified group, Robert Welch of the John Birch Society, was not only against the anti-Semites but against segregation and that he purged the society of both anti-Semites and racists. What was important to the establishment and liberal/leftist press was to let the mud fly, hoping that enough would stick to tarnish and abort the conservative competition to liberalism's hegemony in American politics.

In a nation as large and diverse and free as the United States, you *will* find, of course, a few real Nazis and fascists (though it's a question how many of them are really FBI spies and informants). The liberal media's attack against the burgeoning conservative movement, then, took three forms: (1) Simply *labeling* conservatives as Nazis or fascists; (2) looking desperately for *some* nut who had attached himself to a specific event or organization and spotlighting that barnacle to besmirch the whole group or event; and (3) ignoring mainstream conservatives in favor of spotlighting the most extreme groups, and then leading the reader or viewer to make the desired association between conservatives and extremists.

Bill Buckley himself was one of the first of the new conservatives to find themselves the target of such smears. With the publication of his first book, *God and Man at Yale*, Buckley was accused as follows: " . . . the methods he proposes for his alma mater are precisely those employed in Italy, Germany, and Russia" (*The New Republic*); "[Buckley is] stating the fascist alternative to liberalism. . . . What more could Hitler, Mussolini, or Stalin ask for?" (*Yale Daily News*); and this from the august *Saturday Review of Literature:* "The book is one which has the glow and appeal of a fiery cross on a hillside at night. There will undoubtedly be robed figures who gather to it, but the hoods will not be academic. They will cover the face."

In the coming years, virtually all of us in the conservative movement would find ourselves the targets of such smears, and without mass media outlets of our own, we were virtually defenseless against the charges—our protests simply were ignored. For example, CBS's Mike Wallace asked conservative radio commentator Fulton Lewis Jr. to explain "the attraction the far Right has for crackpot fascist groups in America." "Thunder against the Right," in the November 24, 1961, issue of *Time*, featured attacks by President Kennedy, Attorney General Robert Kennedy, the Department of Social Action of the National Catholic Welfare Conference, and the Union of American Hebrew Congregations (mixing politics and religion was okay when practiced by the Left). The *New York Times Magazine* chimed in with "Report on the 'Rampageous Right,'" or those who have "a deep distrust of democratic institutions and of the democratic process—a distrust, in short, of the people" and who "subscribe wholeheartedly to the conspiratorial, or devil, theory of history." (Unfortunately M. Stanton Evans has never got around to writing one of the books he wanted to write: *The History Theory of Conspiracy*.) *Newsweek* got into the act with "Thunder on the Right: The Conservatives, the Radicals, the Fanatic Fringe," and *Time* returned to the attack with "The Ultras."

Uh, do you see a theme here?

In *The Rise of the Right*, long-time *National Review* publisher Bill Rusher showed the extent to which the liberal media had pursued the smear by analyzing the biennial indexes of the *Readers' Guide to Periodical Literature*. This publication indexed, by topic, all articles appearing in 125 of the nation's leading publications. From March 1, 1957, to February 28, 1959, the listing of articles on conservatism consumed just 1 3/4 inches. From March 1, 1959, to February 28, 1961: 4 inches. From March 1, 1961, to February 28, 1963: 14 1/2 inches of almost entirely hostile articles (not including the 3 1/2 inches listing articles in *National Review* itself, which had become the first conservative periodical to be indexed).

As we said, the procedure was to ignore conservatism as long as possible—then to smear it when the critter refused to die.

The Kennedy assassination:
A new opportunity to smear the Right

Virtually every conservative active in 1963 can remember exactly where he or she was when President John F. Kennedy was assassinated in Dallas—and not only because of the trauma of the assassination itself, which conservatives shared with other Americans, but because of the way blame for the killing was placed on conservatives or "the Right." Most of us got angry calls and insults, the mildest being some variant of "I hope you're happy—you got what you wanted!" The offices of the National Draft Goldwater Committee in Washington, D.C., were closed—the doors locked, lights shut off—because of death threats over the telephone and mobs banging on the door.

By now, Americans were so conditioned by years of "radicals on the Right" propaganda that even some conservatives initially assumed the assassin must have been a right-wing nut. After all, as the Voice of America (your taxpayer dollars at work) would tell the world in its bulletin announcing the shooting, Dallas was "the center of the extreme right wing." Walter Cronkite—"America's most trusted newsman"—would tell television viewers that Barry Goldwater's response to the assassination, at a political event, was a curt "no comment." (The truth was that Goldwater was in Muncie, Indiana, at his mother-in-law's funeral, and he had not yet been interviewed about the assassination when Cronkite made his report.)

The revelation that the assassin was a pro-*communist* nut and a former defector to the Soviet Union was not much hindrance to the liberal and leftist smearmongers. The association between the assassination and conservatives had already been made, so it was only necessary to shift the blame a bit. Bishop James A. Pike would explain that right-wingers "have consistently supplied the fuel which would fire up such an assassin." (Imagine that: Conservatives caused a pro-communist nut to shoot Kennedy!) Senate Intelligence Committee hearings, led by Democratic Senator Frank Church, would blame "a conspiratorial atmosphere of violence." (You can connect the dots.)

As a result of the Kennedy assassination, the Goldwater campaign of 1964 almost didn't take place. Goldwater and Kennedy, at opposite ends of the political spectrum in the Senate, nevertheless were personal friends, and they respected each other. Goldwater was looking forward to a race on the issues. The conservative leader had no such respect for Lyndon Johnson—suddenly the new sitting president. He expected nothing but mud from LBJ (and LBJ wouldn't disappoint him).

In terms of practical politics, too, the assassination meant that a Goldwater campaign—indeed, almost *any* Republican campaign—was doomed from the start. Wounded by the assassination, Americans were unlikely to change the occupant of the White House so quickly. Also, Johnson was not perceived by the public to be a liberal, while Kennedy was, and Johnson was from the South himself—Goldwater's political stronghold.

Here we must note how a traumatic event such as an assassination can change our perception of the victim. Post-assassination, Kennedy became a virtual saint in the sentimental memories of Americans, and most everyone now assumes that Goldwater *never* had a chance to defeat such a "popular" president. Not so in 1963. The very vulnerability of Kennedy, a not-that-popular president before the assassination, helped fire the Goldwater candidacy with many GOP fence-sitters. Just look at what *Time* magazine—as we've seen, no friend of conservatives—had to say on October 4, 1963, just weeks before the assassination:

> Until recently most political observers figured that Democrat John Kennedy was a sure 1964 winner, and that it did not make much difference who the GOP candidate would be. Now, many are changing their minds. . . . A state-by-state survey by *Time* correspondents indicates that at least Republican Barry Goldwater could give Kennedy a breathlessly close contest.

America would never be given the opportunity for a clear, straight-forward contest between a liberal and a conservative. At least not in 1964. Goldwater himself was so saddened by the assassination—and re-alistic about what it meant for his chances—that he was determined to drop out of the race. Fortunately for the movement, friends convinced Goldwater he couldn't let down the thousands of conservatives who had pinned their hopes on him.

The campaign: Mudstorms, as predicted

The Goldwater campaign was not the best performance in history. The candidate himself was all too capable of putting his foot in his mouth without any assistance from liberals, and he too often made it apparent just how unhappy he was to be waging this campaign. And the "Ari-zona Mafia" that ran his campaign was inept. Period.

As this chapter is not a history of the Goldwater campaign, we'll offer just one small example of the ineptitude of the campaign. Three exciting conservative books—Phyllis Schlafly's *A Choice Not an Echo*, John Stormer's *None Dare Call It Treason*, and J. Evetts Haley's *A Texan Looks at Lyndon*—sold millions of copies, mobilizing grass-roots support for Goldwater. Contrast that with the official (and boring) campaign book, *Where I Stand*, which wasn't shipped to bookstores until late Sep-tember, and even then sold only 5,000 copies. The three entrepreneurs were self-published and they promoted their own books; the Arizona Mafia had opted for the traditional New York publisher approach. More on this later.

Having noted the deficiencies of the campaigner and the campaign headquarters, we must add that their performance did not make much of a difference anyway. From beginning to end, most Americans saw the campaign through the lens provided by the mass media—which is to say, the liberal establishment media—and there was no way they were going to elect a "fanatic" to the presidency. That's the way it is when your opposition controls the mass media and you have no alter-native media capable of reaching the masses.

National Review kept track of what it sarcastically termed "Voices of Moderation." When Goldwater was nominated, columnist Drew Pearson reported that "the smell of fascism is in the air at this convention." California's Democratic governor, Edmund "Pat" Brown, agreed: "All we needed to hear was 'Heil Hitler.'" Baseball star Jackie Robinson: "I believe I know how it felt to be a Jew in Hitler's Germany." *New York Times* columnist C. L. Sulzberger: "[if Goldwater is elected] there may not be a day after tomorrow." And Democratic Senator William Fulbright on the Senate floor called Goldwaterism "the closest thing in American politics to an equivalent of Russian Stalinism"—thus earning, once again, the sobriquet "Senator Halfbright."

The Rockefeller-Republican *New York Herald-Tribune* was only slightly less hysterical: "The Republican Party now does face a clear and present threat from the Know-Nothings and purveyors of hate and the apostles of bigotry." And the Anti-Defamation League of B'nai B'rith showed how to defame a movement with an entire book devoted to the *Danger on the Right*.

Basically the only players with fewer scruples than the media were LBJ himself and his chief hatchet-man, Bill Moyers. Rick Perlstein reported in his book, *Before the Storm*, that "Moyers was instrumental in pioneering an innovation in presidential campaigning: the full-time espionage, sabotage, and mudslinging unit. . . . The group met in a conference room directly above the Oval Office, because Johnson wanted to monitor their work closely. This project was his favorite." One of the team members, incidentally, was the CIA liaison to the White House (again, your tax dollars at work). Perlstein says the team also "retained the CIA's domestic covert-actions chief, E. Howard Hunt [later of Watergate fame], to place spies in the Republican National Committee (they delivered daily reports to a dummy office in the National Press Building called 'Continental Press')."

All these nice, moderate, respectable liberals—Pat Moynihan, Bill Moyers, the CIA operatives—reached the pinnacle (or, rather, gutter) of success with their ad campaign against Goldwater. Starting a grand Democratic tradition, one ad showed two hands taking a Social Security card from a wallet and tearing it in two. But the worst were the ones, especially the infamous "Daisy" commercial, depicting Goldwater as a Doctor Strangelove who would blow up the world in a nuclear holocaust. Moyers would later brag that they had "hung the nuclear noose around Goldwater and finished him off."

Conservatives tough it out—and build, build, build

How did conservatives survive in this climate of hate toward us? Quite simply, by toughing it out and never giving up. It was demoralizing to realize all our efforts had little chance of success, but we seemed to sense that something larger was at stake than one year's election, no matter how important that election was. Besides, we lived the Goldwater slogan, "In your heart you know he's right." The more we were attacked as fascists, the harder we worked.

And the results—well, sometimes the most obvious results are not the most enduring ones. We started off this chapter with the obvious results: the numbers depicting the extent of the Goldwater GOP's defeat. Now it's time to look at the more enduring results of the campaign.

First, the Goldwater campaign was the first mass campaign in modern American history in terms of the number of people involved. An estimated four million men and women took an *active* part in the campaign, contacting many millions more. Couch conservatives became missionaries. LBJ had only half as many workers, even though the Democratic voter pool was 50 percent larger.

This Goldwater mobilization paid dividends far into the future: Thousands of those precinct-level workers became the officials and strategists of the movement in years to come. Even today, if you ask a conservative of a certain age when he or she became active in politics, the answer is likely to be, "In the Goldwater campaign." Nearly 40 years after the Goldwater campaign, the novelist Joan Didion—no longer thought of as a conservative—can still proclaim: "I voted, ardently, for Barry Goldwater. Had Goldwater remained the same age and continued running, I would have voted for him in every election thereafter." Such was the attraction of the man.

Second, this populist reach was even more apparent in fundraising. The Goldwater campaign was the first popularly financed campaign in modern American history. The 1960 campaign, with between 40,000 and 50,000 individual contributors to Nixon and some 22,000 to Kennedy, was typical of the approach from previous years. Estimates of the number of contributors to Goldwater in 1964—combining federal, state, and local campaign groups—range from 650,000 to over a million. As you'd surmise from such an explosion in the number of contributors, individual and smaller contributors became hugely important. Only 28 percent of the Goldwater federal campaign contributions were for $500 or more, compared to 69 percent of the Democratic contributions.

Third, a new political star was born. When things were their bleakest, near the end of the campaign, Ronald Reagan's 30-minute narrative, "A Time for Choosing," was broadcast nationwide on television— over the protests, by the way, of the Arizona Mafia—and galvanized all who watched it. Reagan was eloquent, on target, and stirring. Even journalists David Broder and Steve Hess had to admit it was "the most successful national political debut since William Jennings Bryan electrified the 1896 Democratic Convention with the 'Cross of Gold' speech."

Constant rebroadcasts during the final week of the campaign raised millions of dollars. Thereafter Reagan was pretty universally regarded as the most effective spokesman for the conservative cause, and Henry Salvatori revealed that he and other conservative businessmen approached Reagan to run for governor of California largely as a result of "A Time for Choosing."

There were other enduring accomplishments from the campaign, as well. As summarized by *Human Events*: "The Republican Party is essentially conservative; the South is developing into a major pivot of its power; and a candidate who possesses Goldwater's virtues but lacks some of his handicaps, can win the presidency."

The grass-roots nature of the Goldwater campaign changed the face of American politics. The Democrats would continue to rely on labor unions as their chief source of financial support and manpower. Liberal Republicans would remain dependent on fat cats for financing and paid party workers for logistical support. But after Goldwater there would be lists, lists, and more lists of conservative contributors and workers, and the utilization of those lists would propel conservative Republicans to power, as we shall see in Chapter 7.

7

Conservatives Test a New Secret Weapon

For those of us who are old enough to have lived through it, the months following the defeat of Barry Goldwater were the Dark Ages for conservatives—far worse than, say, after Watergate in 1974 or after the Ford-Dole ticket lost in 1976. Watergate was not about family—conservatives had supported Nixon because of who his opponents were, but he was not one of us. Goldwater was family. And his defeat was intensely personal.

In retrospect, of course, we were not as bad off as we imagined while licking our wounds. To begin with the obvious, we had uncovered a hard-core base of 27 million who would vote for a conservative in America. Perhaps the only advantage of running a fervently conservative and also often inept campaign was that it demonstrated that the worst-case scenario for conservatives could still produce 27 million votes. And that meant conservatism didn't have to be consigned to third-party status. With better packaging and delivery, conservatism had a chance in mainstream America.

Another benefit for conservatives was that the Goldwater campaign stripped us of any delusions that we could get a fair shake from

the establishment's mass media. We didn't waste time, therefore, trying to convince the media that we were really good guys; instead we
concentrated on guerrilla warfare—on ways to get around the establishment's mass media.

We already had the answer—direct mail—though it wasn't that
obvious at first. Even in the 1960s, direct mail was an established industry in America and offered businesses a way to sell directly to
consumers. Sears, Roebuck and Co. had become a corporate giant
and trendsetter by putting its catalog into mailboxes all across America.
Reader's Digest had become the world's largest magazine and print
publishing empire by utilizing direct mail advertising. What remained
to be done was to apply those same techniques to politics in a systematic way.

Think of a political movement as a stream that is trying to become
an ever-larger river. Then think about the importance of tributaries and
water volume. The more tributaries and the more volume, the bigger
the river becomes. In a political movement, those tributaries are organizations, campaigns, and issues people will fight over; and, in our instance, direct mail was the rain that fed those tributaries, causing them
to grow individually. Put those tributaries together, and they soon
create a swelling river. In the years between 1964 and 1980, direct
mail was the rainfall that filled ever-more-substantial tributaries—
organizations, campaigns, issues—that in turn, by 1980, had created the
Mississippi River of American politics: conservatism.

Let us be clear that even before 1964 direct mail *had* been used in
politics. It was used sporadically, though, on an ad hoc basis, not sys-
tematically to build a movement. The classic examples are from Senator Robert A. Taft's campaign for reelection in 1950 and General
Dwight D. Eisenhower's presidential campaign in 1952. Both stories
are relayed in *The Solid Gold Mailbox*, written by Walter H. Weintz, the
direct mail guru for *Reader's Digest*.

Taft was the leader of the conservative wing of the Republican
Party, and in 1950 the labor union bosses were pouring money into
Ohio in an attempt to defeat his reelection bid. His chief sin was that he

was the coauthor of the Taft-Hartley Act, which curtailed the power of the union bosses to shut down the nation's industries if they didn't get what they wanted. Unions were the most powerful political force in America at this time, and this was a "do or die" campaign for the bosses.

"Senator Taft was convinced that he should take his stand on the Taft-Hartley Law," says Weintz, "and, of course, we tried to talk him out of that, because we knew that blue collar workers would be against him on the basis of the Taft-Hartley Act." Since the senator was adamant about taking a principled stand, his advisors retreated to the follow-up barricade: "Let's test it." One of the great advantages of direct mail is that it allows you to test what you "know" to be true. Different letters were mailed to Ohio constituents about why they should support Senator Taft, and asking for contributions. Each letter had a "key code" to measure responses. Here is what happened, as Weintz tells us in his informative book:

> We sent out about 20,000 copies of each letter. I was astounded when the letter (written by Senator Taft), which was built around a positive presentation of the Taft-Hartley Act, was far and away the most successful.
>
> We subsequently mailed hundreds of thousands of Taft-Hartley letters into the blue collar worker sections of the industrial cities of Ohio: Cincinnati, Cleveland, Akron, and so on. The blue collar workers responded by voting overwhelmingly for Taft against the urging, advice, and $3 million campaign fund of the union leaders.
>
> In addition, much to our surprise, we received a substantial number of small contributions, which helped us to finance the direct mail campaign. Indeed, the campaign paid for itself!

As far as we can tell, this is the first documented case in American political history in which direct mail was used to bypass the establishment (in this instance the union bosses) and go directly to constituents (the union workers themselves), producing a victory based on conservative principles.

In the 1952 presidential campaign, Eisenhower had defeated Taft for the GOP nomination, but his campaign was stalled for lack of a clear-cut political theme. Again, the candidate's advisors were certain, as Weintz puts it, "that campaigns are won by not taking a stand on anything." They opted for the "it's time for a change" theme. Others thought that letters denouncing Democrat corruption or detailing pocketbook issues would do best. *Reader's Digest* again loaned Weintz's services to the Republican Party, and Weintz tested the issues by writing 10 letters on different campaign themes and initially sending out 10,000 copies of each of the 10 letters.

To the surprise of virtually everyone, including Weintz, the clear winner was the letter on foreign policy, touting the headline, "WILL YOU VOTE TO CONTINUE CODDLING THE RUSSIANS?" and promising to produce results in the seemingly never-ending war in Korea. It pulled about two and a half times better than any of the other letters.

Weintz tells what happened next:

> It was a striking, clear-cut proof that the war in Korea outweighed every other political appeal Eisenhower could make.
>
> The results were so conclusive that we put together a report . . . and showed [Eisenhower] these results. A few days later, Eisenhower made his famous "I shall go to Korea" speech, and suddenly his campaign was off and running.

Using the Korea theme, Weintz got 300,000 small contributions for the Republican Party. The direct mail campaign not only paid for itself but also brought in additional funds to be used elsewhere.

This sort of broad-based political support was revolutionary, considering that up to this time most presidential campaigns—in both major parties—were financed by a relative handful of fat-cat supporters. In effect, the Republicans had discovered a secret weapon—direct mail—but failed to use it in a systematic, sustained way because the party under Eisenhower and Nixon was oriented toward the establishment, not toward a grass-roots base. It would take the Democrats even longer to appreciate the potential of direct mail in politics. Conservatives would be the ones to take the letter and run with it.

As we wrote in Chapter 3, "The Recipe for Creating a New Mass Movement," Martin Luther's "secret weapon"—the printing press— "wasn't *literally* a secret weapon, of course. . . . It had the *impact* of a secret weapon, though, because Luther understood the potential of this new technology and he had the will to use it, unlike his opposition in the Catholic Church."

So, too, with this modern secret weapon of direct mail. Neither the Republicans nor the Democrats, *being* the establishment, understood its true potential or had the will to use it. The conservatives did. They had no choice but to adopt a populist bent, since establishment venues were closed to them.

Conservatives use their secret weapon to create a revolution

NOTE: Richard Viguerie, coauthor of this book, first comprehended the true political potential of direct mail and used it to create the conservative mass movement. The rest of this chapter is presented in the first person, allowing Richard to tell his story directly.

In 1960 I was a young clerk with an oil company in Houston, Texas, fresh out of college and in the Army Reserve. I spent many of my after-work hours in Republican politics. There weren't many Republicans in Texas at that time, and promotions could come fast if you were willing to work hard at thankless tasks. I became chairman of the Harris County (Houston) Young Republicans, then Harris County campaign chairman for John Tower in his quixotic campaign for the Senate against Lyndon B. Johnson, who owned Texas politically at that time. LBJ was running for two offices at the same time—for reelection to the Senate and for vice president with John F. Kennedy. As part of my campaign work, I wrote a fundraising letter for Tower—a one-pager that did well. Little did I know that this would become my life's work!

I was hooked on politics, and wanted eventually to make a bigger mark somewhere, probably in Washington, D.C. My opportunity came in the summer of 1961, but in the street canyons of New York City—a far cry from the Texas prairies to which I was accustomed.

National Review, located in New York City, carried a classified ad searching for four fieldmen for an unnamed national conservative organization. I had become friends with a fellow Houstonian, my present coauthor, David Franke, who was then on the editorial staff of *National Review.* He was also *National Review*'s unofficial emissary to the conservative youth movement, just as the magazine's publisher, Bill Rusher, was its emissary to the adult conservative movement. I flew to New York for an interview with Rusher. With Rusher's and Franke's recommendations, I was offered the job.

As it turned out, there was really only one position—account manager for Marvin Liebman, the young movement's public relations and fundraising specialist. Marvin had been instrumental in creating and funding organizations such as the Committee of One Million, Young Americans for Freedom (YAF), and the World Youth Crusade for Freedom. I hit it off with Marvin, and became his account executive for the YAF account.

Not direct mail, but it worked

I was surprised to learn after arriving on the job that YAF, not one year old, was $20,000 in debt with only a couple of weeks' operating money on hand. Having just received my big break in life, I wasn't about to have it disappear on me. I was determined that YAF would succeed.

Marvin used several methods of raising money for his clients. One was to call wealthy conservatives such as Charles Edison, youngest son of the inventor and former governor of New Jersey; Captain Eddie Rickenbacker of World War II fame; and industrialist J. Howard Pew. Another way was to throw dinners with distinguished speakers, charging a fee substantial enough to bring a profit. A third method was print ads in the *New York Times* and other New York publications. These ads solicited support for his client's cause, and contained a coupon. Readers who supported the cause would clip out the coupon and mail it in with their checks. This approach wasn't as efficient as direct mail later would be, but in the hands of a creative promoter like Marvin Liebman it worked.

I remember my first meeting with Marvin, following my interview with Bill Rusher. We talked for an hour or so in his office, where he showed me a stack of files measuring something like three feet by three feet. These small file cabinets were filled with three-by-five index cards, each providing the name and address of a donor to one or more of his causes. The donors may have given $50, $100, $500, or $1,000— once or several times. All you had to do was ask, and these people would give money! I was like the young duckling that had never seen water, but knew what to do with it once he saw it.

At that time, neither Marvin nor anyone else in the conservative movement did what we now call acquisition mailings—using the mail to acquire new donors. The opportunity was there, because postage at that time was so incredibly cheap, but political people just didn't know how to do it. It wasn't on their radar screens. Marvin dealt with relatively upscale donors, and his system worked, so he didn't feel the need to explore other avenues. Also, to tell the truth, most of us never believed we could be a truly *mass* movement, with the need for mass support; we were comfortable in our ideological niche. As is so often the case, our biggest constraint was in our own heads.

Well, it didn't take me long to discover that I really didn't like calling on people and asking them face to face for money. Asking over the telephone wasn't much better. I found that I had a knack for writing letters, though, so that's what I began to concentrate on, learning as I went and refining my letters as I learned what worked and what didn't work. Soon direct mail was almost my whole focus—for fundraising, subscriptions to YAF's magazine, *The New Guard*, YAF membership, everything.

At some point I left Marvin's employment to become executive secretary of Young Americans for Freedom and run the organization directly. Then YAF moved to Washington, D.C., and I moved my new
and growing family to the nation's capital. Later I asked YAF to hire
someone else as executive secretary and allow me to concentrate on
what I enjoyed doing, and did best—raising money.

In January 1965, during the darkest hour for the conservative
movement, while I had two small children at home, I left YAF's employ entirely to found my own company, with YAF as my sole client.
Then I lost my YAF account in the incessant internecine squabbling
that always plagues youth politics, and had to scramble for new clients.
Throughout it all, I never looked back, and I never lost faith in what I
saw as the future of politics. I was confident that direct mail could and
would become the Big Bertha of political fundraising.

I learn about branding, and my letter to
Ronald Reagan ends up in Ronnie Jr.'s toy box

As I've said, my interest in direct mail began when I was working for
Marvin Liebman, partly because of my shyness in asking people face to
face or phone to phone for money and partly because I saw the potential for direct mail and knew that's what I did best.

Plenty of young conservatives were boning up on conservative philosophy, and many others were studying the techniques of political organization. Nobody, as far as I could tell, was studying how to *sell*
conservatism to the American people. I knew I was never going to be a
conservative intellectual, so for a period of a few years I didn't read the
growing number of conservative books that were being published, and
I barely looked at *National Review* or *Human Events*. Time was too pre-
cious. I decided to spend every spare moment intensively studying
commercial direct mail, so I could apply those techniques to political
nonprofit groups. I would focus on becoming the best marketer I could
be. I read marketing books (and not only on direct mail), psychology

books, and studies of what causes a person to buy or not buy something. I'd pore over every page of *The Reporter of Direct Mail*.

I didn't have to play Lewis and Clark. Commercial direct mail had plenty of giants—people like Claude Hopkins, David Ogilvy, Leo Burnett, Dick Barton. In particular, I considered Ed Mayer and Dick Benson to be my mentors. You need to study the giants because we're not talking about normal, natural skills. You have to learn those skills. It's not normal to think that an eight-page letter is going to pull significantly better than a one-page letter. You have to learn what causes a person, who's moving rapidly in one direction, to stop, sit down, read your copy, take out a checkbook, write a $25 check, put it in the mail, and then keep on going. That takes skills that don't come naturally to you.

And I learned on the job what worked and what didn't work. One of the first things I learned with Young Americans for Freedom, for example, was: *stick to your brand* (to use commercial terminology). I tested two letters against each other, to see which type pulled better. One letter talked about the work that YAF was doing on college campuses; the other (we were getting close to 1964) talked about how YAF was going to help nominate and elect Goldwater, "if only you send us a check." (There were no rules or regulations at that time prohibiting nonprofit organizations from direct campaign work.)

I was able to figure that one out real quick. The help-us-elect-Goldwater letters did very poorly. We were a bunch of teenagers and twenty-something-year-old kids, after all, and the older conservatives with money couldn't be convinced that we had the electoral expertise to make a difference. Besides, there were plenty of other groups that were working the Goldwater pitch, and could do so more convincingly.

On the other hand, we *were* able to convince older conservatives to help our work on the campuses. We were fighting the radical SDS, the liberals, and the communists on college campuses, and *that* was something older conservatives perceived we could do better than anyone else. The Republican campaign groups weren't going to do that. *That was our brand. That was our market.*

I had not understood branding, and the importance of the image your potential customers or donors have of you. But I never again made that mistake. I also learned through this experience that people with disposable money are older—usually 50 years of age or older—and they will go to great lengths to help young people. As long as you stay in your area of expertise, they will support you and respond.

I also learned the ins and outs of getting celebrity signers for your letters. People like Captain Eddie Rickenbacker and Charles Edison would sign our letters, as they had before for Marvin Liebman's other clients. But I also got Barry Goldwater to sign appeals for us, which was great the closer we came to 1964.

The strangest and funniest turn of events came in 1962 when I asked this movie actor named Ronald Reagan to sign a letter for YAF. He was making speeches for General Electric and hosting "Death Valley Days" on TV back then, and this was long before his famous speech during the Goldwater campaign and before anybody thought of him as governor material, much less presidential material.

Anyway, I wrote Reagan a short letter, and attached a sample of the fundraising letter that I hoped he would sign. A week went by, and no response. Two weeks, then a month. I was very disappointed, because with his acting career Reagan was one of the highest profile conservatives I could get to sign a letter.

Eventually, I pretty much forgot about it. Then months later I was reading our "comment mail"—people's responses to you, whether of the "great work!" or "go jump in the lake!" variety. Some people would mark up your letter and say "this is a bunch of junk," and you'd throw it in the wastebasket. One letter seemed to be of that variety, marked up with crayon scribbling. I threw it away, but something made me take a second look. Something was different about this letter.

Then I realized this was the letter I had sent to Reagan. I looked at the bottom of the letter, beyond the crayon marks, and there was a handwritten note from our future president: "Dear Mr. Viguerie, I just found this letter in Ronnie Jr.'s toy box. I apologize! Of course you may use my name if you think that would be of any help."

Reagan's name pulled well, to no surprise, and we used his name for some years. But that relationship almost didn't get off the ground because of an attempted hijacking by four-year-old Ronnie Jr., who liked my letter so much that he used it for art practice and stored it in his toy box!

It all starts with your name (and address)

Of all the problems that I had in these first years as a direct mail fundraiser, number one was the lack of identified conservatives on mailing lists. Today I have, in my desk, a book-size file of several hundred conservative mailing lists. Back then we had only a handful of conservative mailing lists. And lists are the *lifeblood* of direct marketing.

Very few conservative political organizations had mailing lists to begin with, and those few who did weren't about to share them. The John Birch Society was probably the best-organized group on the Right at this time, but I suspect they kept their membership list in a guarded vault somewhere, probably deep underground—no way would Robert Welch make that list available! The other groups weren't much different.

You have to understand that nonprofits and political organizations had never heard of commercial direct mail at this point in history. They didn't even know it was out there. It was happening all around them, but they didn't see it. They were in the world, but not of it. It was like two separate worlds: the secular, or commercial, and the non-secular, the nonprofits. So the idea of renting your mailing list for a fee and paying a fee to rent other mailing lists—it was like talking in gibberish. Over the coming years I would play the role of a mad political dentist, pulling teeth one at a time as I worked to convince these organizations that list exchanges and rentals not only were not suicidal, but they were the way to create an ever-larger movement and enrich everyone's organizations.

I remember my first list rental agreement because it was such an innovative step for us in politics. *National Review* had the same problems I was having—a lack of names to mail to—so I rented my 12,500 names to them for about 3 cents a name (today, that kind of list would go for 15 to 20 cents a name). I sent them a pack of labels, and I remember going to the post office several weeks later and there was a check from *National Review* for around $350. I just stood there, holding the check and saying to myself, "Wow!" That was a lot of money then just to rent your list. I was so elated I took off the rest of the afternoon and went to the movies!

I also worked out a deal with Bill Rusher, exchanging the YAF list for *National Review*'s "expires"—people who had subscribed to the magazine at some point in the past, but who weren't currently subscribers. Obviously that kind of list is not going to be as good as a list of current subscribers because the "expires" list includes people who decided they weren't conservative, or didn't like politics that much, or didn't have the time to keep up with it. But it wasn't until around the late 1980s that *National Review* began to rent their list of active subscribers.

In the primitive political direct mail world of the 1960s, you just did what you could do. One device was the "friend get a friend" approach, where you ask your current subscribers or supporters to send you the names and addresses of their friends who may be interested. It's an agonizingly slow-moving approach.

Without a doubt, my most valuable resource was Marvin Liebman's list of something like 50,000 names of people who had donated to his causes or indicated an interest. Occasionally he would let me mail to that list, or to a portion of it.

Good as gold: The Goldwater names

After several years of living on a near-starvation diet of names to mail to, I saw a (pardon the pun) golden opportunity in the Goldwater campaign. At that time, federal political campaigns had to register, on a quarterly basis, the names and addresses of all persons who contributed $50 or more to the candidate. The list was kept on file with the clerk of the House of Representatives, and you could look at the list in the clerk's office.

I decided to do more than look at the names and addresses. I copied them laboriously by longhand, one contributor after another. This soon turned out to be more time consuming than I could handle, so I hired a half dozen or so women to do this for me. The clerk and his staff eyed us suspiciously, because nothing like this had ever happened before. But there didn't seem to be any law saying we *couldn't* copy the names and addresses. Finally, the clerk decided he had better cover his rear flank and told me we couldn't copy names anymore—he just wasn't comfortable with it. If I had known then what I know now, I would have kept the operation going and said, "Talk to my attorney." But we packed up our yellow pads and complied with his order.

Luckily, we got most of the Goldwater donor names before the clerk's nervousness shut us off. The total list was something like 15,000 names, and we had 12,500 of them. Since they had been reported on a quarterly basis, we had a nationwide list of the early responders—the most ardent Goldwater supporters in the nation. And that list was my treasure trove, as good as the gold bricks deposited at Fort Knox, as I started The Viguerie Company and began raising money for conservative clients.

In January 1965, I took the names and gave them to a friend named Tom Martin. He and his partner Charles Hamby did the computer work for two Catholic charities during the day. At 5 o'clock, everybody else would go home. They got permission to stay and use the computers for their own efforts—to moonlight. They went on to start their own business, CPS—Control Processing Systems—which they sold a few years later for something like $12 million.

I remember that I gave them my names in January 1965, and in February Tom brought me my names on a magnetic tape. I unraveled it, about 20 or 30 feet of tape, and asked him in alarm, "Where are my names?" The only tapes I'd ever seen had holes in them—I had never seen a magnetic tape. So that was my introduction to computers and magnetic tape.

People sometimes say, "It was the computer that allowed Viguerie to pioneer political direct mail." That's not really true. I could have done what I did without computers, using any of the old technology, such as Addressograph or Scriptomatic. *Lists* are the lifeblood of direct mail, and I now was the sole possessor of the best list in the nation for raising money for conservative causes. I also knew what to *do* with that list.

Growing, step by step, under the radar

Conservatives were not a major concern to the establishment in the years immediately following 1964. We were a convenient punching bag, good to beat up on when they needed to show that a particular issue or position was too "radical" to be taken seriously. The Republicans had to throw us a few crumbs, but they didn't consider us to be a serious threat, and for good reason. We had been trounced, and they assumed that was the end of *that*. No more forthright conservatives running for national office.

Under the establishment's radar, though, we kept busy and kept growing. Even if the pace of growth was agonizingly slow, we hoped and trusted that at some point we'd reach a critical mass where we *could* make a big difference in the national political agenda.

I kept adding to my list of conservative donor names. My contract with any client would give both the client and me access to donors' names, which was critical in expanding the base of the conservative movement. It had the effect politically that free trade has economically— it made for easy market access across borders (in this instance, organizational borders) since I was, in effect, the NAFTA framework governing conservative lists. If the donors to group A would also be likely to contribute to group B, group B had easier access to a "ready made" prospect file of conservative activists. Group B obviously would benefit from the additional donors, but this helped group A as well, since it would be just a matter of time before group A would get access to the expanded group B list, not to mention the lists of new organizations C, D, and E. Just as free trade dramatically expanded the world economy in the second half of the twentieth century, so my "common market" of conservative names expanded the conservative universe.

By centralizing access to many conservative supporters, conservative organizations were able to prospect at less expense, not to mention faster and with greater precision. It made the movement—which consisted of multiple leaders and organizations—more efficient as well, because it was easier to target supporters who were shown to be predisposed to conservative issues.

I didn't realize it at the time, but I was a "supply-sider" before that term came into use. I remember vividly how old-line conservatives would tell me there were "only" 125,000 (or whatever number of) conservatives in the nation who would contribute money. Starting new organizations and publications, according to their logic, meant that each conservative cause would get a smaller piece of the finite pie. I said to myself, and to them, that we were in deep cow chips if there were only 125,000 dedicated conservatives in a country of over 200 million people. If that were the case, I might as well sell my business and do what I *really* enjoyed—spending time with my family and playing golf. But I knew that in politics, as in economics, the key is to keep that pie growing bigger and bigger.

(By the year 2000 there were probably 5 million contributors to conservative causes and campaigns, plus perhaps 2 million contributors to the Republican Party, almost all of them solicited by direct mail. I think I've won that argument—indeed, I had won it by 1980.)

At first it was slow going, but with time the pace picked up. In the spring of 1965 I bought a list of some 50,000 names from my friend John Swain—an early direct mail fundraising pioneer—of people who donated to various charities, causes, and campaigns. They weren't entirely conservative, but heavily so. Then around 1966 Marvin Liebman decided to get out of the conservative PR business and pursue his first love—the theater—in London. I bought his entire donor list of about 50,000 names. I remember how my wife, Elaine, and I drove to New

York and filled up the trunk of our car with 50,000 Addressograph/ Scriptomatic metal plates. I now had a total file of over 150,000 conservative donors.

The foremost theme with most of my clients could be summed up as "stand up to communism." This was the big issue of the era that eclipsed all others. Some of my clients worked entirely in the foreign policy arena—among them John Fisher's American Security Council and Ted Loeffler's World Anti-Communism League. But anticommunist issues were also pivotal for broad-based early clients such as the American Conservative Union. In another policy area, I had great success raising money for H. L. (Bill) Richardson's Gun Owners of America and Gun Owners of California, where he was a state senator. The National Right-to-Work Committee and its foundation, as well as the National Rifle Association, were also major early clients.

I wasn't the only conservative utilizing direct mail by the late 1960s, by any means. In New Rochelle, New York, Neil McCaffrey was using his previous direct mail experience with the Macmillan publishing company to build his Arlington House Publishers and the Conservative Book Club. The *National Review* crowd was using direct mail to build the magazine, the Conservative Party of New York, and other vital efforts, such as Bill Buckley's race for mayor of New York City in 1965. California—and particularly Orange County—was a hotbed of conservative political activity, with direct mail playing a role, though not as big a role as it would assume later when I took on Max Rafferty's campaign for the Senate. And out of St. Louis, Phyllis Schlafly was zeroing in on Richard Nixon's front man, Henry Kissinger, for appeasing the communists (this was before the Equal Rights Amendment caught her attention). She was particularly adept at using GOP and women's organizations to grow her movement, but she also used direct marketing.

Although it's true that other conservatives were using direct mail, when it came to broadly funding a mass *movement* through direct mail, I pretty much had the field to myself from 1965 to 1978. Wyatt Stewart had left my firm in 1977 to work for the GOP Congressional Campaign

Committee, and he now offered me an opportunity to raise money for them. I turned down his offer because I wasn't happy with the drift of the Republican Party and didn't want to be co-opted by the GOP establishment; I wanted to be free to criticize the GOP and keep pulling the party to the right. Then Stewart repeated the offer to Steve Winchell, who was my executive vice president. Steve accepted, and went on to raise a ton of money for the Republicans. Stewart and Steve took the various Republican fundraising entities from around 25,000 names in 1977 to about 2 million by November 1980—a phenomenal accomplishment. This played a significant role in Reagan's landslide election and the GOP's capture of the Senate.

Stewart and Steve now gave me serious competition in political direct mail, but we were appealing to two separate but mildly overlapping universes—conservatives and Republicans. As the conservative movement grew, a number of other executives would leave my firm after learning the business to set up shop on their own. I started saying then, as I say now, that I don't run a direct mail agency so much as I run a university.

All of this was a sign that the conservative movement was growing and maturing into a political machine too large to be funded by one advertising agency. We didn't realize how much we had grown—and the establishment *certainly* had no clue—until the pivotal elections of 1978 and 1980.

PART III

The New and Alternative Media Bring the Conservative Movement to Power

8

Using Direct Mail to Build the Movement and Elect Reagan

The conservative movement as we've known it for the past 25 years would not exist without direct mail. Talk radio, cable television, and the Internet have played valuable roles in expanding the power of the conservative movement, but they were johnny-come-latelys—they didn't appear until the late 1980s and 1990s. At that point the conservative movement had already elected Ronald Reagan as president and changed the face of the U.S. Congress. A mature movement already existed in the 1980s that could take advantage of the new alternative media, but it was direct mail that created that movement and helped bring it to power.

In this chapter we will explain *why* direct mail was so powerful—its unique advantages for a political movement shunned and disparaged by the mainstream media. We will chronicle the growing pains experienced by conservatives as they shifted their primary allegiance from Barry Goldwater to Ronald Reagan, and as the original movement leaders of the Goldwater era were eclipsed by the leaders of what became known as the New Right.

Why direct mail is so powerful for insurgents

Since the beginning of the conservative movement, the U.S. mail has been conservatives' principal method of communication. Even today, conservatives may get most of their political *news* through talk radio, cable television, and the Internet—an opportunity not enjoyed by previous generations of conservatives—but most activist communication between individual conservatives and their organizations and causes and candidates takes place through the U.S. mail. In time we expect the Internet to become the foremost medium for activism, but at the present time that's still a work in progress.

Direct mail offers many advantages to conservatives. It:

- Helps to find the conservatives among 292,000,000 Americans.
- Informs conservatives as to which battles must be fought today, this week, or this month.
- Advises conservatives where conservative candidates are running and that they need help.
- Brings the conservative message to tens of millions of Americans who have never read any of the conservative periodicals or Web sites—people who are conservatives in their hearts but don't realize it until they get a letter in the mail that catches their attention and awakens the conservative within.

Let's face it—even today, for all the growth of conservative talk radio and cable television, establishment liberals remain the *dominant* force in mass media. "Old Television" (NBC, ABC, CBS) remains solidly liberal in its composition and outlook, with viewing audiences that dwarf those of "New Television" (the cable news channels). The big weekly newsmagazines (such as *Time* and *Newsweek*) remain liberal, as do the major newspapers (the *New York Times, Washington Post, Los Angeles Times*, and most of the others except for the relatively small-circulation *Washington Times*). Even on the Internet, the largest news outlets are online versions of these liberal media.

In the past two decades, conservatives have developed news outlets on cable and the Internet that now deny liberals their *monopoly* of mass media news. And that's a pivotal, dramatic change. But for all these changes, direct mail remains the foremost communication tool for conservative *activists*.

Now let's return to the years before the emergence of talk radio, cable news, and the Internet, with particular emphasis on the years leading to the election of Ronald Reagan as president. During that era, conservatives thought of direct mail as *our* TV, radio, daily newspaper, and weekly magazine combined. Let's see how it worked to bring conservatism to power, *under the radar* of the liberal media.

Direct mail gave conservatives a way to bypass the liberal "gatekeepers" at the liberal mass media. *We've mentioned this before, and we will continue to emphasize it. It is that important: The liberal news anchors at the television networks and the editors of the* New York Times *and the* Washington Post *were the "gatekeepers" of the news. They decided what was news, and what wasn't. Conservative issues would not pass the test, and conservative leaders and organizations were news only when they could be ridiculed or otherwise used to liberal advantage.*

That sounds too conspiratorial to you? David Keene, who is the long-time chairman of the American Conservative Union, gives an example from 1975, when he was working for Ronald Reagan's campaign to wrest the GOP presidential nomination from Gerald Ford, who had become president as a result of Nixon's resignation over Watergate.

"Herb Kaplow—who was with ABC—very early concluded that the Reagan challenge to Ford was *real*," Keene recalls. "He called me because we were good friends, and said he wanted to film something from the campaign and get it on the evening news."

"I took him to Florida," Keene continues, "and actually allowed him to attend and film what were usually termed 'secret meetings.' He was very appreciative of that. But then he called me a few days later and said, 'I don't know how to tell you this, but it's not going to appear. My news desk says that the Reagan thing is not real—it's not a story.'"

This is an interesting example of how a major conservative campaign was determined to be non-news by a gatekeeper even though an enterprising reporter had an inside scoop at what was going on. But the story gets even more interesting.

Keene continues,

> Several months later, Johnny Apple of the *New York Times* wrote a now-famous column in which he said, in effect, "The Reagan campaign is real." The next day Kaplow called me back and he says, "This is embarrassing, humiliating, but now that the *New York Times* has certified that the Reagan campaign is real, I'm going to be allowed to run a piece on it."
>
> I said, "Well, that footage is still good."
>
> He replied, "I know it is, but not only is the Reagan campaign real, this year the story is direct mail. So what I need is footage of people opening mail!"

It would be hard to fabricate a more precise conspiracy tale of liberal gatekeepers at work. There's no need to fabricate conspiracy theories, though, when this is how the liberal news world really worked—and still does work, to a large extent. And here was where direct mail played one of its most important roles. Conservatives didn't have to wait until the *New York Times* gave its imprimatur to know that the Reagan campaign was real. They had found out, months earlier, when they opened their mail, and were busy at work *making* the Reagan campaign "real." In fact, it was all of their hard work *under the selective radar* of that "news" outlet that finally forced the *Times* to concede that the campaign existed and had to be taken seriously.

In short, direct mail was the conservatives' vehicle to carry their message to the voters without going through the filter of the liberal-leaning news media.

Direct mail greatly expanded the nation's base of active citizenship and gave conservatives a voice in setting the nation's political agenda. Political direct mail has created a revolution in America by greatly expanding the number of people who are actively involved in choosing their government. No longer do a handful of backroom politicians set the agenda, as they once did, telling us whom we can vote for in November. Voting is merely the last act in the process of selecting who governs us, and it is not the most decisive part of the process. By the time people vote at the polls in November, the candidates have been selected and the issues debated (or obfuscated). This is the most important part of the process because it determines what choices we have in November. And this is where direct mail has had its greatest impact: It gives conservatives a voice in setting the nation's political agenda.

Today we take it for granted that hundreds of thousands of Americans, even millions, will contribute to the campaign of at least one presidential candidate. And contributing your hard-earned money is much more of an active civic commitment than is answering a public opinion poll or watching the presidential debates on television. We also take it for granted that dozens, even hundreds, of political organizations and committees—from Right to Left—will take an active part in the campaign; and that millions of Americans will join in the efforts of those groups and contribute to them. *All of this is democracy in action.* We take it for granted, but it was not always so. It is a recent development, spanning a mere half century of our nation's history. And direct mail is what gave us this modern world of mass citizen involvement in the political process.

For more than four decades, several million conservatives have become involved in countless political efforts through the medium of direct mail. The same process occurs on the Left, too—George McGovern's presidential campaign and the lobbying efforts of the

Sierra Club and Handgun Control are examples. Citizens across the political spectrum have been empowered by direct mail.

The potential for mass participation in politics was awakened by the candidacy of Barry Goldwater in 1964. He inspired millions of Americans to get off their couches and join in political action for the first time. They gave money—mostly small amounts—*en masse,* too. In 1960 somewhere between 40,000 and 50,000 people contributed to Richard Nixon's campaign, even fewer to the Kennedy campaign. In 1964, as Goldwater later wrote in *The Conscience of a Majority,* "The best count ever made of the individual contributors to my campaign . . . put the total at 661,500." Of that huge number, only 15,000—as we've seen—gave more than $50 to the federal campaign and therefore were reported to the clerk of the House of Representatives. This was truly a campaign financed by the "little people."

The Goldwater campaign occurred right before The Viguerie Company institutionalized ideological direct mail. But what happened with those 661,500 names is illustrative of the difference between the Old Right and the New Right.

Old Right: The "Arizona Mafia"—the insiders who surrounded Barry Goldwater—created an organization to carry on the senator's work. As William Rusher relates in his book *The Rise of the Right,* it was "a rather scholarly little group called the Free Society Association. . . . This organization, which concentrated on publishing conservative pamphlets and other materials, had control of some (though not all) of the mailing lists generated by the campaign, so it could not be ignored . . . " What did they do with this valuable resource? Not much—publish some pamphlets. And where is the Free Society Association now? It has long bit the Arizona dust.

New Right: Consider what The Viguerie Company did with its base of just 12,500 Goldwater donor names, compared to how the Free Society Association used its hundreds of thousands of names. The Arizona Mafia's tight control of the association resulted, in Rusher's words, in "the creation of a rival and more broadly based organization, to be called the American Conservative Union . . . " Unlike the long-defunct

FSA, the ACU has been a vital player in the conservative movement to this day. Its actions are fueled by direct mail.

Thanks to direct mail, conservatives—and their candidates—were able to become an independent, vibrant force, free of the fetters imposed by the Republican political hierarchy and the liberal media. With this independence, conservatives could concentrate on advancing the conservative agenda rather than the Republican agenda. The two agendas most definitely were not always the same.

An excellent example of this divergence (because of the Republican treachery involved) was the matter of the Panama Canal giveaway in the late 1970s. According to the polls, about 70 percent of Americans opposed the proposed treaty returning the canal to dictator-run Panama. Probably over 85 percent of registered Republicans opposed the giveaway. But the business and political establishment wanted it, so the Republican hierarchy just wished the issue would go away—"ignore it, forget it, and we'll vote for the treaty when nobody's looking." It was left to the conservatives to lead the fight against the treaty.

The GOP "treachery" to which we referred? Well, the conservatives made such a ruckus over the Panama Canal treaty that the Republican hierarchy *couldn't* ignore it. Its solution? The Republican National Committee mailed millions of letters signed by Ronald Reagan asking people to contribute to the RNC to defeat the Panama Canal treaty. Then RNC chairman Bill Brock refused to spend any of the money raised by Reagan's anti-treaty letter on any anti-treaty activities. He even refused a modest plea by one of his own Republican senators—a request by Republican Senator Paul Laxalt for $50,000 to help underwrite the cost of an anti-treaty "truth squad."

Laxalt and Reagan insisted on talking with Brock. When they did so on December 15, 1977 via a joint telephone call, they came away very angry. Brock would not budge. Someone present during this conversation said he heard Reagan use words that he hadn't thought Reagan knew.

Almost immediately, Senator Laxalt and Congressman Phil Crane, then chairman of the American Conservative Union, called Richard Viguerie, who volunteered to raise the $50,000 by direct mail in two weeks' time. But instead of $50,000, over $110,000 came in. Viguerie's success was dramatic proof of the reduced importance of political parties, and of the New Right's ability to engage in and finance important political activity outside a major political party.

Direct mail also helped conservative *candidates* remain independent of GOP institutional inertia. At that time the standard nomination and election procedure was for a potential candidate to be vetted by his local hierarchy, after putting in years of work doing the bidding of the party organization. By then, this potential candidate would be tamed, or perhaps "neutered" is the better word, and would pose no threat to the party hierarchy. For presidential candidates, the liberal mass media also expected to be part of the vetting process—and you can guess who would and would not get the media's seal of approval.

Direct mail changed all that.

Conservative candidates learned to use direct mail to win election over the GOP hierarchy's choices. Here we'll let a professional political periodical tell one such story: "Conservatives complain that national Republican strategists are too willing to run campaigns through local GOP officials—even if those officials have a record of losing in the past," reported *Practical Politics.* "They point to Indiana's 4th Congressional District, where Republican Dan Quayle ran in 1976 against veteran Democratic Rep. J. Edward Roush."

Practical Politics continued: "Quayle, nominated for the House because more prominent Republicans declined to run, found the local GOP organization relatively cool to him. Some party regulars privately felt comfortable with Roush. Quayle, using a considerable amount of money and help from the Viguerie-linked Committee for the Survival of a Free Congress, built an independent organization and won. New Right spokesmen love to cite that race as an example of Republican flabbiness and their own potential."

As for presidential candidates, the American Conservative Union's David Keene recalls what it was like "when [he] came to Washington in the early 1970s, before the explosion of alternative media, including direct mail."

"Look at the way presidential candidates were selected," Keene says.

> They had to undergo vetting—with the collapse of the party system in the early '70s—by journalists. There was actually a sort of track of dinners you had to go to, and if these couple of dozen journalists—David Broder and others—thought you were worth consideration, you could become a serious candidate. In those days, if you didn't have any impact with ABC, NBC, CBS, the *New York Times*, the *Washington Post* and the *Los Angeles Times, Time* and *Newsweek*, you might as well forget it—you were out. Because there really was no other way to reach people on a mass basis.

That sort of vetting veto is *real political power*, and explains why the establishment media have never been favorably disposed toward direct mail, which stripped them of that power, and why they could barely disguise their contempt for someone like Ronald Reagan, who rode the direct mail train to victory despite their disapproval.

Direct mail freed conservatives from dependence on the big corporations that had traditionally financed GOP and Democratic politics (and which expected to be paid back with favors). Donald J. Devine has been a conservative activist all his life and was a key Reagan administration official in the '80s. In his book *Reagan Electionomics: How Reagan Ambushed the Pollsters,* he notes how direct mail "allowed conservatives to outflank both the mass media (so we could present our message directly to individuals) and corporate America (so we could obtain contributions directly from the grass roots)."

This is an aspect of direct mail and conservatism that is often ignored by the liberal media, which like to pretend that conservatives are the lapdogs of big business just because they believe in free markets.

The truth, of course, is that it's the liberals who are the major beneficiaries of big business largesse—either directly (the way environmental
groups blackmail an oil giant like BP, for example) or indirectly by hijacking foundations (which were set up by super-wealthy, mostly conservative individuals).

The big corporations do not fund conservative groups. They fund
liberal organizations. Necessity is the mother of invention, and out of
necessity conservatives learned how to stay alive financially through
direct mail. The truth is that big business has become far too cozy with
big government. And big government, in turn, protects big business.
It's a sweetheart arrangement. Big business is comfortable with red
tape, regulations, bureaucracy—these things freeze the status quo, im-
pede newcomers, and hold down competition. If you see a business effort against stifling government regulations, you can bet it's led by the
National Federation of Independent Business and the other small-
business groups that use direct mail themselves to mobilize support.

Conservatives haven't been successful in getting big business to
stop funding liberal groups because (a) the Left poses more of a direct
threat to the big corporations via boycotts, shareholder campaigns, and
eco-terrorism; and (b) there are too many points of ideological divergence between grassroots conservatives and big business, whose leaders are more comfortable with the elitist social circles of Manhattan
and Aspen than with traditionalist and religious conservatives. Where
conservatives *have* been successful, however, is in guiding the *political
contributions* of corporations in a more conservative, or at least Republican, direction. *Because conservatives were able to wrest control of the
GOP, the presidency, and much of Congress through direct mail, without
significant corporate support, big business of necessity had to shift its political donations rightward in order to retain its influence in Washington. Call
it Practical Politics 101.*

In the pivotal 1980 election, Ronald Reagan was at best the fifth
choice of the big-business establishment Republicans. Their first, second, third, and fourth choices were Connolly, Bush, Dole, and Baker.
Reagan won without their support, though, by utilizing direct mail and

by tapping the conservative movement that had been built with direct mail. Reagan's nomination and subsequent victory served as a riveting wake-up call to big business, and the results can be seen most directly in donations from the conduits of campaign funds, the political action committees (PACs).

The Reagan campaign first got started in 1976 and just kept on growing, with grassroots support for conservative Republican candidates. Business lobbyists couldn't help but note the changed environment. Morton Blackwell's analysis in the *New Right Report* shows the percentage of big-business PAC money given to liberals in contested U.S. House and Senate races between 1976 and 1978:

Percentage of Big Business Contributions Going to Liberal Candidates

	1976	1978
Chicago and Northwestern Transportation Company	92.9% liberal	27% liberal
National Forest Products Association	100.0	39.0
Weyerhaeuser Corporation	61.9	17.0
Georgia Pacific	44.8	16.0

The important point to remember is that big business's political support for liberals began to wane only after conservatives wrested control of the Republican Party *by utilizing direct mail.* Big business will play ball with anyone willing to play ball with them—be they conservative or liberal, Republican or Democrat, or communist for that matter. It was the independence generated by direct mail that propelled the conservatives into the ballpark.

Direct mail made fence-straddling Washington politicians more accountable to their conservative grassroots constituents. During the 1950s, 1960s, and most of the 1970s many politicians mastered the art of acting and voting liberal in Washington while sounding conservative to their constituents back home. They could return to their home districts on weekends and make speeches calling for a strong America, attacking waste in Washington, and complaining about big government. Then, on Monday, they could go back to Washington and vote to block new weapons systems, to give away the Panama Canal, to increase taxes, and to create new government agencies.

Occasionally, liberal politicians would visit communist leaders like Fidel Castro and return to the United States with words of praise for the Cuban dictator, praise that most voters in South Dakota or Idaho never heard. Politicians could get away with this double life because most of the national (and some of the local) media weren't about to expose them. If the end result was to advance the liberal agenda, then— the media reasoned—the end justifies the means.

"Our problem," Paul Weyrich explained to the readers of *Conservative Digest,* "is that we have permitted these people to get by with that. We have permitted them to talk one way in the district and vote another way in Congress. It's got to stop. And we think that we can make a contribution towards stopping that."

Direct mail exposed those cozy arrangements to the sunlight. Conservative political organizations and PACs could—and did—organize intensive mailings to constituents of a state or Congressional district, letting them know the *real* voting records of their senators or representatives and making politicians' duplicity an issue in campaigns.

Direct mail can't end the hypocrisy, but at least it can curb it somewhat by exposing it. The politicians' charade can get quite sophisticated without exposure. The American Conservative Union's David Keene recalls how it was when he came to Washington in the 1970s:

> The average representative or senator had three response letters ready on any issue of importance. If you wrote and said, "We need a missile defense" he'd send you a reply saying "I agree completely and I've done this, this, and this." If you wrote that you didn't want a missile defense, he'd reply saying "I agree with you and I've done this, that, and the other." If you indicated

you were undecided or in the middle, he'd reply that
he was "giving the matter serious study."

On any big issue, so many votes and parliamentary maneuvers are involved that a resourceful Washington politician can find *something* he
did that will mollify the constituent. Indeed, he often arranges his
votes so he can point to a "yea" vote and a "nay" vote, as needed. "But
that isn't *as* successful now as before," Keene says, "because of the impact of the alternative media. Now, if you do something duplicitous like
that, you risk being exposed." The Internet has boosted the honesty-in-
voting cause, but the exposure process began with direct mail.

*Direct mail can bring a conservative candidate over the top to vic-
tory, by adding a critical 5 percent of the vote based on single-issue
appeals.* Most competitive races for the House, Senate, or presidency
are won or lost with somewhere between 45 percent and 55 percent of
the vote. A switch of 1 percent to 5 percent of the vote—or getting an
additional 1 percent to 5 percent of voters to the polls—can turn an
election.

Single-issue direct mail can make that difference.

For years conservatives dominated the issues, but lacked access to
the country's microphones. So for years conservatives lost elections,
often having secured somewhere between 45 percent and 49 percent of
the vote—tantalizingly close, but not enough. Then the New Right leaders said, "We're not going to talk only about the economy and national
defense anymore. We're also going to talk about social issues like abortion and pornography and prayer in the schools." Of the people likely
to vote for the Democratic candidate, 1, 2, or 3 percent could be in-
duced to switch over (and contribute $10 or $20) because of one issue—
busing, prayer in the schools, whatever.

The New Right began working for the people concerned with those
issues, getting the resources they needed to communicate with the
country. And the New Right got these single-issue leaders to increasingly think in terms of coalitions—scratching each other's backs. And

in election after election, single-issue voters made the difference, propelling conservative candidates to victory.

With the New Right's success in using single issues came howls of indignation, of course, from the Left. But it was selective indignation. Conservatives were merely copying what liberals had been doing successfully for years. Hubert Humphrey attained national prominence on the single issue of civil rights, while for George McGovern the single issue was Vietnam, and Ralph Nader has been nothing if not a coalition of single-issue groups and causes.

Direct mail: More than fundraising

Imagine how you would become a credible candidate for federal office without the help of direct mail. One possible route would be to serve as a toady of your local GOP or Democratic organization for years and hope to get their support; presumably that party support would then bring in enough funds to pay for those expensive television ads to get your message to the public. Alternatively, if you have enough money—if your name is Steve Forbes or if you're married to Teresa Heinz Kerry, for example—you can take a shortcut around the party organization and spend your excess millions on TV ads, hoping that the TV ads alone will generate workers for your campaign as well as general public support.

Thanks to direct mail, those are no longer your only options. You don't have to be a multimillionaire or an ideological agnostic to run for office.

To this day, too many people persist in thinking of direct mail only as a fundraising method. It's really mostly advertising—and often the most efficient form of advertising.

Raising money may be one purpose of a direct mail campaign, but it's only one of several purposes. A letter may ask you to vote for a candidate, volunteer for campaign work, circulate a petition among your neighbors, or write letters or send faxes to your senators and representatives. To encourage you to take action, a direct mailing will tell you about some of the compelling issues in the campaign and where the candidate (and his opponent) stands on those issues.

That is advertising, and it is far cheaper than television advertising—in both the initial outlay required and the net cost. Television ads cost so much because the message is going to everyone who turns on the tube, whether they're interested or not (and most won't be, instead using your ad as an opportunity to channel surf or quickly grab a snack). Political direct mail advertising, in contrast, through wise list selection goes almost entirely to people who are *predisposed* to agree with you on the issues or candidates, people who are open to persuasion to support your cause.

That's not all. Direct mail is the form of advertising that is most effective at paying for itself. In effect, the people whom the campaign mails to will pay for the advertising themselves, by responding with a check. With TV, in contrast, the outlay cost is much higher (for reasons we've already given) and it's not likely that any of that cost is going to be underwritten by the people watching your commercial. A 30-second or 60-second spot simply is not enough time to convince a person to write a check. A good eight-page letter will beat a TV spot every time because it gives compelling reason after reason after reason for someone to part with their money. So, if you want to go the expensive TV-ad route, you have to foot the bill yourself or find some rich folks to fork up the money. And you know the saying about paying the piper.

These are some of the reasons that direct mail is the advertising medium of the underdog and the non-establishment candidate. It enables organizations or causes not part of the mainstream to get funding.

The irony is that so few self-styled "consumer" groups or publications understand how direct mail works or appreciate its importance for the underdog. In most cases, the "consumer advocate" tag is a means for getting subscribers and then most of the funding comes from the big-bucks advertisers who take out ads in the publication to reach the subscriber. The publication's real allegiance is to those big-bucks advertisers. In other cases, the explanation is ideological—you can safely bet your milk money, for example, on the proposition that any time the liberal AARP talks about conservative direct mail, the operative word will be "expose." But even a generally sound consumer publication can get confused.

Kiplinger's *Changing Times*, for example, once wrote about conservative direct mail efforts in an article entitled "Dear friend, Send money": "Using the mail is an expensive but increasingly popular way to raise money for political causes and candidates." This statement begs the question: If it's so expensive, why is it increasingly popular? The answer, of course, as we've shown, is that direct mail is the *cheapest* form of advertising and fundraising, and *that* is why it is "increasingly popular." The times indeed were changing, but *Changing Times* just didn't get it.

The two main reasons some otherwise smart people didn't "get it" then and still don't get it now are (1) they don't understand that direct mail is as much advertising as fundraising, and (2) they don't understand another critical marketing concept: *the lifetime value of a donor or customer.* We've paid attention to the first misunderstanding. Now let's take a look at the concept of lifetime value.

Any successful business has to take "lifetime value" into account. This simply means that your first contact with a customer is likely to be a loss; you start making money when the customer is pleased enough to return and do business with you again and again, many times in the future. If all your customers patronize your business only one time, you'll soon run out of customers and will have to close shop.

A successful small business owner recognizes this imperative by providing friendly, helpful customer service, convenient hours of operation, and competitive prices. With a big business manager, the experience may be less personal, but the lifetime value concept still holds. When Marriott builds a hotel for $10 million, it doesn't check the receipts for the first night the hotel is open and say, "Well, we only brought in $10,000 and it cost us $10 million, so let's blow it up. It doesn't work." Management recognizes that it may take six, seven years to recover its investment.

People generally understand this principle when it's practiced by high-profile businesses. Jeff Bezos of Amazon.com understands the lifetime value of a customer—that he may have lost money the first time you bought a book or CD from him, but over time you may spend thousands as a customer. America Online floods America with those "1,000 free hours" disks. It's prepared to spend a dollar and bring in 20 cents at first, losing 80 cents, because it's buying a share of the market and your lifetime value as a customer.

We go into the concept of lifetime value in detail because some people seem to think that marketing rules change when the "business" is a nonprofit cause. But the rules don't change if you desire long-term success for your cause or movement. When The Viguerie Company applied direct mail to ideological politics, it also applied the business concept of lifetime value to politics. Neither had been done before, so some people simply didn't understand what was going on. And of course *some* people had a vested interest in spreading misunderstanding—such as the TV behemoths and big-city papers, which were losing advertising money to direct mail, and the liberal media gatekeepers, who were losing their political vetting clout.

In politics, as with business, of course, the more long term your outlook is, the more important lifetime value becomes. If you are selling Christmas trees by the highway, or setting up in a vacant space at the mall to sell new year's calendars, you don't worry much about lifetime value. In a month or so you're going to be out of there. It's the person who wants to *stay* in business come January 1 who should be concerned about lifetime value.

The political equivalent of the Christmas tree stand, you might think, would be a candidate's political campaign—here for a couple of months, then over. But the analogy only partially works. First, the candidate naturally hopes he will win, so he'll want to get his "customer" (the donor) to support him again in his future re-election efforts. Even if he loses, he may have campaign debts to pay off, and he may plan on running a larger, more effective race in the next campaign season, so current donors still have lifetime value.

When dealing with short-term political campaigns, it's important to remember that you generally don't make money with your first mailings, but rather with repeat mailings. It is, therefore, critically important that the candidate start his direct mail campaign as soon as possible—before the formal campaign launch date, with a "draft" or "exploratory" direct mailing that can be rolled over into the campaign effort after launch.

In direct mail parlance those initial mailings are called "prospect" or "acquisition" mailings: You are mailing to lists assumed to be sympathetic to find the good folks who will actually contribute. They always constitute a relatively small portion of the list, which is why these "prospect" or "acquisition" mailings will likely "lose" money. But you then add those donors to your campaign "house list," and when you mail to your "house list" in a few weeks you are mailing to people who have already demonstrated their willingness to support you. That's when you make the money with which to run your campaign. Today a 2-percent to 3-percent response may qualify a prospect mailing as a success, whereas a mailing to your "house list" can generate a 10-percent to 20-percent response, or even more.

In politics, the lifetime value concept is *most* important, of course, for organizations, groups, and causes that hope to be around for a while. Conservative organizations recognized this early on, and used direct mail to build a long-term political movement. Since liberal organizations, as well as the Republican and Democratic parties, learned from the success of the conservatives, it is fair to say that the "lifetime value" concept has now been firmly established in the realm of American politics.

Growing pains: From Goldwater to Reagan

As the conservative movement grew, fed by a rising tide of direct mail, it experienced growing pains. That's probably inevitable. Part of the pain involved a switch over the years from Barry Goldwater to Ronald Reagan as the movement's titular leader.

Barry Goldwater had not wanted to be a movement leader—or presidential candidate—in the first place. But after being drafted for the job and going through the pain of 1964, he didn't seem to want to vacate the post, either. That, too, is probably just human nature and inevitable. The growing movement needed a more involved and activist-oriented leader, though, and it knew where to look—California.

Actor Ronald Reagan, at that point Governor Reagan, had no hesitation or second thoughts about assuming leadership of the conservative movement. He was willing to speak anywhere that conservatives gathered. He helped raise funds and visibility for conservative organizations, candidates, and issues. And he accomplished all this through direct mail as well as his eloquent podium presence.

Matters between Goldwater and Reagan came to a head in 1975 when Goldwater said, in a Los Angeles TV interview, "I happen to believe that Nelson Rockefeller would be a good president. . . . I believe Rocky would be a damn good president now that he has ended his liberal drift." Nobody but Barry had noticed that end to Rockefeller's liberalism, and this was a stab in the back to conservatives, who were already envisioning a promotion for Reagan from governor to president.

Conservative Digest, a monthly published by The Viguerie Company, had grown in little more than a year—utilizing direct mail, of course—to become the political journal with the largest circulation in the nation, Left, Right, or center. It now took the lead in encouraging conservatives to honor Goldwater as a legend but to look elsewhere for leadership. The Arizona senator objected to some of the things said about him in *Conservative Digest,* but the magazine backed up its statements. William Loeb, editor of the influential *Manchester Union Leader* in New Hampshire, wrote to thank *Conservative Digest* for "a very fine service to the conservative cause for being so kind and polite about [Goldwater], but at the same time pointing out what had to be pointed out."

At the National Press Club in November 1975, Goldwater had stated, "I don't want those 27 million [who voted for me] to think I'm trying to lead them. . . . I never for any moment assumed I had a position of leadership over anybody." Conservatives decided to take him at his word, and turned to Ronald Reagan for energetic leadership. It was a bloodless revolution as these things go.

Growing pains: From Old Right to New Right

An ascending movement needs an energetic leader to serve as its most visible spokesman and to promote the cause. But we're not a banana republic, so we need a lot more than one supreme leader at the top. A mass movement in a democratic republic requires lots of organizational leaders, pooling their energy and their complementary skills to push the movement ever forward.

That sort of *movement* leadership emerged in the 1970s, and gradually became known as the New Right. The phrase "New Right" had first appeared in a different context in 1962, when Lee Edwards wrote an article for the Young Americans for Freedom magazine, *The New Guard,* called "The New Right: Its Face and Future." Conservative columnist M. Stanton Evans then used the phrase in 1969 to describe the emerging conservatism on college campuses, contrasting it with the New Left. But John Filka of the *Washington Star* was the first, in 1975, to use the term in talking about the "social conservatives" who were reshaping the conservative movement.

At the heart of the New Right leadership were six energetic and creative individuals—Richard A. Viguerie, whose direct mail fueled the movement; Paul Weyrich, founder of the Committee for the Survival of a Free Congress; John (Terry) Dolan, chairman of the National Conservative Political Action Committee (NCPAC); Howard Phillips, founder and national director of the Conservative Caucus; Morton Blackwell, who trained young activists nationally; and Ed Fuelner, president of the Heritage Foundation. The growing movement had other key activists as well—such as Phyllis Schlafly in St. Louis, Tom Ellis in North Carolina, and H. L. "Bill" Richardson in California—but these six and their allies were all located in the Washington, D.C., area, where they could meet frequently and regularly to organize the conservative agenda.

This New Right represented a sharp break with the inherited conservative leadership of the founding days and the Goldwater movement. It's true that the Old Right had emphasized economic issues and anti-communism while the New Right added social issues to the mix, but there really wasn't much outright *disagreement* between the two groups on issues. Their key differences were in temperament and operational style—in short, they implemented different types of activism.

Temperament. The first generation of conservative leaders—the Old Right—did heroic work defining conservatism and defending it against insuperable odds. The arduous nature of that task, though, tended to make them more defensive than aggressive in the political arena. They often seemed more interested in *being* right, more interested in winning the debate than in winning the election. The second generation—the New Right—was younger, more impatient, and more aggressive, or proactive. For them the goal was winning campaigns and gaining power. They were more interested in winning the election than in winning the debate.

Operational style. As we've already mentioned, the Old Right tended to see the conservative movement as a pie with a fixed size. Adding new organizations and causes meant all the existing groups (run by Old Right leaders) would get a smaller share. The New Right leaders were supply-siders before that term came into vogue: We can constantly grow the pie, they said, allowing everyone's slice of the pie to grow along with the overall movement. The Old Right was suspicious of the new political medium—direct mail. The New Right embraced it. And the Old Right took a rather lackadaisical approach toward political organizing, while the New Right planned and organized at a feverish pace. As one New Right leader put it, he would wake up every day thinking, "What meetings can I call today? What six things can I do today to weaken the Left and strengthen the conservative cause?"

Someone who understood well the difference between the Old Right and the New Right was Wesley McCune, director of the AFL-CIO front, Group Research, Inc., one of the Left's top conspiracy hunters. McCune saw a threat to democracy in everyone to the right of Nelson Rockefeller. You could sense his grudging respect for the New Right as he told a reporter: "The Old Right didn't fight, it opposes. The New Right members are fighters, scrappers. And the difference between 'old' and 'new' is mainly a difference in their pragmatism."

"We organize discontent," explained Howard Phillips of the Conservative Caucus, "just as all successful movements do." He added, on another occasion, that "there are an awful lot of [Old Right] conservatives in America who think their role is to lose as slowly as possible."

The leaders of the New Right unhesitatingly adopted and adapted some of the techniques used successfully by liberals for years—a process called reverse engineering. Japanese products after World War II provide a good example of reverse engineering. At first Japanese products were poor copies of American products. Then, Japanese products became better copies. And then, a lot of their products ended up better than ours. In the same way, the New Right learned from the liberals and the Left. The Left had foundations—so the New Right started the Heritage Foundation (and others) at this time. The Left had political action committees—so the New Right started the National Conservative Political Action Committee (and others). The Left had an array of single-issue groups—so the New Right started dozens of its own. A spokesman for the AFL-CIO's Committee on Political Education admired his opponents' methods. "After all," he said to the *National Journal*, "the New Right is just using all the techniques we've used for years."

The one thing that the New Right brought to the table that the Left had *not* was the marriage of computerized direct mail and the political process. Use of this new technology would make the New Right's foundations and PACs and special interest groups far more effective than those of the Left over the course of the Seventies.

The person most responsible for the New Right's deliberate policy of reverse engineering was Paul Weyrich of the Committee for the

Survival of a Free Congress. He told the *National Journal* how he had come to Washington as an aide to Colorado's Senator Gordon Allott and soon begun

> wondering why liberals were constantly winning victo-
> ries and conservatives were not. Then, one time, I got a
> rare opportunity to sit in on a strategy session on some
> civil rights matter with other Senate aides. There be-
> fore me were all the different liberal groups, inside and
> outside Congress, the journalistic heavies, and it was a
> magnificent show. They orchestrated this particular bit
> of legislation in a very impressive way, each group
> playing its role—producing a study in time for the de-
> bate, drafting an amendment, planting stories. I saw
> how easily it could be done, with planning and deter-
> mination, and decided to try it myself.

So, Weyrich started the Committee for the Survival of a Free Congress in 1974 to counter the liberal National Committee for an Effective Congress. House Republicans started a Republican Study Committee in 1973 as a counter to the liberal Democratic Study Group. A conservative Senate Steering Committee was started the following year to counter the liberal GOP's Wednesday Club. The Heritage Foundation was created in 1973 to counter the research conducted by the many liberal study groups, including Ralph Nader's organizations. The Conservative Caucus was founded in 1974 to counter the Left's Common Cause. And the National Conservative Political Action Committee was formed in 1975 to counter the AFL-CIO's Committee on Political Education and other liberal PACs. All of these private conservative groups except Heritage were partially or totally funded by direct mail through The Viguerie Company.

"I've jokingly said," Weyrich observed a few years later, "but there's some truth to it, that I'm sort of a Japanese mechanic of the New Right, copying—and hopefully making a little better—the operations of the Left."

All of this planning and organizing, involving so many groups (and we've given you just a sampling of the *major* organizations), requires, of course, a lot of meetings to coordinate everything for the greatest impact. *Lots* of meetings. The top operatives mentioned here began meeting in the '70s for breakfast every Wednesday at the McLean, Virginia, home of Richard and Elaine Viguerie. Then most of these top operatives would hold their own regular meetings, extending the networking. Weyrich held his "Kingston Group" meetings for conservatives on Friday mornings, "Library Court" sessions for pro-family activists every other Thursday, and "Stanton Group" meetings on alternate Thursdays to discuss foreign policy and defense developments. Rep. Philip M. Crane (R–IL) held monthly "ecumenical luncheons" at the Capitol Hill Club. And Morton Blackwell convened "PAC lunches" every two weeks. To stroke the fears of liberals who saw all these meetings as evidence of a grand conspiracy, Terry Dolan deadpanned to the *Baltimore Sun:* "It's very extensive. We have meetings every 15 or 20 minutes."

(As a side note, during the Reagan years, the Viguerie inner-sanctum meetings morphed into two weekly sessions. The organizational operatives continued their Wednesday breakfasts at the Vigueries' McLean home, and this was followed by another gathering that evening where they were joined by six or seven key Republican congressmen, with Newt Gingrich as their leader. The organizational leaders thought of themselves as the movement's "outside" leadership group, with the congressmen as the movement's "inside" leadership group—and there were never that many congressmen who thought strategically, the way Gingrich did. "I remember one session in particular," Viguerie recalled. "Everyone had left except for Gingrich, Howard Phillips, and myself, and we were sitting on the sofas in my living room as Gingrich laid out his strategy for how he would run for president." Obviously, not *all* of the New Right's goals have been accomplished.)

Throughout this period, the leaders of the New Right consciously thought of *themselves*—not the Republican Party—as the alternative to the Left and the Democrats. And thanks to the independence provided by direct mail fundraising, none of their organizations depended upon the Republican Party or a handful of big business donors for their existence. The great majority of these leaders were people who did not hold public office, and had never held public office. Conservatives did not look to elected officials for their leadership. The politicians were necessary to organize votes for or against something, of course, but generally they did not provide the leadership on key issues. That came from the New Right leaders, who utilized alternative media. You could say the New Right was funded by the post office because it depended on the post office to get its message out.

It's important to understand, too, that Watergate allowed the development of the conservative movement to transpire without too much resistance in the Republican Party. President Nixon became preoccupied with Watergate in 1973, and the Republican Party was in disarray or simply drifting throughout the two years of the Ford-Rockefeller White House and into the Carter years. Politics, like nature, abhors a vacuum, so the conservatives filled that vacuum and provided leadership for the Right in America.

Viguerie recalled:

> It was as though we were on an airplane, and that plane was meandering in all directions. We the passengers were getting increasingly nervous and unhappy, so five or six of us walked up the aisle to the front of the plane and knocked on the cockpit door. You know, we wanted to suggest some ways to fly this plane better. There was no answer, so we opened the door. And what did we find? *Nobody* was flying the plane! The cockpit was vacant! So we put down our coffee cups and legal pads, and we had a blast for six or seven years—*flying the plane!*

Creating the Religious Right with alternative media

No discussion of this era would be complete without recognizing the importance of the Religious Right in the expansion of the conservative movement. In the 1960s the conservative movement had benefited from the widespread conversion of Catholics from the urban Democratic machines to an increasingly Republican-based conservatism—largely over the issue of communism. Now, in the 1970s, it was the Protestants' turn to mobilize politically and expand the reach of the Right. A number of issues spurred this development, but none was as important as the legalization of abortion with the Supreme Court's *Roe v. Wade* decision in 1973.

The Rev. Jerry Falwell and his Moral Majority were the first to put the Religious Right on the map. Falwell is a Southern Baptist preacher who, almost from the beginning, used radio and television in his ministry—at one time his "Old Time Gospel Hour" was broadcast over as many as 500 radio stations across the nation. But its message was entirely nonpolitical—until that 1973 *Roe v. Wade* decision. Falwell determined that conservative and independent Christians had to get involved in politics—something most of them shunned, or at least kept separate from their religious witness.

The Moral Majority was formed in 1979. Falwell hired Cal Thomas, now a top syndicated columnist, as moderator of his radio program and Bob Billings as the group's first national director. When Reagan was elected president, he appointed Billings to the Department of Education in recognition of the support he had received from the Moral Majority, and Dr. Ron Godwin subsequently became the Moral Majority's national director. Godwin had been associated with Falwell for years, traveling weekly from Lynchburg, Virginia (Falwell's home base), to Washington, D.C., to attend the New Right meetings in Richard Viguerie's home.

"Dr. Falwell is what you'd call a self-made media figure," Godwin told us.

> He got his message out to the nation through the aggressive use of alternative media. He did it by buying television and radio time, by the use of the news conference, by faxes, by special events in auditoriums and convention centers across America. And by direct mail.

> At our height we were probably the largest religious direct mailer in the country. We had some 500 employees involved, from the mailing house to the cash receiving and the data processing.

A monthly tabloid, the *Moral Majority Report,* became a key part of that direct mail campaign. "I built its readership up to a million a month through direct mail," Godwin told us. It was both a fundraising vehicle and an educational tool. "I remember that when we first took on the issue of prayer in schools," Godwin recalls, "our donor base was totally lukewarm to it. We began carrying a series of articles about the importance of school prayer in the *Report,* and five months later we had outstanding support from our donors." Godwin continued:

> As time passed, the fax machine came into active play. Even today, [Falwell] faxes his *Falwell Confidential Report* to almost 300,000 people, including almost 200,000 ministers. He's turned the minister's pulpit into a bully pulpit. Until Dr. Falwell broke the barrier, you almost never heard anything political from a conservative Evangelical pulpit. Today, on any given Sunday, there may be 50,000 churches where you'll hear the pastor say something that he got from the *Falwell Confidential Report* or from Dr. Gary Bauer's daily fax report. That's as radical a change as the fundamentalist side of Christianity has seen in a hundred years.

(The humble fax machine has played other important roles in world politics as well. Your coauthor Richard Viguerie and his then-teenage son Ryan attended a World Freedom Fighters conference in Prague, Czechoslovakia, the week of July 4, 1990, where the hundreds of attendees from the West were asked to bring a fax machine and leave it for the Freedom Fighters to use behind the Iron Curtain.)

Direct mail: Under the radar—like a water moccasin

By January 1978, the New Right was creating enough commotion to be noticed occasionally, but it was still regarded mostly as a nuisance that refused to go away and leave the political ballgame to the pros. As the *National Journal,* the Washington insiders' journal of record, put it: "[The New Right] is, in short, an anomaly on the political scene, but one that both the press corps and the politicians in Washington are watching—if not yet taking too seriously."

By the end of the year, they would all be whistling a different tune. The anomaly would soon morph into a threat to the civilized (i.e., liberal) world.

For the next few months, though, only a few Washington political analysts took the movement seriously enough to investigate at the source. One of those analysts was the dean of Washington correspondents, the *Washington Post*'s David Broder. Broder paid a visit to Richard Viguerie full of questions, for he was mightily perplexed. This was years into the Carter presidency, when the Democrats also held an almost two-thirds majority in the House and Senate. Yet Carter couldn't get his key proposals passed. Nothing was going through. Why weren't Democrats able to implement their agenda? Broder had just talked to people in Vice President Walter Mondale's office, and they had not been able to provide a plausible explanation. Perhaps Viguerie had a clue to unlock this mystery. And Viguerie did, as he explained how his direct mail operation was sending perhaps 70 million letters a year at that time, for conservative organizations, opposing Jimmy Carter's initiatives. Broder was given the mandatory tour of the Viguerie computer room, housing thousands of computer tapes with the names and addresses of all those millions of conservatives on the mailing lists.

Tom Brokaw also interviewed Viguerie, on his Thursday show following the November 1978 election. Viguerie assumed they would be talking about the debut of the New Right, with all those new senators and representatives, but that wasn't what interested Tom Brokaw. No,

Brokaw whipped out Viguerie fundraising letters for two clients, Congressional candidates (and brothers) Philip and Dan Crane. Two separate candidates but the letters were almost identical—how could Viguerie be that deceptive? The conservative revolution was beginning to triumph all around him and Tom Brokaw couldn't see it. He didn't have a clue.

Then came the 1980 elections. The New Right had targeted six powerful Democratic senators—and five went down to defeat, to be replaced by conservatives. In the House, the "Newt Gingrich class" of conservative candidates—about 35 of them—were sworn in as congressmen. More of the liberal media became interested in how this was happening under their radar (they hadn't been alerted by the *New York Times*). But they still, for the most part, didn't get it.

The biggest achievement of the 1980 election, of course, was Ronald Reagan's landslide victory and the conservative siege of Washington. Seventy-five percent of the money for Reagan's campaign was raised by direct mail, and behind that was the more than 1 billion pieces of conservative mail that had gone directly to voters in the preceding six years.

The political pros were beginning to understand what had happened. Eddie Mahe, a well-known Republican political consultant who had taught at the Kennedy School of Government at Harvard University, put it this way: "If you ranked political institutions in this country, organized labor would be first. The Democratic Party is second. The Republican Party is third. The Viguerie network is unquestionably fourth."

The establishment media still didn't get it, though, so Viguerie was again called upon to explain what had happened. This time it was to one of the breakfasts regularly hosted by Godfrey Sperling, the chief Washington correspondent for the *Christian Science Monitor.* These breakfasts were for print media only—no electronic guys allowed.

"Mr. Viguerie," Sperling began, "Ronald Reagan was elected in a landslide last Tuesday, beating an incumbent president. Republicans took control of the Senate and had big pick-ups in the House, in

governors' seats, and in the state legislatures. We had a political earth-
quake last Tuesday. No one saw it coming. What happened?"

"Excuse me, sir," Viguerie replied, "*you* didn't see it coming, but we
tried our best to tell you beforehand. I can't tell you how many press
conferences we called, and none of the people here in this audience
showed up. Ever. We put out countless press releases and tried every
way we could to tell you what was happening. You had zero interest in
what we were doing."

Then, out of curiosity, Viguerie asked to see the hands of the reporters present who had ever heard of the Rev. Pat Robertson. Only
about two or three reporters' hands out of 25 went up. Point made.
Robertson at this time hosted the *700 Club* on religious television and
was on his way to becoming an 800-pound political gorilla, but they
had no idea who he was. The establishment media guys obviously
weren't watching the *700 Club*. They preferred to watch each other. It's
an incestuous practice still in vogue in Washington.

Probably never before in American history had a political movement advanced so far in so short a period of time, and yet been so ignored by the establishment. The interesting thing about direct mail is
that when it's professionally done, it has a devastating impact. It's like
using a water moccasin for a watchdog—very quiet and very effective.

Phyllis Schlafly Uses Alternative Media to Stop ERA

On October 12, 1971, the U.S. House of Representatives passed the proposed Equal Rights Amendment (ERA) to the Constitution by the lopsided vote of 354 to 23. The Senate then shouted its approval in an 84 to 8 vote on March 22, 1972. Explaining the lack of meaningful opposition was the seemingly innocuous language of the proposed amendment:

1. Equality of rights under the law shall not be denied or abridged by the United States or by any State on account of sex.
2. The Congress shall have the power to enforce, by appropriate legislation, the provisions of this article.
3. This amendment shall take effect two years after the date of ratification.

That was it. Sweet and simple—it seemed. All the usual liberal suspects were for it, but so were prominent conservative politicians like Strom Thurmond, George Wallace, and Spiro Agnew. Conservatives had opposed most of the civil rights legislation of the '60s on constitutional grounds, only to find themselves smeared as racists even as they lost the battle. The conservative *politicians*, at least, weren't going to make that mistake again—especially when the supposed beneficiaries of this wonderful gesture constituted half their electorate (women) and the feminist movement was at the height of its power.

Having passed in Congress, the amendment now needed the approval of three-fourths (38) of the states. And the states were rushing to see which could ratify the fastest. Fourteen states ratified the ERA in the first month after Congress's approval, and by the end of the first year 30 states had done so. Only eight more states were needed, and the ERA would be part of the United States Constitution.

The Equal Rights Amendment clearly was unstoppable.

Until an Alton, Illinois, housewife got into the picture, that is.

Granted, Phyllis Schlafly was not your ordinary housewife. As we've seen, her first book, *A Choice Not an Echo*, had sold more than 3 million copies in 1964 and probably was instrumental in securing Goldwater's victory in the California GOP primary—and, with that, the party's presidential nomination a few months later. Since 1964 she had become an expert on national defense, writing books such as *The Gravediggers* and *Kissinger on the Couch*. But she had little interest in ERA until a friend convinced her to look into its ramifications. She did that, and was horrified by what she found.

In February 1972, Phyllis Schlafly spelled out the hidden dangers in the Equal Rights Amendment in her monthly newsletter, *The Phyllis Schlafly Report*. In this and nearly 100 subsequent issues, she noted that ERA wouldn't give women any real new rights—the 1964 Civil Rights Act forbids discrimination against women, and ERA pertains only to government actions, not private actions, so it wouldn't (for example) guarantee equal pay for equal work. On the other hand, ERA *would* take away rights and privileges women already had—first and foremost, by requiring drafted women to serve in combat on an equal basis with men. ERA would also transfer vast powers to the federal government and make taxpayer funding of abortion and same-sex marriages constitutional rights. Clearly it wasn't exactly the innocuous proposal it seemed.

It is doubtful that the feminists even noticed that first anti-ERA issue of the *Phyllis Schlafly Report*. They had all—*all*—the nation's mass media on their side. Why should they care about the opposition of some obscure letter with a circulation of around 3,000! They would quickly learn to care a great deal about Phyllis Schlafly's new crusade.

How Phyllis beat Ms. Goliath

"In regard to alternative media," Mrs. Schlafly told us, "when we got into the ERA fight all we had was the telephone and the *Phyllis Schlafly · Report.*"

In 1972, her four-page, two-column newsletter had about 3,000 subscribers. They were Republican activists—"the women who went to Washington to support me for president of the National Federation of Republican Women, an election I lost because they stole it from me."

Those 3,000 subscribers took her anti-ERA issues to their state legislators. The first tangible result was in Oklahoma. "I got a call at 8 o'clock in the morning from my friend in Oklahoma. 'So, Phyllis,' she said, 'I took your newsletter to the state legislature and they rejected ERA!' Then I realized I had something."

In September 1972, Phyllis called around a hundred women from 30 states to meet in St. Louis to form a one-issue movement—Stop ERA. She told us in an interview:

> I appointed a Stop ERA chairman in a lot of states, but we didn't go for any organizational structure beyond that. It was all without pay, so the ones who worked the hardest got to the top. I laid down the party line on how to argue ERA, and how to debate it. And then everybody who wanted to defeat it pretty soon saw that my arguments were reliable and effective, as opposed to other arguments that other people would think of, like "God wants you" or "the UN plot," or something like that.

Over the next three years, five more states ratified ERA but three states that had already ratified it had second thoughts after Phyllis's female warriors went into combat and they rescinded their support (states can do that). The ERA movement, once thought unbeatable, was stalled.

Phyllis didn't stop working, however. "By 1975," she related, "we realized we wanted a real organization. That's when we morphed into Eagle Forum. People were interested in a lot of other issues as well, and there were plenty of states where ERA was no longer an issue."

But she also led the troops in yet another significant battle, in her home state of Illinois—which had scheduled an ERA ratification hearing for April 27, 1976. In that battle, she broke the spirit of the ERA movement and showed conservatives *how* to wage a one-issue fight. In the process, she opened up a new front for the conservative movement that would be a key factor in the movement's future growth—the pro-family religious coalition.

When the Illinois legislature convened in Springfield on April 27, 1976, they were confronted with a thousand women waving placards outside the legislative building and urging them to turn down ERA. This was no longer your tiny band of Republican activists. "Nobody in Springfield had seen anything like that," she recalled. "And they came out of the churches. Many of these people had never been to Springfield before—they didn't know what the capitol looked like. We were bringing people out of the churches into the political process."

In the early days of Stop ERA, Phyllis explained, "the only respectable organization that had taken a position against ERA was the National Council of Catholic Women. The national office was a bunch of liberal Democrats, and they were no help, but the organization had—before I got into the picture—published a nice flyer on what was wrong with ERA, how it was an attack on the family and so forth."

The liberals in the national office, Phyllis continued, "tried to make people believe they didn't have that flyer, but I had a copy of that flyer and I reprinted it to look exactly like the original—I think it was a pale green color or something—and distributed it widely. I also was able to get the local members—you know, the ones in the states—to come and testify at the ERA hearings. But they were the only respectable ally we had."

Phyllis is a Catholic herself, but she knew that one religious group wasn't enough. When she organized the Eagle Forum, which would continue the Stop ERA fight, she invited Evangelical Protestants onto her board: "Particularly prominent among the Protestants was the conservative branch of the Church of Christ. Members of the Lutheran Church–Missouri Synod were also very helpful."

Today, after the growth of the Christian Right, we take interdenominational action for granted. In the early to mid-Seventies, however, Phyllis was opening new territory. Leftist church groups had long worked together for their statist causes, but rarely before had churches on the Right collaborated.

"It was very funny at our Eagle Councils [the annual meetings of Eagle Forum]," Phyllis recalled. "These people had never been in the same room before, and I'd say, 'Now, the person sitting next to you might not be "saved" but we're all going to work together to stop ERA.' Getting the Baptists and the Catholics to work together, and getting *them* all to work with the Mormons—this was something! I made them do it!"

"It was very tolerant of the newcomers to accept me as their leader," she laughed. "I think a lot of them didn't know I was a Catholic back then, but when they found out they didn't feel threatened by me. They accepted me. Some of them tried to convert me, but they finally gave up on that! They worked together, and that was a real achievement."

And they weren't all Christians. "Orthodox Jews were with me from the start," she told us. "From the very beginning there was a Chicago rabbi who testified at our first hearing. And then there was a leading rabbi, Rabbi Hermann Neuberger—people called him 'Phyllis's rabbi'—and he was extremely supportive."

Phyllis's coalition reached out in other directions as well: "In Illinois, a very strong black contingent—headed by the Rev. Hiram Crawford, who is now deceased—supported us. When we were having our rallies, they sent busloads of blacks to join us. People who had to take a day off from work.

"We also had good support from blue-collar union women. A woman from Ohio was our leader in adding that contingent. We had all kinds."

We noted to Phyllis that it seems that one element of her success is that she concentrates on the issue, rather than making it a party or even an ideological fight.

"It was never about party or ideology," she responded. "I always say I'm very tolerant. I let a person support my issue for the reason of his choice."

"In Illinois," she continued, "our opposition misread us as a subsection of the conservative movement. It was not that. After I won, the conservative movement was glad to take credit, but it wasn't, and in Illinois we always had a complete mix of conservative and liberal Republicans, conservative and liberal Democrats, the downstate rural guys as well as the Chicago machine Democrats."

We asked, "Supporters from the Daley machine?"

Phyllis responded, "A lot of these machine Democrats were God-home-and-country people. Although the scale of values for some of them was that the machine comes first, then the party, and then God and country are after that. These are people who thought they'd die and go to hell if they voted Republican. A lot of these people knew that ERA was wrong, but they'd play a certain game of musical chairs, voting yes one time and no another time."

"And then we had the chief AFL-CIO representative in the Illinois legislature," she recalled, breaking into a smile. "He was a flashy Irishman known as 'Terrible Tommy Hanahan,' and he's the one who called the ERA crowd 'a bunch of brainless, braless broads'! George Meany personally called him to tell him to switch to yes, but he wouldn't do it. I mean that's the kind of people we had!"

Lessons from the Stop ERA fight

Phyllis Schlafly has been one of the most successful activists in the conservative movement, and her success lies in her ability to motivate both the hard-core conservatives—the cadre of the movement—and the masses, including those who have never thought of themselves as conservative or Republican. But she needed the alternative print media, made possible by Gutenberg's printing press, in order to achieve her full impact.

A Choice Not an Echo was a tract with amazing "pull"—with perhaps the closest example in our day to the repercussive effect of Tom Paine's *Common Sense*. *A Choice Not an Echo* appealed to two cadres— the Goldwater precinct captains who passed them out to all voters in their precinct, and the delegates to the 1964 Republican convention. But it also appealed to the grass-roots masses—selling over 3 million copies, convincing political couch potatoes to become activists, and converting many Rockefeller and LBJ supporters.

With the Stop ERA movement, Phyllis's first task was to motivate the cadre—those 3,000 activist Republican women—into battling the feminists at the height of their power, on an issue that was sweeping the nation with virtually no opposition. She admits they didn't start out really *expecting* to win.

She explained:

> In the post-Goldwater decade or two, conservatives fought battles without any real expectation of winning. I mean, we had to do what was right. Conservatives had a very defeatist mentality—I'm going to pass out my literature, but we're just waging a holding action.
>
> If I had known it was going to be 10 years and all that money and all those people, I don't know if I would have started it. But, initially we picked it up because it was the right thing to do.

There's a lesson there for all of us.

Later, after Stop ERA's initial successes, Phyllis demonstrated how to broaden the appeal, as we've relayed in detail. She was successful by keeping on message—focusing on the *issue*, not partisan politics or ideology. We could all profitably adopt her standard of tolerance: "I let a person support my issue for the reason of his choice."

The irony is, once you've opened up the channels of communication between disparate groups, you are likely to find that you all agree on other issues as well. Phyllis didn't start out by trying to convert those Evangelicals, blacks, Orthodox Jews, and blue-collar Democrats to the conservative movement or the Republican Party—all she wanted them to do was to defeat ERA. But countless numbers of them went on to *become* conservatives and Republicans. Their eyes were opened politically by the ERA fight.

Those are pretty amazing results considering that she started out, as she says, with just two alternative media at her disposal—the telephone and her newsletter. It's worth noting, though, that today she has become a master of all the other media that now are open to her—countless TV and print interviews with the mass media (now that conservatives can no longer be marginalized), her own radio commentaries six days a week, and an Internet site with a massive amount of information and interactive content.

The ERA movement has never simply disappeared—it is formally introduced in each new session of Congress, and there continue to be fights on the state level. But there is no realistic hope of it getting anywhere in today's political climate, and probably its main purpose today is as a fundraising issue for liberals among *their* hard-core cadre. The Equal Rights Amendment has effectively been taken off the political agenda. That is the highest level of political success, and for that we can thank Phyllis Schlafly.

9

Liberals Wake Up

The main theme of this book is how conservatives used new and alternative media to take power in America. A secondary theme, beyond that, is how the use of new and alternative media has changed *all* of American politics, Right and Left.

Regarding direct mail, The Viguerie Company had a decade's head start in using the mailbox to build a political movement. Liberals were caught asleep at the wheel, and it cost them dearly. The exact moment when they were jolted awake was the evening of November 4, 1980, when Ronald Reagan was elected president and the GOP captured the Senate. The New Right barbarians had captured Washington largely with direct mail as their principal weapon. Thereafter, the liberals pursued direct mail with dedication and marketing smarts. Thanks in large part to the people we interviewed for this chapter, they have now leveled that particular playing field. In our considered opinion, they have probably even *surpassed* conservatives in the effective use of direct mail.

Mind you, the Democrats are far behind the Republicans in *party* use of direct mail, but that's because of the Democrats' longstanding and disastrous dependence on labor unions and big special-interest donors. When it comes to independent liberal *causes*—the environmental, pro-choice, consumer watchdog, civil rights, and other groups—the liberals are definitely no slouches.

For conservatives, the first massive, nationwide, grassroots fundraising effort involved the presidential campaign of a senator from a small state, basically an outsider within his party who was too honest and blunt for his own good, who rode a populist crusade to get his party's nomination but then lost disastrously in November against the other party's ruthless sitting president. Now change the year from 1964 to 1972 and that's exactly what happened on the Left, too. Senator George McGovern of South Dakota was the liberals' counterpart to Barry Goldwater, and his nemesis—Richard Nixon—was the liberals' equivalent to Goldwater's nemesis, LBJ. McGovern used direct mail to finance his campaign and in the process changed liberal and Democratic politics in America as surely as Goldwater's campaign had changed conservative and Republican politics in America. So, let's begin with that story.

Morris Dees plays a fast one on George McGovern

Morris Dees, a poor boy from the Alabama cotton fields (don't get him started on that!), raised money to get through college by obtaining a list of his fellow students' birth dates during the school year, then writing to their parents: Just send me a check and I will deliver your son or daughter a birthday cake from the local bakery. From that humble beginning, the 'Bama Birthday Cake Service, Dees built a direct mail empire in the South. As Dees told us, "When I graduated from the University of Alabama with a law degree five years later, I had a Ph.D. in direct mail!" For a while, he and Millard Fuller (later founder and president of Habitat for Humanity) were partners in a direct mail company; then he bought out Fuller. From 1960 to 1970 Dees was involved in his direct mail business as well as a civil rights law practice, but the law always remained his first love. So at a still-early age Dees sold his direct mail business and started the Southern Poverty Law Center.

Dees had no particular interest in national politics, but in 1970, on a trip to Indiana to conduct legal research for a case, he found himself at a gathering where George McGovern was the speaker. McGovern was considering running for the Democratic presidential nomination, but polls at this time showed that he had only 1 percent support, and Dees hardly knew who he was. When Dees was introduced to McGovern after the speech, the senator asked what field of work he was in, and Dees mentioned the law center and his direct mail background. McGovern asked for Dees's telephone number and jotted it down.

Unbeknownst to Dees, several years earlier Senator McGovern had asked Richard Viguerie to raise money for him by direct mail for his 1968 Senate campaign. Viguerie had politely declined, citing their ideological differences on virtually every issue. Apparently McGovern was still looking for direct mail help, for six months after that speech in Indiana he called Morris Dees and said: "I want to write a letter to announce my presidential campaign. Would you handle it for me?" "He really had not heard of me or from me or anything," says Dees. "He just kept good notes, I guess. So I was kind of flattered."

Dees flew to Washington and sat down with the senator and Gary Hart, his campaign manager. They presented Dees with a one-page announcement letter (no fundraising) they had written. "It was just awful!" Dees told us. "And it was on red, white, and blue stationery!" The two politicians obviously had very little understanding of direct mail, and they confused Dees's role with that of a printer who would just take the letter and get it out. Instead Dees asked for a batch of McGovern's speeches and brochures so he could learn what the senator was about, and he retired to his hotel room to write a real letter. Then he flew to New York to get the help of direct mail writer Tom Collins, and finally they had a seven-page letter for Dees to give to McGovern and Hart.

The culture clash between politicians and marketer continued. (This happens all the time on the Right, too.) Dees explained that as long as they were going to spend money sending out a letter, they should raise money with it. And he explained that a longer letter would almost always draw better than a short one. They weren't convinced. They gave the letter to Harvard economist John Kenneth Galbraith and former Kennedy speechwriter Richard Wade for a critique. When it came back from the "brain trust" it was again one page long.

Dees was in a quandary. He knew the one-pager wouldn't work. He knew his would. "So I didn't use the letter that McGovern had given me back with his approval. I sent my letter. I figured, I didn't work for McGovern, you know. He couldn't fire *me*. I was just a volunteer."

"Why did I do it?" Dees asks himself. "I'm not sure. Maybe it was because everyone I had seen in Washington was so timid around politicians, acting as if senators were gods. Maybe I just wanted to prove the Beltway crowd wrong."

Back home in Alabama, Dees heard nothing for a couple of days. Then he got a phone call from McGovern assistant Pat Donovan: "The senator wants to see you *right now!*" With the inevitable return of bad-address letters, they had found out which letter Dees sent. "I'm in the middle of a case, so I'll be there in a few days," Dees replied. He wanted time for the responses to the letter to start coming in.

"Well, money started *pouring* in," Dees recalls. "When they called me again, it was in a voice that had totally changed. 'Oooooh boooy! C'mon up!'"

That first letter had a phenomenal 15-percent response rate. Gary Hart, in his campaign memoirs, wrote: "In the first three weeks of February we received $305,000. This money financed the campaign through the middle of 1971. . . . This was unquestionably the first financial turning point of our campaign. I cannot imagine surviving politically through 1971 under the financial restrictions of 1970."

Dees was asked to be the campaign's fundraiser, and he accepted. He conducted a fundraising campaign with many innovations, among them a special club for donors who would pledge monthly contributions—a great success. "The club idea itself proves," says Dees, "that Alexis de Tocqueville was right when he observed almost 150 years ago that America was a nation of joiners."

"The entire direct mail program during the race for the nomination brought in $4,850,000," Hart wrote. "After subtracting costs of approximately $650,000, the net amount made available to the campaign was $4.2 million."

With that, Dees told us, "we got the nomination away from all the powers to beat—Ed Muskie, Hubert Humphrey, 'Scoop' Jackson . . . everybody. Direct mail gave people a chance to vote with their checkbooks."

As for the national campaign that followed: "We raised $26 million to $27 million for McGovern, netting about $20 million. And those are 1972 dollars. In today's dollars it would be like *netting* $100 million easy, which is a lot of money." And it produced a list of 600,000 contributors.

Dees told us:

> We ended with a surplus, not a deficit. We paid back every single loan everybody made us. And I had about 15 wealthy people who trusted me after they saw results, and if I needed a million dollars to mail a lot of mail, I just called 'em up, got a hundred thousand from each, and paid 'em all back when the money came in. And that was possible back then because you didn't have any restrictions on campaign funds except for corporate contributions.

Gary Hart showed unabashed appreciation in his memoirs: "In the judgment of many, including myself, Morris was one of the very few bona fide geniuses involved in the McGovern campaign and, on more than one occasion, probably its savior."

McGovern showed his appreciation in two ways. He let Dees use the 600,000 names for as long as he wanted, to raise money for Dees's Southern Poverty Law Center. And he signed letters himself for that effort. Dees went on, politically, to be Jimmy Carter's fundraiser in 1976, using direct mail to defeat George Wallace in the pivotal Florida primary. And, on the personal side, he used direct mail to turn his

Southern Poverty Law Center into one of the nation's top success stories in ideological nonprofit fundraising. Today it has a half-million donors. "There would be no Southern Poverty Law Center without direct mail," Dees says without hesitation.

George Wallace, by the way, had also asked Morris Dees to be his fundraiser. Dees declined because of their differences on civil rights, but introduced Wallace to the person he thought should do the job— Richard Viguerie. Viguerie at first declined, considering Wallace too liberal for his tastes. ("I knew what you meant by that," Dees recalls today, "because Wallace *was* a liberal. He was a real populist liberal.") But then Viguerie, seeing an opportunity to throw a monkey wrench in the Democratic Party's machinery, came to agreement with Wallace, and the hundreds of thousands of names of Wallace contributors he amassed were later used to help conservative Republicans take over the South. Morris Dees is well aware of the irony in that turn of events.

Roger Craver jump-starts liberal activists

In 1970, the Sierra Club—which had been around for 70 years or so— had 14,000 members. To join, you had to get an existing member to vouch for you and sign your membership application. Then, if you passed muster, they'd let you in. Planned Parenthood had 8,000 donors. The League of Women Voters, another venerable old organization, had 20,000 members. And the American Civil Liberties Union had 10,000 on its rolls.

Then Roger Craver got ahold of them, turning them into the awesome giants they are today. And he did it all with direct mail.

Craver caught their attention when he took charge of fundraising for a newly created organization, Common Cause. "In five short months," he tells us, "it went from zero to 250,000 members and $5 million, which in those days was an enormous amount of members and a fairly enormous amount of money." Suddenly everyone on the Left wanted to be the *next* Common Cause.

The impetus to start Common Cause in 1970 came from John

Gardner, former secretary of health, education, and welfare under LBJ, then chairman of the National Urban Coalition, which had been formed in response to the burning of cities after the assassination of Martin Luther King, Jr. Gardner explained to Craver that the coalition was funded by unions, some Fortune 500 companies, and big churches. "Consequently, every time John Gardner wanted to make a change," Craver explained to us, "he had to deal with Walter Reuther, R. J. Reynolds, or what have you. And the reason he called me was that he wanted to figure out, 'How do I get the money I need for social change by getting people—a lot of people—to give a little bit of money, so I'm not dependent on any of them?'"

Gardner's fundraisers at the National Urban Coalition were big-gift oriented and thought that supporting Common Cause through small donations was a crazy idea. And they had families to feed, kids in college, so they weren't looking for a challenge they thought likely to fail. Someone recommended Gardner talk to this young, single guy who was director of development at George Washington University. That was Roger Craver.

"Well, in fact," Craver tells us, "when Gardner put the idea in front of me, 'Could you raise lots of money from lots of people in small amounts?' I was frankly too dumb to say 'No.' I said, 'Sure, why not?' And so, that was the way we started on the Left."

Craver sees direct mail as a way "to make an end run around the centralized sources of money and power, the big institutions. The important thing for both the Right and the Left and the middle is that this technology of direct mail, which today looks so simple and so fundamental, was really the first personal form of mass communications. It was a way of identifying people, holding a conversation with them, and watching them respond. It created millions of involved citizens."

Craver continues: "Ben Wattenberg, the political analyst and commentator, once said the two greatest American contributions to political democracy were the primary election and direct mail. The primary election because the people had a choice in choosing who the candidates would be, and direct mail because this was where a $15 involvement made a difference."

Ideology aside, Craver sees functional similarities between what The Viguerie Company does on the Right and what his firm, Craver, Mathews, Smith and Company, does on the Left:

> What's been happening in the democratic sense is that you've been servicing people who had enormous frustrations and gave them an outlet. And I was doing the same thing. It became possible for the passionate on both sides of the political spectrum to organize and mobilize, and it knocked out the institutional "middle" that always tried to move everything to the center, squashing both the Right and the Left. So the ability to get more spectrum, more ideas into the democratic process, is what direct mail has made possible. And the rest is history.

Back to the initial success of Common Cause, Craver reflects:

> Suddenly, here was Common Cause with 250,000 members, and John Gardner and I were assaulted by groups that were just beginning to get an idea that they should get into this medium of direct mail. I was starting to take off so much time helping Nader and NOW and all these other groups. Finally Gardner said to me, "Why don't you go off and do this commercially, and I will make sure you have enough resources to survive so you can build this business." So that's how I got into the direct mail agency business.

Common Cause was the original client of his new firm, of course. Next was the National Organization for Women (NOW), "which," Craver says, "did not have an office, and had only 3,000 members when we became associated with it. They held their meetings in taxicabs as they drove around Washington because they were worried about security and privacy." In very quick succession, Craver's firm helped found or build a number of other organizations—Greenpeace, Public Citizen, Handgun Control, the Sierra Club, Planned Parenthood, the American Civil Liberties Union, Amnesty International. In short, a Who's Who of the Left in America.

If you will recall our Chapter 7, recounting the birth of The Viguerie Company, a major problem on the Right was finding and accessing lists to mail to. We asked Craver: How about on the Left?

"There weren't any lists on the liberal side," Craver responded. "So I went to the Library of Congress and looked at magazines, at newsletters. I'd ask myself, 'What type of person would buy this?' And then I'd check to see whether any of the appropriate subscriber lists were available."

Very few were available. "In those days," Craver recalls, "people didn't exchange. They didn't swap their subscriber lists; they didn't *lend* them. I mean, they just used them themselves."

To break the impasse, Craver decided to use some professional negotiators:

> At Common Cause John Gardner had access to a lot of Foreign Service people who admired him, and they were retired. Through Gardner I organized a corps of them, and my first volunteer was the retired U.S. ambassador to Jerusalem—we still had an embassy in Jerusalem in those days. His name was Evan Wilson, and I remember the day he showed up. I looked at this guy in a pinstriped suit and he said, "I'm reporting for duty. What do you want me to do?" And I said, "I want you to get your guys to go around to this list of organizations and magazines and see if they have a list we can use." And that's how I put those diplomats to work negotiating the use of mailing lists.

"And I remember the two best lists we used," Craver continues. "The first was the customer list of something called 'Kozak Auto-Dry Carwash'—they ran an ad in *Parade* every Sunday. It was a cloth that you wiped your car down with, and for whatever reason that list worked better than anything in those early days of Common Cause."

The second list also was car related: "We had a meeting with early members of Common Cause, and I walked outside to talk to one of them. When we got to the end of the parking lot I noticed that it was filled with an extraordinary number of Volvos. So I rented a Volvo list, and that worked. So it was a very deductive trial-and-error process."

We pushed back further in time and asked him: Who taught *you* direct mail? How did you learn? Roger Craver's answer was as intriguing as Morris Dees's story of the 'Bama Birthday Cake Service.

"I learned direct mail when I was 13," Craver responded.

> My father was a florist in Gettysburg, Pennsylvania, where we had a national cemetery. During the Korean War they brought back a lot of the boys who died there and buried them in Gettysburg. My father did most of those funerals. My mother had a business sense, which most florists don't—they like beautiful things, but they don't particularly know how to make money. She got the names and addresses of the parents of the vets who were buried there, and my job was to write them on the anniversary of their son's death or burial, and again on the anniversary of his birthday. We built quite a business of putting flowers on graves, using my direct mail letters.

That's an even better story than Morris Dees's birthday cakes, we said. Craver snapped back:

> Same experience! Same experience! I mean, he dealt in sugar, I dealt with death, but I guess it just shows that parents love you. I'll never forget that experience—not the technical experience of writing the letters and seeing the results, but the experience of having these families come back to Gettysburg and stop by the flower shop to talk to us and say "thank you." They'd tell us about their son and bring pictures of him when he was

a little boy. It taught me to appreciate the power of a letter that connects directly with someone's feelings. It taught me what passion is all about.

Finally, we asked: Just how important is direct mail to liberals today?

His pithy reply: "They love to piss on it, but when you look at liberal causes, it still represents between 70 percent and 95 percent of the funding of all the mainstream causes."

A view from the Left Coast

California has been a hotbed of liberal/Left activism since at least the 1960s, so it was natural for us to turn to Mal Warwick, whose Berkeley-based fundraising firm (Mal Warwick & Associates) has handled clients like the Feingold Senate Committee, NARAL, the National Council of La Raza, and the Union of Concerned Scientists, as well as numerous cause-related charitable organizations. His firm specializes in direct mail, telephone, and Internet fundraising. Warwick is also one of the most prolific and well-regarded authors of how-to fundraising books and newsletters.

Warwick explains, "During the '70s, I was an activist in Berkeley and surrounding cities here in California, and worked primarily in connection with Congressman Ron Dellums, who had first been elected in 1970 from the Berkeley-Oakland area. I was on the campaign staff for [Dellums's] first campaign and throughout the decade."

In the 1980 campaign, the National Conservative Political Action Committee marked Dellums as its number-one target and vowed to raise a million dollars to defeat him. As Warwick explained to Dellums, "It was pretty clear that for the first time ever, we were going to have to do some serious fundraising." Dellums's response was typical of so many politicians in the '70s, regardless of ideology: "Well, *I'm* not asking anybody for money. . . . That's for *you* to do."

That need to raise money led Warwick to direct mail. "I went around to my better-heeled friends, got them to open up their

Rolodexes, and I started writing letters to people asking them for $500 or $1,000 at a pop. To my utter astonishment, they sent checks!" He raised about $18,000 this way, enough to launch the direct mail campaign. Then his first general mailing—a letter signed by George McGovern—cost something like $25,000 and brought in "well over $100,000. First-ever mailing." Warwick was hooked, and began to study how to write copy, learning quickly.

Soon he was in business on his own, leaving Parker, Dodd and Associates, where he had been introduced to direct mail. "From the outset," he told us, "I made this firm decision not to open branch offices. The fateful decision, really, was not to move to Washington. Since my business was initially very largely political, it would have been a real advantage for me to move to Washington. But I like it here, and this is home. The upshot is that we've never grown very large at all, and I don't regret that at all." Others would point out that, with total employment at around 40 and maybe 25 or 30 clients at a time, his is not a *small* direct mail operation. And in California in particular it has had an impact.

Despite staying in Berkeley, Warwick has been involved in a number of presidential campaigns, starting with "Alan Cranston's ill-fated run in 1984. That didn't go very far." Next, Warwick says, "I signed up with Gary Hart in 1986, and we actually raised most of the money in his short-lived campaign. The money we brought in actually kept the campaign alive. It was about $2 million altogether."

Warwick tells us:

> About a month after Hart managed to sink himself into oblivion, we signed up with Jesse Jackson. From a direct mail perspective, that was certainly the most successful of the efforts. We raised about $7 million for Jackson. Here, too, that was the lion's share of the money for his campaign. In the final analysis, including all the matching funds, he brought in close to $20 million. But an enormous proportion of the matching funds came in the final couple of months, and most all

of the organizing, staff salaries, and television that were used in his successful primary races came from our direct mail campaign.

Warwick also raised money for the presidential bids of Tom Harkin ("again," Warwick says, "we raised most of the money for his race; he didn't have much luck with major gifts"); George McGovern in his second race ("George wanted to run yet another race, and he was really such a nice guy, it was so hard to say 'no'"); and Paul Wellstone ("a long-time client and good friend. . . . We raised the money for his exploratory committee in 1998—almost all of it").

We asked Warwick: "How important has direct mail been for the liberal cause, for liberal organizations?" He replied:

> It's not a simple picture. Certainly there are many sizeable national organizations—starting with Common Cause, and going through organizations like Amnesty International, the ACLU, and others—that would not exist as we know them were it not for direct mail. NOW, NARAL Pro-Choice America—quite a few large, influential, national progressive organizations owe their fortune to direct mail fundraising.

Warwick continued:

> However, in some ways direct mail has been a mixed blessing for the Left, as I see it. It's much more difficult to raise money by direct mail for some issues than for others, so that has helped to shape the agenda—not always for the better, in my opinion. The fact is, many organizations have become so dependent on direct mail that "the tail wags the dog"—only those issues that appeal in the mail will raise them the funds they need to thrive. So they're captives of their audience, rather than playing the role that some of them would prefer to play, of shaping the agenda through their own planning processes.

"Also," Warwick added, "direct mail has had a deadening effect on many individual donors who otherwise might be activists. It has become much easier for a person who supports a progressive agenda to simply write a few checks and send them in the mail, rather than play a more active role."

We asked for examples of issues that did not respond to direct mail appeals on the Left. "It's very difficult to raise money for international issues," he replied. He had considerable success raising money for organizations fighting U.S. intervention in Central America in the 1980s, but with the end of the Cold War international issues dropped off the fundraising map—even if not on the geopolitical map. Iraq as an issue probably happened too fast to become a direct mail issue. "But the truth is," Warwick said, "we couldn't find a client who wanted to mail on it. I thought that was shameful, but there it was."

Even in the environmental arena, where liberals have had so much success, Warwick sees nuances others might miss: "Certain issues strike a responsive chord with the public, and others *don't*. I mean, some of the worst problems we face in many communities in this country come from toxic spills and solid waste management. Yet it is virtually impossible to raise money around those issues—at least in 'cold mail' [prospect mail]. Whereas, if you want to save the rainforest, or cuddle pandas, it's another story altogether."

Finally, we asked Warwick for his guess at how many people in America contribute to liberal and progressive causes through the mail—assuming, of course, that it would be possible to cut out all duplications between the various organizations. He told us, "Most of the work I've done has been with more specialized programs where we really haven't attempted to reach out to the entire liberal universe. But I'm led to believe by others who have thought about this a lot more than I have, that there's probably something on the order of 4 or 5 million people. But I'm sure that it doesn't run more than 5 million."

Our own estimate of how many people contribute to conservative causes by direct mail would be around 2 million "hard-core" donors and activists, plus perhaps another 4 million who are interested in one cause but not much beyond that. So there you have it—rough parity between the Left and Right in the mail. And taken together, Right and Left, roughly 10 million Americans—about 4 percent of the population—are setting a lion's share of the nation's political agenda through direct mail.

High-tech targeting: The Democrats' future?

Back in 1999, Dana Milbank in *The New Republic* described Hal Malchow as "a sort of mad political scientist [who] pushes the boundaries of technology with 'Chi-Square Automatic Interaction Detection,' or chaid analysis, which he believes improves on conventional polling. Instead of using small samples and guesswork, this software can use mounds of empirical data to predict the juiciest fundraising targets, the easiest voters to persuade, and the likeliest to vote."

Have no fear—we won't be giving you a course here in Chaid Analysis 101. But over lunch at Washington's Signature Restaurant, in March 2003, we did pick up some insights from Hal Malchow that we'd like to pass on to you. And, we might add, he came across in person not at all like a mad political scientist, but rather a genial Washington insider who has learned how to combine two of his great interests, politics and technology.

The three partners in Malchow's firm—Malchow Schlackman & Hoppey—specialize in "targeted political communications." Together they have helped elect 14 governors, 16 U.S. senators, and more than 40 members of the House. They also create political mail for the AFL-CIO, the National Education Association, the Sierra Club, NARAL Pro-Choice America, and a number of other institutions on the Left. Malchow explains their techniques in detail in his book, *The New Political Targeting*.

Malchow has been doing the direct mail prospecting for the Democratic National Committee (DNC) since 1994, so many of our questions to him zeroed in on the Democratic Party, more so than with the others we interviewed for this chapter.

Probably the juiciest bit of insider knowledge we got was that the Democratic National Committee list of dependable donors is a mere 300,000—small stuff compared to the Republicans' list. (This brings us back, again, to the Democrats' dependence on unions and big donors.) Hillary Clinton, on her own, has a donor list of 250,000. Think about that. This one U.S. senator (admittedly a rather special U.S. senator) has a donor list almost as large as the Democratic National Committee! That one fact alone tells you a lot about where power resides in the Democratic camp today.

"The Democratic National Committee made a mistake in deciding not to let the 2004 candidates have access to the DNC list," Malchow told us. Each of the primary candidates could have rented that list, used it to boost their campaigns, then added their own donor names to the core that existed before. "That way the DNC would have had a big harvest."

We had a number of questions for Malchow when we interviewed him for this book in March 2003.

> Q: Liberal organizations have such good direct mail programs going, so why do you think the Democrats have done such a poor job compared to the Republicans?

> A: You know, the problem is not so much about Democrats and Republicans as it is about liberals and conservatives. There are twice as many angry conservatives in this country as there are angry liberals. Liberals, by their very nature, don't get as angry as conservatives do, and that puts the Democratic Party at a great disadvantage.
>
> In 1995 and '96, when Gingrich and the Republicans took over Congress, those were big, golden days [for fundraising]. I did 50 million pieces of prospect mail for the DNC those two years, and I thought, "Well, we've caught up with the Republicans on direct mail." But I looked and the Republicans' bump was even bigger than the Democrats'. We lost ground during that period!

Q: A large part of your constituency consists of inner-city people, and they're just not responsive to direct mail. Don't you start with a big disadvantage there?

A: Yes, but it's not as big as you would think. The very bottom [by income] is a problem area, but only the very bottom. People at the 20th or 30th percentile are better than the ones at the 98th percentile for us. It may be the type of mail we send out, you know? [He laughs.] But every time I write something that's motivating and inspirational and principled, we get terrible returns.

A lot of the liberal groups like Amnesty International or the Audubon Society are really kind of middle of the road in their appeal, so their donors trend upscale. Not the DNC, not the DNC. I've always wondered about that. In fact, I did some analysis once and found that the higher-income zip codes or neighborhoods, based on census data, performed worse for the DNC.

A few peace groups are in the mail now [March 2003] and their returns are staggering—they're doing really well. But for obvious reasons this isn't translating as well for the Democrats, because the Democrats are sort of straddled on this issue. In fact, it's hurting us because the anti-war crowd is angry at the Democrats.

Q: What kinds of lists do you use for the Democratic National Committee to prospect for new donors?

A: We had a great year in prospecting last year [2002]. We did around 8 million pieces, but the only way we did it was with three different packages going—one for voter files, one for the liberals, and one for the seniors.

If we had to live off the liberal market, we'd be nothing because it's really shrinking. There's been a clear trend these past few years, and that has been that the size of the donor list on the liberal side has been shrinking. A lot! The basic liberal universe that's available to the DNC right now is probably around a half million to 600,000 unique names that we don't have yet as donors. Ten years ago it would have been a million, million and a half names.

That doesn't count all the environmental lists. They're pretty tricky, and they're always tricky for the DNC. Because some Democrats will sell out the environmentalists, and the environmentalists know that's not a good place to go to see their aims accomplished. But we do better on some lists than others. The Sierra Club works fairly well for us.

Q: You mentioned seniors. Do their lists work well for you?

A: No. *One* seniors list works well for us, but it's a big one—the National Committee to Preserve Social Security and Medicare. It's the best list, but it's not as big as it used to be. It used to be 4 or 5 million names. Now it's down to about a million or so—maybe even a little less.

The package we were using was about privatization of Social Security, but that package wouldn't travel anywhere else. It worked only on the seniors list. It wasn't working on liberal lists. People with more money—with money in the stock market—weren't as uptight about this. We did get the package to work on voter lists, but we had to put a ceiling on the income level we mailed to. The higher the income we'd go to, the worse the package would do.

Q: Conservative fundraisers have an easier job when the other side is in office. Is that true for liberals too?

A: No. You know, there is a fundamental message difference between Democratic and Republican mail. I have never, ever seen a piece of Republican mail that did not have the words "liberal Democrats" on the reply card. And there is a much more negative tone.

I don't know how many times I've been on some seminar panel and a Republican on the panel will say to me: "You guys don't know what you're doing, because your mail is too positive." But our letters work better with a positive message.

In 1995 and '96, when we did so well, Newt Gingrich and the Republican Congress obviously were driving our returns. But if we put Newt's picture on the front of a piece or made it about Newt or directly attacked him, the returns would go way down. It didn't work. Well, sometimes . . . you could probably attack Jesse Helms more directly.

Our best time was when Clinton became president. When Clinton went in, the DNC returns went through the roof. And it was no negative thing—it was about helping us bring our principles to fruition. That 1993–1994 period was just golden.

You have to remember that the Democrats hadn't had a president that really inspired them since Jack Kennedy. And here was this guy, and—he had the juice. He could get up there and move people, and people wanted to be a part of that.

So much of the DNC mail to donors was just Clinton trinkets. We did a Clinton photograph. Another time we got some cheesy artist to paint a picture of the White House and sent that—their "official" White House print. *Huge* returns. And I remember the next year, my partner said, "Well, we're going to do it again." I go, "Why? They got one last year." He replied: "It doesn't matter." So we went and painted the *back* of the White House. And it did great! And then they painted the Lincoln room. The donor mail was almost devoid of issues.

Q: Does a negative approach, or fear, work better for liberal organizations than for the Democrats?

A: Yes. For the issue groups what works is bad news and harvesting the bad news. When the Supreme Court didn't overturn *Roe vs. Wade* in 1990 or 1991, NARAL went from a million to 200,000 donors in no time. And it was because our threat was gone.

Even so, when you do mail for them, the best letters try to keep some idealistic tone to them. But if you're a candidate or the Democratic Party, it's really the positive stuff that works.

Q: How about the impeachment trial?

A: Well, that was really good. I did the Clinton Legal Expense Trust, and that was the most successful mail I ever did. I was getting as high as 11 percent returns on prospecting the liberal lists. And not even the Democratic Party—using Daschle's list or Kennedy's list or something like that—could get returns in that range.

So, obviously, when impeachment came around, people rallied to his side.

Q: Conservative groups don't seem to get as involved in elections, as opposed to issues, as liberal groups.

A: I think the NRA [National Rifle Association] obviously does a lot. Yet we don't see as many of your issue groups out there playing in the elections. But *we* do. I'm talking about election mail for candidates—voters' guides, comparisons, that sort of thing. Each of the unions—a lot of the big unions have their own programs besides what the AFL-CIO is doing. The National Education Association has a big membership. NARAL, in an ordinary year, will spend a lot of money.

Q: Do the Democrats understand and appreciate the importance of direct mail more today than they did 10, 15 years ago?

A: I think there was always appreciation for it. I mean, they're more *desperate* today, is what they are, now that they've cut their own throats with campaign finance reform. On the whole, I think the party has been very supportive. It's just never going to produce for the Democrats what it produces for the Republicans.

Q: Do you see a general lesson from all this?

A: You tell me if I'm wrong, but there's almost a certain level of irritation about a conservative coming to politics. A conservative is coming to politics because there's something they have to stop. Democrats come to politics because there's something they want to create. And I think in that distinction lies the fundamental difference in attitude and what they respond to.

Morton Blackwell Trains Tomorrow's Cadre

If there really were a vast, right-wing conspiracy outside of Hillary Clinton's fevered imagination, one of its hubs would be 1101 North Highland Avenue in Arlington, Virginia, a suburb of Washington, D.C. The only problem is that Webster's defines a conspiracy in terms of *secret* schemes, and there's no secret about what the Leadership Institute is doing at this address. It's training tomorrow's conservative leaders, most of them young, with a heavy emphasis on media savvys.

Sometimes your best compliments come from the other side. So it is with the Leadership Institute, which can quote Alan Colmes, the liberal co-host of Fox News' *Hannity and Colmes*: "I wish there were people on my side of the aisle doing what you're doing."

Morton Blackwell, one of the key New Right leaders we portrayed in Chapter 8, started the Leadership Institute in 1979. Today it owns the five-story Steven P. J. Wood Building on North Highland, thanks to the generosity of 9,675 donors acquired by direct mail. The first floor consists of the lobby and a restaurant that leases its space; the four floors above are dedicated to training, training, and more training. In the basement is a dormitory for Institute students. Since 1979, and through 2003, the Leadership Institute has trained 37,696 students for success in media and the public policy process.

At the Institute, there is no clear demarcation between media success and public policy success—each exists to serve the other. In today's world, as Morton Blackwell and the Leadership Institute staff fully understand, only media-savvy politicians can survive and succeed. Take the Institute's "boot camp of politics," its Youth Leadership School. "The school is not a series of lectures on political theory and philosophy," says Blackwell. "*It is a crash course on how to win.*" (Not that Blackwell overlooks the thought behind the action. Students and interns get that from his *Read to Lead,* an introduction to 25 classic conservative books, and guest speakers from academia and Washington's think tanks.)

Communication skills are as much a part of the Youth Leadership School's curriculum as election-organizing skills.

Similarly, the Campus Election Workshops train student activists in electing fellow conservatives to student government. Part of election success is organizational smarts—"choosing the right candidate" and "building an effective campaign staff." The rest is media smarts— "forming a message that resonates with students" and "generating catchy, unique literature to gain public support."

Here, briefly, are some of the Leadership Institute's programs dealing with communications and the media:

- Its **Broadcast Journalism School** provides "the training necessary to obtain positions and build careers in the highly competitive, liberal-dominated field of broadcast journalism," according to the Leadership Institute's program review. Started in 1992, it has had 2,448 students through 2003. Of these, some 97 Leadership Institute graduates are working professionally in TV news at networks and local stations, and another 214 are working elsewhere in the news media.
- The Institute's **Effective Television Techniques Workshops** "teach conservatives how to communicate effectively on television." And not just youth leaders—conservative academics, state legislators, and even members of Congress come here to hone their skills. The Heritage Foundation has

sent several dozens of its public policy experts here to re-ceive television training, and the American Legislative Ex-change Council has also made good use of this program. Genevieve Wood, herself a veteran of television and of the culture wars (she's with the Family Research Council), is the Leadership Institute's technical consultant for this program.

- The **Student Publications School** "gives conservatives the expertise and skills required to start and run successful inde-pendent, conservative campus newspapers," reports the Insti-tute's program review. The May 25, 2003, issue of the *New York Times Magazine* looked at the explosion of campus con-servative publications and credited the Leadership Institute's training of budding journalists, along with programs from other organizations such as the Young America's Foundation (see Chapter 12) and the Intercollegiate Studies Institute (see Chapter 5). In 2003 this program helped launch a record 21 new campus publications, including ones at Michigan State University, Johns Hopkins University, and Brown University.

    In total, around 80 publications got their start here in the form of training and small start-up grants. The goal is to help students get started *and* teach them how to stay afloat finan-cially with the help of alumni and conservative foundations, by using direct mail and other skills. The *California Patriot* is now in its sixth year of publication at UC Berkeley, and the *Northwestern Chronicle* has been going for more than 10 years.

- The **Capitol Hill Writing School** gives conservative staffers a review of the basics of good grammar and effective con-stituent and colleague correspondence. The Institute started this program when a survey by its employment placement office revealed writing to be the skill highest in demand by Congressional offices.

- It's easy to guess the focus of the Institute's **Direct Mail School**, **Advanced Direct Mail School**, and **High Dollar**

Direct Mail School. As we've stressed in this book, direct mail is the media used by conservative organizations to raise most of their operating funds, and these programs at the Institute teach the skills necessary to continue and expand the reach of these organizations.

- The Leadership Institute's **Public Relations School** and **Advanced Public Relations School** teach its students: "Your success often hinges on how well you articulate your message through the media. This is a tough challenge for many conservatives already disadvantaged by a major, hostile media."

- In the Institute's **Public Speaking Workshops** and **Advanced Public Speaking Workshops** "students learn how to give speeches to motivate action, to be at ease in front of an audience, and overcome common mistakes."

- And the Institute's **Internet Leadership School** "teaches conservatives how to use the Internet to communicate messages in the public policy arena," including "how to create and maintain an effective Website for their cause, campaign, or organization" and "the newest ways to use the Internet to organize and communicate."

In these media schools and workshops, students don't just listen to teachers—they work together with state-of-the-art equipment in the Institute's **Sacher Multi-Media Center.** In fact, the studios and equipment here are so advanced that numerous conservative organizations in the Washington area—among them the Alliance for Marriage, 60 Plus Association, and Free Congress Foundation—regularly come here to produce their television or video programs. Graduates of the Broadcast Journalism School also use these facilities to create their resume and portfolio tapes.

Nor does this exhaust the litany of Leadership Institute programs. More firmly in the political techniques area are its **Capitol Hill Staff Training School, Legislative Project Management School,**

Candidate Development School, Campaign Leadership School, Foreign Service Opportunity School, Grassroots Activist School, and **Freshman Legislator Training School.** This being a book on the media, however, we've had to place our emphasis on the programs more directly involved with media and communications.

"Friends of liberty," Morton Blackwell observes, "should rejoice that there is, in fact, no vast, right-wing conspiracy. If all good groups were united in one tightly led, disciplined organization, that organization would have all the efficiency of the old Soviet economy. Adam Smith's invisible hand works in changing public policy as well as in creating wealth."

And a very visible helping hand from the Leadership Institute makes sure that the work of Adam Smith's invisible hand is translated into action in Washington and across the nation.

10

The Talk Radio Revolution

Conservatives dominate talk radio to such an extent today that it's easy to forget (if we ever knew) that radio's first impact on national politics was as a tool of the liberal establishment. A quick glance back in history will reinforce our observations that: one, the emergence of a new medium brings great benefits to the political faction that first recognizes that medium's capabilities and moves decisively to utilize those capabilities; two, a key value of the new medium is its role as an alternative to the old media, a way to bypass the gatekeepers of those old media; and, three, the flirtation between entertainment and politics is no new affair.

Indeed, the first scheduled radio broadcast was on an election night, in November 1920. Since only a mere 500 or so households had equipment to receive that first radio broadcast, its immediate impact was minimal, but it ushered in a new era. By 1930, 45 percent of American families had a radio, and that figure continued rising to 80 percent by 1940. By then the United States had more than half of the world's radios, and more homes had radios than had telephones.

Politics abhors a vacuum, and began filling the vacuum tubes of

America's radio receivers in the 1930s, big time. Herbert Hoover missed the boat: He didn't realize radio's political potential, and he didn't have a personality suited to exploit radio. Franklin Delano Roosevelt did have the personality, and became America's first "radio president." Radio didn't *make* him president—the Great Depression did that—but it played a key role in his ability to win four terms as president.

When FDR was elected in 1932, inaugurating the New Deal, America had two radio networks. CBS was liberal from the get-go under the leadership of William Paley. NBC, on the other hand, had close ties with the Hoover administration. Once FDR was elected, however, NBC did its best to outdo CBS in its fealty to the new president and the New Deal. The result was a united front for the New Deal.

Douglas B. Craig, in his *Fireside Politics*, reports that "NBC broadcast over 12 hours of speeches by administration figures during Roosevelt's first week as president but gave the Republicans no times at all. . . . During 1933 FDR spoke 20 times over NBC's network, and his cabinet spoke 107 times between them. NBC also paid Louis Howe, FDR's closest adviser, $900 per week to give its listeners an inside view of Washington affairs, and even Eleanor Roosevelt earned $4,000 for hosting NBC broadcasts during 1934." And this was the more "conservative" network!

In Europe, Adolf Hitler and Benito Mussolini were ruthlessly using radio to attain and keep power. In the United States, FDR (an early admirer of Mussolini) did not hesitate to use government power to bring the radio networks in line and keep them there. One of his most controversial programs was the fascistic National Recovery Administration (NRA), and the radio networks' regulator, Commissioner Harold Lafount, warned them that it was their "patriotic" duty to refuse to sell airtime to advertisers who did not abide by the NRA codes. He added: "It is to be hoped that radio stations, using valuable facilities [their broadcast wavelength] loaned to them temporarily by the government, will not unwittingly be placed in embarrassing positions because of the greed or lack of patriotism on the part of a few unscrupulous advertisers." The radio stations had no difficulty interpreting the meaning of the phrase, "using valuable facilities loaned to them temporarily by the government," and by mid-1934 the NRA alone had received some $2 million worth of free air time.

Liberals sometimes try to deflect attention from this New Deal co-opting of radio by countering: "But look at the popularity of that right-wing radio priest, Father Charles Coughlin of Detroit." First we should note that Coughlin was no conservative Republican, but a populist who melded together a crazy quilt of leftist and rightist views. The attempt to make him into a conservative is part of the campaign to portray anti-Semitism, which Coughlin embraced later in his career, as a right-wing rather than socialist movement. In reality, Coughlin viciously attacked Herbert Hoover and urged his listeners to vote for FDR in 1932. And the Hoover administration had pressed CBS to drop his program, forcing Coughlin to broadcast on independent non-network stations from 1931 on.

Roosevelt not only was the first to recognize the political potential of radio, he understood *how* to utilize it to bond directly with the American people and he used it to bypass the conservative gatekeepers at the predominant, established medium of that day, the daily newspapers. *Broadcasting* magazine wrote in 1939: "Because the bulk of the dailies are predominantly anti–New Deal, it has long been an open secret in Washington that radio more and more was being relied upon to disseminate administration views." Radio also helped FDR bypass Congress in appealing to the public: He gave more than 300 radio speeches and "fireside chats" during his tenure as president, while Congress was on the air only on special occasions, such as the opening or closing of each annual session.

Hollywood and the entertainment industry shamelessly backed the president on radio, just as they overwhelmingly back liberal politicians and causes today. Dozens of top stars and entertainment figures endorsed the president and the New Deal on radio programs, among them Humphrey Bogart, James Cagney, Groucho Marx, Danny Kaye, Judy Garland, Lana Turner, John Huston, and Claudette Colbert.

As the nation passed from the New Deal era to the second half of the century, when the conservative movement was born, radio shed most of its political role—the liberal TV networks were ready to assume that responsibility—and became predominantly an entertainment medium. A few conservative voices could be heard—commentators such as Fulton Lewis, Jr., John T. Flynn, Dean Clarence Manion, and the Rev. Carl McIntire—but these were commentaries sponsored by business advertisers. Conservatives never had the luxury of using the iron fist of government to get their views on radio, the way the liberals did. These radio voices were a valuable morale booster for grassroots conservatives who felt lonely and powerless, but in the big scheme of things they were voices in the wilderness. The liberal television networks and a press corps that was now solidly liberal maintained control over the news presented to Americans for some four decades—until radio was reborn as a political medium in 1987.

The talk-radio explosion begins

In 1949, the heyday of socialism disguised as liberalism, the Federal Communications Commission enunciated its so-called Fairness Doctrine. It required broadcasters to (1) give adequate coverage to issues of public importance, and (2) ensure that such coverage accurately reflects opposing views. This became known as the "equal time" doctrine—if someone attacked you or your favorite position on air, you had the right to equal time for a rebuttal. In 1959 the good Democratic and Republican members of Congress passed legislation stipulating that this doctrine didn't apply to coverage of political conventions. Broadcasters could cover the Democratic and Republican conventions without giving equal time to third-party conventions. Equal time, it seemed, had its limitations after all.

The whole doctrine was a statist concoction. It was based on the unarguable premise that the radio spectrum is a scarce resource, but then everything of value is a scarce resource. In America we ration scarce resources by putting a price on them—selling the resource in a

free market. In socialist countries the government allocates the resources. The FCC opted for the socialist approach.

The Fairness Doctrine also made second-class citizens of broadcasters compared to their printing cousins when it came to the free speech
protections of the Constitution and the Bill of Rights. No less a liberal
than CBS-TV's Dan Rather testified before the FCC in 1985:

> When I was a young reporter, I worked briefly for wire
> services, small radio stations, and newspapers, and I fi-
> nally settled into a job at a large radio station owned by
> the *Houston Chronicle*. Almost immediately on starting
> work in that station's newsroom, I became aware of a
> concern which I had previously barely known
> existed—the FCC. The journalists at the *Chronicle* did
> not worry about it; those at the radio station did. . . .
> Once a newsperson has to stop and consider what a
> government agency will think of something he or she
> wants to put on the air, an invaluable element of free-
> dom has been lost.

Stations faced four threats if they did something deemed "unfair" by
the government bureaucrats: (1) outright revocation of their license; (2)
non-renewal of their license; (3) a license challenge at renewal time by
a complainant; and (4) the chilling financial costs of defending themselves before the government. The results were exactly what people of
common sense—i.e., people not in Congress or the bureaucracy—
would have predicted. The Fairness Doctrine, invoked supposedly to
protect and foster free speech, instead stifled free speech. Rather than
run the risk of those four threats, most stations opted to have no commentary on public issues at all, or only the blandest commentary
possible.

By the 1980s the ideological tide was turning away from socialism
and state planning, in favor of freedom and free markets. Ronald Reagan reigned in the United States, Margaret Thatcher in England. In
1985 the FCC decided that the Fairness Doctrine invoked obsolete no-
tions of spectrum scarcity, chilled free speech, and violated the First

Amendment. The FCC declined to abolish the Fairness Doctrine, however, because it was unclear (for legal reasons we don't have to go into
here) whether the Fairness Doctrine was law or regulation at that
point. The FCC asked Congress or the courts to act.

The following year the D.C. Court of Appeals ruled that the Fairness Doctrine was not law, and the Supreme Court upheld that decision. In 1987 the FCC then abolished the Fairness Doctrine, the
Democratic majority in Congress passed legislation to make the Fairness Doctrine law, President Reagan vetoed the legislation, and the bid
to override his veto failed.

The Fairness Doctrine was now history, and radio stations could air
controversial commentaries without fear of being run out of business.
The modern era of talk radio began and grew with an explosive force.
In 1993, with a Democrat in the White House, the Democrats thought
they had a chance to bring back the Fairness Doctrine. As the *Wall
Street Journal* put it: "Members of Congress just don't like the wide interest in public policy matter that talk radio generates." But they were
too late. In a brief six years, over a thousand radio stations had
switched to a talk-radio format—*because that's what their listeners
wanted.* Talk hosts picked up the fight and won, swamping Congress
with angry messages from listeners who also happened to be voters.

Rusty Sharpe quickly becomes talk-radio's top star

When the Fairness Doctrine bit the dust in 1987, radio broadcast officials sighed in relief but few people in or out of the industry expected
the revolution that quickly ensued. After all, the big action—including
soap operas and variety shows—had long since shifted from radio to
TV, with daytime radio now dominated by thousands of local disc jock-
eys interrupted occasionally by network news reports. In an effort to
cut personnel costs, local stations ran nationwide shows at night and
on weekends, when the radio audience was much smaller. A hit nationwide *daytime* show was not on anyone's horizon. The mantra for daytime radio was "local, local, local."

A former ABC network executive named Ed McLaughlin saw opportunity, however, where others saw only ratings and financial disaster. He found his on-air vehicle in DJ Rusty Sharpe, and within two years Rusty had become a nationwide sensation and would soon be credited with "saving daytime radio."

"Who the heck is Rusty Sharpe?" you ask, incredulously. "I've never heard of him."

Oops. We forgot to mention that he changed his on-air name to Jeff Christie.

"Whoooo?" you repeat.

Enough already. We've been teasing you, using the former DJ names of the man whose *real* name is Rush Limbaugh.

The tease has a purpose, though, because a key element of Rush Limbaugh's rise to stardom lay in his background as a disc jockey—an entertainer. After he demonstrated the potential of talk radio for conservative commentators, scores of other conservatives would make it big too, enjoying audiences larger than virtually any print journalist. But none of them came anywhere close to his audience size. Rush the DJ, Rush the entertainer, has been the Big Enchilada of talk radio ever since he launched his national show in the summer of 1988.

Limbaugh himself understands the keys to his success quite well. In a 1990 interview with *Talkers Magazine*, the talk-format trade publication, he explained that "being a DJ teaches you the elements of broadcasting that are crucial, no matter what kind of show you're doing—timing, brevity, quickness, get in and get out. It just gives you the basic fundamentals of broadcasting that you need." And he confessed to *Radio & Records:* "A turning point in my career came when I realized that the sole purpose for all of us in radio is to sell advertising. I used to think radio was for me to become a star and get my ego thrills. I wasn't listener-oriented, I was me-oriented. As I got a little older, I realized the key to my success was making the audience *want* to listen to me."

"I don't have a high-brow attitude," Limbaugh told *Newsday's* Paul Colford. "I have always as a broadcaster felt that a cheap and easy way to get an audience's attention is to say 'f—k.' I've desired a long-term career, one that is cycle-proof. Now, we're seeing the combative cycle in talk radio, while I strive for a good, entertaining program that has controversy without spitting on people." Or, as he told *Talkers Maga-zine*: "You'll have no problem as a talk show host being controversial and hosting a controversial show as long as the controversy comes from the substance of the discussion, not the behavior of the host."

A choice example of Limbaugh's sense of humor came in December 1989 when he called for a halt to women "farding in their cars" because "farding on the highway is very dangerous, as well as offensive to others." The general manager of the broadcast studio panicked and pulled the show off the air until he consulted a dictionary and learned that to *fard* means to paint with cosmetics.

Add to that sense of humor, good judgment about the types of stories that will interest your audience—and passion. Here's how he described that process to *Talkers Magazine*:

> My show is totally what's on the front page of the newspaper first, and then whatever is interesting to me. . . . Even if it's not interesting to them [his audience], it's up to me to make it interesting. If I'm passionate about something—there's something magnetic about passion. You listen to a guy talking about how much he loves bowling. If it's with passion, you listen. You're fascinated by, not so much the content, but the emotion that gets involved. I have a lot of people say, "Well, Rush, when are you gonna tell us about the S&L scandal?" I'll tell you about the S&L scandal when it becomes interesting to me. . . . I think the key is knowing when you shouldn't talk about something. . . . My philosophy is I'm here to acquire an audience. I'm not here to serve any public affairs requirements.

That perceptive attitude explains why even most liberals who hate his politics enjoy his show, and why top broadcasting professionals like Ted Koppel and Tim Russert count themselves as Limbaugh fans. You can't win them all, of course, so you had NBC's John Chancellor sniffing in 1992 about how it "was not a good year for the mainstream political press" but a very good year for "Rush Limbaugh and dozens of others who would in *no way* be called members of the mainstream political press."

Arching his elitist nose ever upward, Chancellor found it rather disgusting that presidential candidates were now catering to "talk-show America" and its "world of communication with ordinary folks . . . without the intermediation of professional political journalists. I think ordinary folks are wonderful, the salt of the earth [sure, sure, John—*in their place*, right?], but ordinary folks are not trained to conduct a serious dialogue with presidential candidates."

Rush Limbaugh—even a top comic writer like P.J. O'Rourke—would be hard put to create a caricature of liberal elitism as damning as John Chancellor did with that unintentionally revealing true confession.

The 1990s as the golden age of talk radio

Two events in the late 1980s foreshadowed the pivotal role talk radio would play in American politics during the 1990s. The first was Rush Limbaugh's rush to the top of the mountain in talk ratings, creating a massive audience unlike any that had existed before. The other was the "tea bag" rebellion of 1988–89, which demonstrated the clout simultaneously available to talk radio hosts whose names were *not* Limbaugh, and whose audiences—while much smaller than Limbaugh's—were still considerable.

In 1988 the Democratic-controlled House of Representatives voted to increase their salaries by 51 percent, from $89,500 to $135,000. On December 14, an irate citizen—Tony from Roseville, Michigan—called talk host Roy Fox of Detroit's WXYT to suggest that voters send tea bags to Washington "and attach a little message to the end of the string that says 'No pay increase.'" Here's what happened next, in the words of *Washington Post* media critic Howard Kurtz in his book *Hot Air: All Talk, All the Time*:

> "I thought it was a moronic idea," Fox says. But the next day, after realizing that the anniversary of the Boston Tea Party was approaching, he urged listeners to join a tea-bag protest. Mary Fox, his wife and producer, lined up a dozen other talk show hosts around the country. Fax machines were just coming into widespread use, which simplified the task. Jerry Williams in Boston and Mike Siegel in Seattle joined the effort, as did deejays in Washington, Los Angeles, Cleveland, San Antonio, Des Moines, and West Palm Beach. They interviewed each other on the air and trumpeted the protest. They joined forces with Ralph Nader and the National Taxpayers Union, which established a Washington post office box for the tea bags. When congressional Democrats held their annual retreat at the Greenbriar in West Virginia, Roy Fox gave out the hotel's fax number over the air. Greenbriar officials were so inundated with faxed protests that they had to shut down their machines.
>
> "What really surprised me was how little it took to turn the tide," Fox says. "It just shows how little impact there is from the public."
>
> Within weeks, organizers were dumping 160,000 tea bags in front of the White House. The tea-bag revolt sparked so much adverse publicity that Congress withdrew the pay raise. "The talk show hosts and Ralph Nader won this round at the expense of the long-term interests of the country," fumed Tony Coelho, the House Democratic whip.

Talk host Roy Fox had put his finger on a key element behind the success of this protest: the lack of input from the American public on most issues before Congress. Most members of Congress understandably would prefer to reign without having to worry about what the peasants want or don't want. But direct mail had already changed that game, and now talk radio was getting into the act. The difference was timing. While it takes weeks to get a mail campaign going, radio could do the job in a matter of hours or days.

The new giant in the alternative-media stable took another step forward in the 1992 presidential election. Arkansas's Governor Bill Clinton, challenging President George Bush, "played talk radio like a piano," said *Talkers Magazine* editor and publisher Michael Harrison. And talk TV too. An example was Clinton's lighthearted appearance on Don Imus's show in New York City, just in time to help him win the important New York primary. When it came to talk, Bill Clinton was no bashful slouch.

The talk-savvy new president had plans to continue exploiting talk radio once he became president. He did 82 radio interviews during his first two years as president, while Hillary did 80. Another major radio initiative centered around his 1993 call for guaranteed national health care—otherwise known as "Hillarycare" because of the First Lady's central role designing and promoting it. This was the first really big thrust of the Clinton agenda, with a lot of political capital on the line. To help sell the proposal, the president invited more than 200 talk hosts from all over the nation to Washington. They received a briefing on September 21, followed by a lawn party two days later where they could broadcast their shows "direct from the White House." Catering to the talk hosts were Hillary herself—who confessed to being a "talk show junkie"—as well as Ira Magaziner, the administration's health care expert, Secretary of Health and Human Services Donna Shalala, presidential adviser David Gergen, and Tipper Gore, the vice president's wife. The president himself made an appearance, too. This was pretty heady stuff for local talk hosts more accustomed to being treated like the hillbilly relatives the family doesn't like to acknowledge.

All that effort to woo the talk hosts had an initial impact, but it soon turned south. By October, *Talkers Magazine's* Michael Harrison was reporting that "the initial infatuation with the health care plan is fading as a majority of those who choose to express themselves don't trust Clinton, don't trust government, and don't trust anything that smacks of socialism." Rush Limbaugh was leading the on-air charge against Hillarycare, and in Washington journalist Bill Kristol (formerly Vice President Dan Quayle's chief of staff) channeled that popular revolt into legislative opposition. Part of that campaign was very public—Kristol seemed to be on every TV talk show around—but the most important part may have been behind the scenes. Kristol sent a barrage of faxes to thousands of conservative leaders, providing talking points against Hillarycare as well as practical advice on defeating the measure in Congress and in the court of public opinion. Each new fax would be on opinion-molders' desks the very first thing in the morning. The fax machine, first used between a mere dozen talk hosts in the "tea bag" campaign, now became a full-fledged member of the alternative media.

Direct mail also played a key role in the fight against Hillarycare. Dozens of conservative organizations—such as the American Conservative Union, under the leadership of David Keene and Don Devine, and the United Seniors Association, led by Sandra Butler—mailed tens of millions of letters.

Thanks largely to talk radio, Bill Kristol, and the direct mail campaign, Hillarycare turned into a nightmare for the Clinton administration. It stalled Clinton's legislative agenda just as the scandals began multiplying. When the Kaiser Foundation surveyed members of Congress and their staffs, 46 percent said talk radio had been the most influential media source during the health care debate, and many of them noted Rush Limbaugh in particular. In contrast, only 15 percent mentioned the *New York Times* (how far the liberal giant had fallen!), 11 percent cited the *Wall Street Journal*, 9 percent said television (oh yes, how far the liberal giants had fallen!), and the *Washington Post*, the *Los Angeles Times*, and the *Washington Times* were each named by 4 percent. Talk radio had arrived on the political scene and it wasn't going to go away anytime soon.

One of the most amazing testimonials to the power of the new media came in the October 3, 1994, issue of the *New York Times*. Liberal reporter Adam Clymer wrote the article, "Hillary Clinton Says Administration Was Misunderstood on Health Care" after two interviews with the First Lady. "This battle was lost on paid media and paid direct mail," she complained.

Explaining in more detail, Clymer wrote: "Most of the administration's defense [of Hillarycare] was carried in newspapers and on television . . . " Then he quoted Mrs. Clinton as saying, "I think in general the press rebutted a lot of claims, but if you don't rebut it in the forum in which the message is delivered, it goes unrebutted. So, that means if you don't have a radio campaign and a TV campaign *and if you don't even know about the direct mail campaign,* the people who are being influenced by that kind of opposition are going to remain influenced" (emphasis added). (See Chapter 8 of this volume, the section titled "Direct mail: Under the radar—like a water moccasin," pp. 134–136.)

In short, the press and network television did their best to defend the Clinton administration, but they were no match for talk radio and direct mail.

Why did talk radio "work" for Bill Clinton the insurgent candidate, only to turn on him full force as president? On the surface the pantheon of Clinton scandals could take the credit—they were just too juicy for a populist medium not to exploit. But behind the scenes there was a more fundamental explanation, and it was provided by one of the most intriguing politician-philosophers of the 1990s, Newt Gingrich.

In an interview with *Talkers Magazine,* Gingrich noted that political advisers see talk radio as "a wide open, rough and tumble, pretty high-risk environment. If you're an insurgent, if you're the guy without money and without name ID, talk radio is perfect for you because you have to take lots of risks. But if you're the front-runner, there's a certain virtue to being a little careful, because . . . one minor mistake could become the story." In other words, front-runners and incumbents prefer a more stage-managed environment.

With their appetite whetted by the "tea bag" campaign and the fight against Hillarycare, talk hosts found plenty of new causes. In 1994 President Clinton pushed for a measure disguised as an anti-lobbyist bill, as in "those big, bad money people in Washington," but the real

Chart 1
Why Listeners Turn on Their Radios
Lively Talk More Important than the Weather or Breaking News

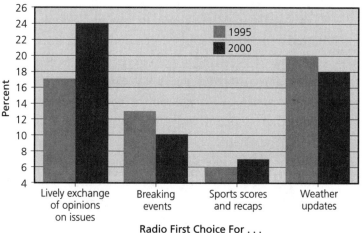

Radio First Choice For . . .

According to a January 2003 Gallup Poll, 22 percent of Americans rely on talk radio as their primary news source. Respondents answered the question: "Please tell me which one—TV, radio, online sources, newspapers, etc.—you are most likely to turn to first for each of the following reasons."

SOURCE: Radio-Television News Directors Foundation, "The American Radio News Audience Survey." This chart is adapted from *The State of the News Media 2004*, a report by the Project for Excellence in Journalism, an institute affiliated with the Columbia University Graduate School of Journalism.

story was that the bill wasn't confined to paid lobbyists. It would have required civic and political groups to disclose the names and addresses of their volunteers, and those who failed to comply could face fines of up to $200,000. Rush Limbaugh denounced it as "anti-American and unconstitutional." On his *700 Club* program Pat Robertson called the bill "one of the most shocking attempts to limit your freedom of speech and the rights of Christian people and other groups concerned about out-of-control government." Conservative activist Paul Weyrich got his network of activists on board. Soon Congressional offices were receiving thousands of calls and messages a day against the measure. Forty-four senators switched their votes to defeat the lobbying bill.

So, too, with President Clinton's $30-billion crime bill. Behind the scenes, conservative media consultant Craig Shirley was unmasking the bill as pork-barrel politics, while Newt Gingrich talked to Rush Limbaugh. "I briefed him on a provision of the crime bill that establishes quotas for murderers and quotas for the death penalty, and he spent twenty minutes on the air describing it," Gingrich recalls. "What was at first fairly obscure for millions of people now became very real." The Democratic-controlled House did an aboutface and defeated the crime bill, forcing the president to compromise. Similarly, *The Nation* magazine blamed talk radio for defeating President Clinton's plan to end the military ban on homosexuals, and for leading the successful fights against Clinton's attorney general nominees Zoe Baird and Kimba Wood.

Direct mail, C-SPAN, and talk radio together were now having an unprecedented impact on national politics. The result was the upheaval of 1994, with the Republicans taking control of the House of Representatives for the first time in more than four decades and electing Newt Gingrich as Speaker of the House. Forget Clinton's agenda. The agenda now was the GOP's Contract with America.

Speaking on Rush Limbaugh's show, Gingrich gave the alternative media full credit: "Without C-SPAN, without talk radio shows, without all the alternative media, I don't think we'd have won. The classic media elite would have distorted our message. Talk radio and C-SPAN have literally changed for millions of activists the way they get information."

The political love affair between the two Republican giants was unabashed. Limbaugh on Gingrich: "rock solid, decisive, committed, unwavering," and one of the "great leaders" in history. Gingrich on Limbaugh: "Rush has made it significantly more expensive to be liberal and significantly easier to be conservative. . . . He does for conservatives what NPR does for liberals."

"Rush Limbaugh is really as responsible for what has happened as any individual in America," said Republican Rep. Vin Weber. "Talk radio, with [Limbaugh] in the lead, is what turned the tide." The freshman Republicans in the House named Limbaugh an honorary member of Congress, and a Harris poll showed 5 percent of Republicans supporting Limbaugh for president—more than the support for Newt Gingrich, James Baker, Lamar Alexander, or Dick Cheney. Even former president Ronald Reagan got into the act, telling Rush: "Now that I've retired from active politics, I don't mind that you've become the number one voice for conservatism in our country."

Even President Clinton seemed to think of Limbaugh—rather than the Republicans in Congress—as the leader of the opposition. At one point he raged about "Rush Limbaugh and all this right-wing extremist media just pouring venom at us every day." On another occasion he fumed, "After I get off the radio with you today, Rush Limbaugh will have three hours to say whatever he wants, and I won't have any opportunity to respond, and there's no truth detector." Clinton seemed to imply that the bully pulpit of the presidency had been trumped by the bully pulpit of talk radio.

To solidify the relationship, Speaker Gingrich rolled out the welcome mat to talk radio in Congress. "We opened the Capitol up to talk radio," he told *Talkers Magazine*. "We had a tremendous outpouring of talk radio hosts who'd routinely come in and broadcast . . . " Indeed, during the last week of the implementation of the Contract with America, more than 40 talk shows originated at the Capitol. (Another Gingrich radio venture didn't fare that well. The Speaker started an Hispanic outreach project, but an early translator carelessly described him as "el bocon de la casa"—"the big mouth." That was the end of *that* project.)

As the decade commenced, the Clinton scandals took the spotlight away from less entertaining policy squabbles, and talk radio was often upstaged by the newest alternative media, the Internet, in exposing those scandals. For his part, Rush Limbaugh seemed to enjoy being leader of the opposition more than being just an entertainer who was conservative. His relationship with the Republican Party became tighter than ever before, and he was committed to George W. Bush and against John McCain. It was getting harder to distinguish between the "alternative" media and the new Republican establishment.

Conservatives actively court talk radio

Conservative organizations in Washington, D.C., have not been bashful about courting the 4,000 or so talk radio hosts across the country. The media director of any right-of-center group has to have the names and telephone numbers of receptive hosts in the Rolodex to contact when a new story breaks, and the organizations make staff officers available for interviews—that's taken for granted. Some groups go far beyond that, though, in their outreach to the talk-radio industry.

For example, the Heritage Foundation, the leading conservative think tank in Washington, is also a leader in courting talk radio. Joseph Dougherty was in charge of this operation at the time we interviewed him, and he gave us a tour of Heritage's two state-of-the-art radio broadcast studios and an overview of their activities in this regard. We have also attended several of the Talkers Forums held twice a year by the Heritage Foundation in conjunction with *Talkers Magazine*. For those sessions, Heritage brings a dozen or so hosts to D.C. to discuss politics on talk radio. "The purpose," Dougherty says, "is to create a free-flowing discussion among some of the top talk radio talent that's not yet appearing nationwide."

The two radio broadcast studios are available to talk radio hosts "of any political stripe" to use for their programs and interviews when they're in Washington—for free. "We provide the equipment, the coffee, the in-house support," Dougherty says. "They can bring in their guests to interview—we've had Ted Kennedy come in. Some of our biggest fans in talk radio are on the Left because when they walk in the doors we treat them so well (as we would do with anybody)." There's no requirement for them to interview a Heritage staffer on their program—but they almost always do. They don't even have to mention Heritage—but they do, of course, usually with some variation of "broadcasting live from Washington, D.C., at the studios of the Heritage Foundation."

To keep this offer in the minds of visiting hosts, Heritage takes out an ad in each issue of *Talkers Magazine*, calling itself "The Talker's

Think Tank." "If you're planning to be in Washington," one ad says, "consider the Heritage Foundation your home away from home. Use one of our studios to do your show. Or just come by for a cup of coffee." Even if you're not doing a broadcast, "Heritage's new Media Visitor's Center—complete with phones, computer workstations, and Internet access—is also available to you . . . free of charge."

The numbers also tell how quickly Heritage's national talk radio outreach has grown. In 2000, staffers gave slightly more than 400 radio interviews, by telephone, to hosts around the country. In 2001, more than 800. In 2002, just short of 1,200. And by 2003, some 2,000 interviews. A surprising number of these interviews were with NPR affiliates around the country. When they want a conservative opinion on an issue, they know who to call.

Another service to hosts is the "Heritage Hot Sheet." A weekly heads-up prepared exclusively for talk hosts, it tells them (via e-mail or fax) what's hot on Capitol Hill, where to get background information on these issues, and whom to call for bookings. *Hot Sheet Extras* are issued as needed in response to breaking news.

The Family Research Council is another conservative organization with extensive talk radio outreach and an all-digital broadcast studio in Washington available at no cost. Its ads in *Talkers Magazine* stress the technological features available to the hosts—ISDN units, microphones, headphones, booms, Internet connections, audio mixers, and more.

Paul Weyrich's Free Congress Foundation runs an audio service for radio stations called "FCF News on Demand." Every weekday, items are posted which can be used in newscasts and which reflect a conservative viewpoint. More than 1,800 radio stations now use this service.

The National Federation of Independent Business (NFIB) is yet another basically conservative organization that pays a lot of attention to talk radio. NFIB media coordinator Angela Jones explains that her "membership loves talk radio and identifies to a large degree with many of the hosts who express, through their political philosophies, support of independent business in America."

To emphasize that connection, a highlight of the NFIB's 2002 Small

Business Summit, held in Washington, D.C., was a 75-minute panel discussing "Talk Radio on Politics, the Economy, and the Future of Small Business." *Talkers Magazine* publisher Michael Harrison moderated the nine-member panel. A recurring theme was the need for ethics and decency, regardless of what is happening today with larger institutions. Armstrong Williams, host of "The Right Side," echoed the audience's distrust of large institutions. "I have worked for networks where the kinds of things they produced were not for me," he told them. "I had to decide if I was willing to walk away from that to build something for myself. Now, I am my product and I decide what goes on the air. If it does not have socially redeeming value, it does not go on the air."

And Jim Blasingame, host of "The Small Business Advocate," got the audience's support with his analysis: "The 20th century was the century of the corporation. But if you take the broad view, that was an anomaly. That was a 70-year period that is essentially gone. The 21st century is and will be the century of the entrepreneur."

Speaking of entrepreneurs, several conservative entrepreneurs of the 20th century saw opportunities utilizing satellite technology to start conservative radio networks. In 1985 Jim Roberts founded Radio America, which provides its more than 400 affiliates with programming that includes news, talk, documentaries, and short features. It achieved full network status in 1997 when it began broadcasting 24 hours a day, seven days a week. Among its programs are "The Michael Reagan Show," featuring the eldest son of the former president; "News Beat" with Blanquita Cullum, featuring regular reports from the White House, Capitol Hill, and the Pentagon; "WorldNetDaily Radioactive," a news-driven talk show hosted by Joseph Farah, the founder and editor of the Internet newspaper; the libertarian "Harry Browne Show," "the first step to discovering freedom in an unfree world"; and Bob Barr's "Laws of the Universe" show, featuring the former congressman and Clinton Impeachment Manager.

And the USA Radio Network also provides 24/7 coverage of news, sports, and business news, plus a couple of talk shows, to more than

1,100 radio stations in the United States as well as around the world via the Armed Forces Radio Network. USA was founded by Marlin Maddoux, who died on March 4, 2004. Maddoux was a conservative/ Christian news talk host in Dallas when he identified a need for a national news service for independent radio stations not affiliated with the major networks. Among those continuing the Maddoux tradition of "family friendly" broadcasting, under news director Bob Morrison and assistant news director Judy Hydock, are anchors Russ Rossman (afternoon drive newscasts), John Scott (morning drive), Allen Stone (midday), and Jason Walker (graveyard shift); religion editor Charlie Butts; and Washington correspondent Connie Lawn, who is the senior White House correspondent after Helen Thomas, who does not do daily reporting.

The culture wars on talk radio

The conservative presence on talk radio deals mostly with politics, but national culture and religious values are close behind.

The leading radio host in the culture wars is, of course, Dr. Laura Schlessinger. With more than 8,500,000 listeners each week, she is talk radio's third-ranking star. Her Paramount Television show was short-lived, thanks to a boycott of prospective advertisers by the Gay & Lesbian Alliance against Discrimination (GLADD). But her radio audience has grown throughout the anti–Dr. Laura campaign—a dramatic indication of how television is much more "politically correct" than radio is. As Ellen Ratner put it in *Talkers Magazine*: "Radio stations *Talkers* interviewed have a different take. No one is particularly bothered by protests. As a matter of fact, radio—unlike television—seems to thrive on controversy . . . the more the merrier."

Dr. Laura's success indicates that the radio audience is more diverse in what it wants to hear than the television audience—or at least the radio audience can get what it wants more easily than TV's audience. During the Iraq war, it was difficult to find coverage of anything else on cable TV. The pressure was there in radio, too. But as David Hall of the Premiere Radio Network told *Talkers Magazine*, "We tried to recast Dr. Laura's show to focus on the war, but the callers just wouldn't cooperate." Dr. Laura herself explained:

> I said, you know what, I don't want to make plans to do war-oriented stuff because frankly everybody's lives are still going on. In spite of the fact that our country is dealing with this, on an individual level everybody still has a life. And they still need to deal with their parents, with their kids, what have you, with their marriages, with their religion. They still need to struggle with that and perhaps even more so, because they're scared now.

Dr. Laura told *Talkers:*

> Sean Hannity and I are buddies and we talk the same way. We're both experiencing success in all these arenas . . . and yet we're extremely similar. . . . We don't do it to become stars. We do it because we have a mission. And our missions are similar, in a way, in terms of philosophy and values. He handles it politically and I handle it sort of sociologically and psychologically. But we don't get up in the morning and say "What can we do to manipulate the media so that we'll be stars and make a lot of money?" We do it, we get up in the morning and ask, "What's the battle we're fighting today?"

Speaking of missions, one of the greatest "unseen" impacts on radio is the growth of religious broadcasting. It flies under the radar largely because the establishment media, mostly secularist in its outlook, doesn't ever consider listening to religious programs; indeed, wouldn't know where to find them. But it also escapes notice because Arbitron doesn't measure religious programming audiences. Just because it doesn't appear in the "official" ratings, however, doesn't mean it isn't out there and having an impact.

Christian radio has grown along with the explosive rise of contemporary Christian and gospel music—another cultural phenomenon largely ignored by the secularist media. Some Christian radio networks

(K-LOVE, for example) are virtually all music; some, all commentary; and others a mixture. Get the audience to listen to the music, these seem to say, and hopefully most of the audience will stay tuned for the commentary.

A pioneer in modern Christian broadcasting is the Crawford Broadcasting Company, founded in 1959 and based in Denver, Colorado. Today it operates 29 AM and FM stations in a dozen markets throughout the nation. Politics doesn't seem to be a major focus of its programming, though some stations carry "Conservative Talk," described as a mixture of topics including "a healthy helping of talk with a conservative world view."

The largest operation, Salem Radio Network, is a satellite radio network based in Irving, Texas, serving more than 1,500 radio stations. Run by Ed Atsinger and Stu Epperson, it distributes daily and weekly programming for more than 40 ministries and organizations. It describes itself as "the only Christian-focused news organization with fully equipped broadcast facilities at the U.S. House, Senate, and White House manned by full-time correspondents—ensuring timely, on-the-spot coverage of breaking news." Among its talk hosts are conservative commentators Cal Thomas, Michael Medved, and Dennis Prager.

Perhaps the hardest hitting and fastest growing of the smaller networks is American Family Radio, based in Tupelo, Mississippi, and started by the Rev. Donald Wildmon in 1991. In little more than a decade it has grown to encompass nearly 200 stations, using the latest satellite technology to create "satellator stations" at a great cost savings. According to AFR, "A single FM station in a large city will cost more than it will cost AFR to construct those hundreds of stations across America."

Patrick Vaughn, the network's general counsel, explained to us that American Family Radio has 188 full-power radio stations (the kind with call letters you'd recognize), 65 translator, or repeater, stations (their call letters are more complicated, so they usually just advertise their wavelength to the public), and 16 affiliates, which are not owned by the network but carry its programming. Translators can't generate their own content, they merely rebroadcast a signal from somewhere else—

in this case, by satellite. Most translator stations are in small towns and are found on the noncommercial part of the radio spectrum, below 92 on the FM dial.

Translators are considered a secondary service by the Federal Communications Commission (FCC), so when there's a contest for a specific frequency between a full-power station and a translator station, the full-power station gets it. And that's what happens all the time: A translator station develops a market in a small town, only to be bumped by a full-power station once that market is evident. That's why American Family Radio has spent the last five years changing many of its translators to its own full-power stations—to protect its turf. Also, since the full-power stations obviously have more broadcast power, the network's programs then reach a larger population.

One local battle got National Public Radio so upset that both the *New York Times* and the *Wall Street Journal* devoted front-page stories to it. Lake Charles, Louisiana, had a translator station that carried NPR programming, and it was bumped by American Family Radio's full-power contender for that frequency. "NPR has a mentality of 'we own the noncommercial educational band' on the dial," says Rick Snavely, general manager of the Family Life Network. "But it belongs to the public."

So, who's on top now?

Talkers Magazine bases its Talk Radio Research Project on "Arbitron reports supported by other reliable indicators." Its estimates of talk radio audiences by size show Rush Limbaugh to be king of the talk mountain with a steady weekly audience of 14.5 million both in 2002 and 2003. No big surprise there.

What is interesting, though, is the steady and fast rise of Sean Hannity as radio's second-ranked host. In 2002 he had a weekly audience of 10 million, and 11.75 million a year later. Considering that *Hannity and Colmes* is the second-ranked show on Fox News Cable, after Bill O'Reilly, Hannity is that rare example of a success in *both* radio and TV. Limbaugh wasn't a success on TV; O'Reilly is puttering along at 1.75

million on radio (small potatoes for him); and Laura Schlessinger says, "I didn't fail on television. I was assassinated." But Hannity is a success on TV and within striking distance of Limbaugh on radio.

Rounding out the megastars other than Limbaugh and Hannity are Dr. Laura Schlessinger (8 million in 2002, 8.5 million in 2003), Howard Stern (also 8 million and 8.5 million), and Michael Savage (6 million and 7 million).

Still big, but below those megastars, are Jim Bohannon, Dr. Joy Browne, and Don Imus, each with 4.25 million listeners per week in 2002, down to 4 million in 2003. George Noory is a new name in 2003 with 4 million listeners. Art Bell had 4.25 million listeners in 2002, but then dropped out of the talk business.

Here are the others ranked among the top 25 or so talk radio hosts, with their estimated weekly audiences in 2002 and 2003:

More Top-Ranked Radio Hosts

Host	2003 Audience	2002 Audience
Neal Boortz	2.50 million	2.50 million
Mike Gallagher	2.50	2.25
Clark Howard	2.50	2.50
Glenn Beck	2.00	1.50
Ken & Dana Dolan	2.00	2.50
G. Gordon Liddy	2.00	2.25
Doug Stephan	2.00	1.75
Kim Komando	1.75	1.75
Bill O'Reilly	1.75	
Jim Rome	1.75	1.75
Bob Brinker	1.50	1.25
Rusty Humphries	1.50	
Michael Medved	1.50	1.50
Dave Ramsey	1.50	1.50
Dr. Dean Edell	1.25	1.25
Phil Hendrie	1.25	1.25
Laura Ingraham	1.25	
Tom Leykis	1.25	1.75
Bruce Williams	1.25	2.25

The vast majority of these hosts are conservatives. The Dolans and Bob Brinker talk on financial topics, while Dr. Edell covers the medical front from a liberal AMA perspective. Michael Medved covers the media, but from a conservative perspective.

"Who's listening to these talkers?" is another interesting question. The talk radio audience broken down by political philosophy shows few liberals, as expected, and a more moderate and libertarian (fiscal conservative/social liberal) streak than perhaps imagined from the stereotype. Here's the breakdown.

The Political Bent of Talk Radio Listeners (%)	
Ultra Conservative	12%
Conservative	25
Moderate	23
Fiscal Conservative/Social Liberal	21
Liberal	9
Ultra Liberal	2
Depends on Issue	8

Audience breakdown by political party again shows a strong independent streak, with a higher population of libertarian listeners than in the general public.

The Party Affiliations of Talk Radio Listeners (%)	
Republican	25%
Democrat	12
Libertarian	6
Independent	53
Other	4

Why don't liberals do better on talk radio? Will they ever?

We put that question to Roger Craver, founder of the liberal direct response firm that brought liberals into the direct mail age, Craver, Mathews, Smith and Company. Craver has undoubtedly raised more money than anyone else around for liberal causes—Common Cause (his first client, which he helped start), the National Organization for Women (NOW), Greenpeace, Public Citizen, Handgun Control, Planned Parenthood, the Sierra Club, the League of Women Voters, the American Civil Liberties Union, the Southern Poverty Law Center . . . you get the picture. If anybody knows what makes liberals tick, as well as their limitations, it's Roger Craver, the man who has been selling liberals and their causes to the American people for more than 30 years.

"Quite frankly," he began, "I think one reason liberals haven't done well in mass communication is that they have this Y chromosome that looks for balance and dignity and decency, and whatever adjective they want to come up with. And they don't know how to go for the jugular."

We all laughed, but it soon became apparent this wasn't just an off-the-wall remark. Craver continued:

> I used to always say, if we could get in, we really ought
> to go to one of the Viguerie or Buchanan barbecues be-
> cause those right-wingers have a hell of a lot of fun,
> and we have these wine and cheese parties to listen to
> this insufferable bullshit on the part of the liberals.
> And I think that translates into the media. I think
> every liberal commentator wants to explain how we
> can work our way out of whatever problem's being dis-
> cussed, whereas the right-winger will just say, "Well,
> the way we can work our way out of this problem is to
> kill the bastards!"
>
> It's a difference of tone, a difference of style, a dif-
> ference between black-and-white . . . and gray. The
> conservatives have always been much more willing to
> view things through the lens of what I call a "morality
> play." I mean, they basically have been able to say,
> "This is good. This is evil. There is no in between."
> Whereas the liberals will say, "Well, I see this is good,
> and this is bad, but you really ought to look at the
> background of these underprivileged children" or
> whatever. It's just a whole different mindset.

But the most effective communication on either side of the political spectrum is black and white. When you get right down to it, all this alternative media is simply professional wrestling. That's all it is. There's good and there's bad. You pick who in your audience are the good, and you vilify the bad. And the Left ought to do the same thing.

We've looked at what various other liberals and conservatives have said about "the liberals' talk-radio problem." While their statements may not be as colorful as what we got from Roger Craver, they all contribute to the answer.

Overreliance on NPR. Barry Lynn, of Americans United for the Separation of Church and State, told *Inside Talk Radio* author Peter Laufer that part of the problem is that the Left has abandoned talk radio. "I think there is a sense in the liberal community that they *have* their radio in National Public Radio, that that belongs to them." And, at this time (1995), Lynn was not impressed with NPR:

> I suppose if you like to hear six-minute pieces about ballet on radio, which frankly has never turned me on, if you like that, then NPR is just for you. I don't think NPR is as innovative as it could be. It has enough staff to do almost any damn thing it wants, yet it doesn't produce extraordinary investigative pieces. . . . But liberals still think if they can listen to it, they'll get their side of the news. I don't think there's much evidence of that. I think increasingly even the commentators on National Public Radio are moderate to conservative.

Our reaction: Forget his very last sentence, and Lynn's point about overreliance on NPR is valid. That's what happens when you rely on federal subsidies rather than the marketplace for your support—federal subsidies become a crutch. Maybe even more of a straitjacket. Rush can say anything he wants, but the NPR folks have to maintain *some* semblance of objectivity. That's why even so many liberals find NPR to be disappointing.

It's the same situation that the Democrats face with another alternative media: They've relied on the labor unions and government agency funding for so long that they've never developed the potential of direct mail fundraising the way Republicans have. The Republicans *had* to—there was no equivalent of the labor unions on the Right. For the Democrats the unions became a crutch, to their long-term detriment.

There is no Left left in America. Howard Kurtz, the *Washington Post's* media critic, says in his book *Hot Air:* "There is . . . no real left wing in today's talk show environment, largely because the Left has faded as a political force in America."

Our reaction: So we're all a nation of conservatives now? Hardly. We're still pretty much a 50-50 divided nation, no matter which side wins a particular presidential election—the Republicans and conservatives have just gotten better at organizing themselves than they were before. It's true that the extreme Left has faded in America, but there's a sizeable and passionate liberal audience of various hues that is not being served by liberal talk hosts on radio.

In fairness to Kurtz, though, his book came out in 1995, when Clinton the "centrist" had routed the hard-liberal wing of his party. Today, the situation is more complicated, with the Democrats in transition to who-knows-where and the Republicans as the party of big government, which Clinton had declared dead. If Kurtz's thesis ever did stand up, it doesn't now.

Liberals have plenty of other outlets for their viewpoints. This is Howard Kurtz again: "There can be no liberal Limbaugh because there is no comparable hunger on the Left for alternative sources of information."

Our reaction: This time Kurtz is much more on target in his assessment. Obviously this is a major theme of our book: Conservatives turned to alternative media because the establishment media were closed to them. With the establishment media in their hands, liberals had no comparable need or desire to exploit the alternative media.

Ditto: We've got TV—who needs radio? Jim Hightower, the Texas populist who is himself a radio talk host, seems to agree with Kurtz's general point. "What happened is the progressive side forgot radio. My generation looked to television and mass demonstrations and other ways of communicating, whereas the conservatives . . . hung in there and continued to build an audience. Now it's just follow the leader. People [program managers and station managers] look across the street and say, 'If that sucker is doing well with a conservative, that's what I need, too.'"

Our reaction: Yes, liberals overwhelmingly dominated *the* most influential media in the '70s and '80s—TV and mass-circulation print. To the hungry go the spoils of the new alternative medium, and the liberals weren't hungry. Conservatives were.

Even the core liberal constituencies can't be counted on anymore. Alan Linder, assistant publisher of *Talkers Magazine*, asked "Who are the liberals?" and looked at their core minority constituencies as they relate to radio.

Blacks are *the* most Democratic segment of the voting public, of course. "Today," observes Linder, "there are a number of African-American talk show hosts who espouse liberalism . . . but one can no longer assume that being black means being liberal. Conservative black hosts such as Ken Hamblin of American View Radio Network, Larry Elder of KABC, Los Angeles, Armstrong Williams of Talk America Radio Network, and Ed Buggs of WJBO, Baton Rouge, fly in the face of that notion quite effectively."

And increasingly this seems to be the case with the black audience as well. Cincinnati's Lincoln Ware told *Talkers*: "Probably 95 percent of African-Americans are liberal or at least they vote Democrat. . . . Then

again, you'd be surprised at the number of [black] listeners you get
who are more moderate or on the conservative side."

As for Latinos, Lisa Evers, a talk host on New York's leading hip-
hop music station—HOT 97-FM (WQHT-FM)—knows that audience
well. Regarding Latinos' liberal-conservative breakdown, Evers finds
that

> the lines are very blurred. With Latinos, the largest
> growing ethnic group in the country and a big part of
> my audience, I see those lines being redefined. As a mi-
> nority group, it's common to assume Latinos side with
> liberal points of view such as the opposition to school
> vouchers. But I've seen hundreds of Latino parents jam
> a public school auditorium in the South Bronx to find
> out how they can get vouchers for their children and
> get them out of the failing public schools. Bottom line:
> If it's a choice between liberal and conservative posi-
> tions, the most immediately practical idea will win out.

Our reaction: Amen! And if a straight liberal approach no longer
works with the most hard-core liberal/Democrat constituencies, where
will it work?

Stuck-in-the-mud radio management. *Talkers Magazine's* former
columnist, "The Lone Liberal"™, offered this as an explanation for why
he was so lonely as a liberal on the airwaves: "Radio management has
a history of only going with what they think works until it doesn't
work anymore. That's why many PDs and GMs [program directors and
general managers] aren't ashamed to state that they don't believe liberal talk show hosts can get ratings. Many of them are so sure of this
assumption that they wouldn't hire Jesus if he showed up at their door
and offered to do the overnight show for free."

Our reaction: "The Lone Liberal"™ always remained anonymous
and went with a Lone Ranger–type mask over his eyes when he made
public appearances—a neat and fun way to dramatize the supposed

dangers of being a liberal in the conservative talk-radio environment. From everything we've heard about radio management, he undoubtedly has a valid point here. Hey, there are five radio managers out there somewhere who won't tell us who they are—because each of them fired Rush Limbaugh when he was still "Rusty Sharpe" or "Jeff Christie"!

That's the nature of the business. But Rush Limbaugh had a super-smart *entrepreneurial* business partner in Ed McLaughlin, who figured out how to get around the then–universally accepted notion that daytime radio had to be local, local, local. It would seem to be a relatively simpler task to convince someone that the 51 percent of the American people who voted for Gore or Nader constitute a potentially lucrative radio audience. Maybe the Left has a dearth of talent not only in radio hosts, but also in entrepreneurial minded business marketers. In fact, we'd bet on it. But more on those points below.

Lack of liberal talent. Ron Kuby is the leftist counterpart to host Curtis Sliwa, the right-wing founder of the Guardian Angels, on New York City's WABC. He expressed to *Talkers Magazine* a variant of the Roger Craver/Barry Lynn complaint: "The Left looks down on talk radio—it's too loud, it's too brash, it's not a bit like NPR." But that was just warm-up for this: "Liberals make shitty talk show hosts. I think Curtis Sliwa said it best when he said that liberal hosts work with a six second delay in their head, pre-filtering everything to make sure they don't offend anybody."

Our reaction: Hey, *he* said that, not us, and the least we can do is agree with him!

In fact, "The Lone Liberal"™ seems to agree with Kuby: "There is *not* a lot of liberal talent out there to prove management wrong. Just as there are not too many Democrat politicians worth voting for, there really aren't that many talented liberal talk show hosts worth hiring—and the ratings do go to the talented among us. Let us not forget, we are broadcasters—not politicians—and *talent* is what drives success in this business. Believe it or not, leftness or rightness are secondary considerations!"

Liberals are too insular to succeed in talk radio. One of the most intriguing analyses comes from Neal Boortz, a libertarian/conservative talk show host on Cox Radio. We're going to quote extensively from his article in *Talkers Magazine*, "Why Liberals Fail in the Talk Business."

Boortz begins by conceding that liberals obviously thrive in other media—as editorialists, columnists, reporters, TV anchors and reporters, and elsewhere. "So," he asks, "why do liberals thrive—even dominate—in these areas while they just can't make the grade on talk radio? The answer? One word. Insulation. They are protected and isolated from the readers, viewers, and listeners."

Boortz explains:

> A leftist editorialist can write his piece, see it published, and then retreat into the safety of his office surrounded by his like-thinking colleagues who proceed to slap him on the back for a job well done. The columnist doesn't have to discuss the contents of his column, his philosophical base, or his ideas with the readers. He doesn't have to defend his logic or substantiate his position. He writes, they read, and that's about as far as the interaction goes. He is, if he desires it, completely insulated from his readers. Ditto for TV anchors, reporters, and commentators.
>
> It is this ability to avoid direct, in-your-face interaction with readers and listeners that protects leftists in the media. . . .
>
> Liberals thrive when the communication of ideas goes only one way. Open a dialogue and they wither. The liberal ideology is, after all, based principally on emotion. Logic and fact are to the liberal what salt is to the slug. . . . If [a dialogue] happens, liberals are going to come out on the worse end.
>
> That brings us to talk radio and the failure of liberals in this medium. Sadly, for the Left, you just can't do

commercially successful talk radio while seeking to avoid interaction with your listeners. They're there and they must be engaged. The talk show host presents an idea, states a position, and then sits there waiting for the telephone calls to begin.

Examples: Tom Daschle can slam Bush's tax cut proposals because they favor the rich. He doesn't have to respond to a housewife from North Zulch, Texas asking him if he happens to know what percentage of all income taxes is paid by the top 1 percent of income earners. Let a liberal talk show host adopt the Daschle line, and the well-informed North Zulch matron becomes a telephone threat. Dick Gephardt can brag that the majority of Americans aren't concerned about a tax cut. Try and see if you can get through to tell him that's no surprise, since his party has managed to free the majority of Americans from any real income tax liability at all. Gephardt can hide from the question, the talk show host can't.

So, here comes the hot shot liberal ready to do his talk show. The 50,000-watt signal carries his leftist ideas to the listeners. The phone lines carry the listener rebuttals right back to him. Fact overwhelms emotion, logic trumps feelings, and the talk lefty starts to sputter and lose credibility. Without some unique "schtict" to sustain him, he's soon gone, the victim of pitiful ratings.

Boortz ends with a note of consolation, however: "Despair not, my leftist friends. There will always be jobs out there for you. . . . There's always that career journey into a world where logic, fact, and common sense have no place at all—you could always become a professor at some liberal arts college."

Our reaction: Whew! We couldn't have said it better ourselves, which is why we let him explain it to you at length.

All of the above statements provide a partial explanation for the dearth of liberal hosts on talk radio, though Neal Boortz's comments seem especially to the point. Boortz's analysis also explains why liberals fare better on cable TV talk shows, since most of those—while appearing on an alternative medium—still remain isolated from their viewers in the way Boortz describes. For better or worse, radio is the most intimate of the alternative media. For conservatives that's better, for liberals that's worse.

What surprised us was the nearly unanimous opinion that there's some inherent reason why liberals don't do well on talk radio, and (the supposition goes) never will. You'd expect the conservatives we quoted to say something like that, but the liberals were equally damning of their colleagues.

Of course there are liberals who disagree, who think liberals *can* do well on talk radio if only . . . if only (fill in the blank). Foremost among these are the persons who hope to do something about it by starting liberal radio ventures, so let's hear from them next.

A new day for liberal talk?

Thom Hartmann is a nationally syndicated talk show host with the i.e. America Radio Network—a liberal venture. In an article for *Talkers Magazine* he writes: "Just as Bill Clinton was the best thing that ever could have happened to Rush, driving demand for radio voices that questioned authority, so too has George W. Bush set the stage perfectly for the emergence of AM radio's second big wave: Democratic/liberal talk."

The key, for Hartmann, is to recognize liberal talk as a separate market niche. Don't make sacrificial lambs of a couple of liberal hosts by using them to balance an otherwise conservative cast. That won't work because "unlike TV, experience shows that talk radio listeners reflect the bias and politics of the particular host, rather than the diversity of the larger marketplace." Liberals mostly want to listen to liberals, just as conservatives want to listen mostly to conservatives.

AUTHORS' NOTE: It seems it's not only liberal hosts who have trouble on talk radio, but liberal politicians as well. Ellen Ratner, described as "a died-in-the-wool Democrat and supporter of Al Gore," wrote the following perceptive analysis for *Talkers Magazine* on how Al blew it. We reprint by permission the three of her 10 points that seem most directly related to the subject of this chapter. "They" refers to Al Gore and his advisors and staffers.

Top 10 Reasons Why Al Gore Didn't Win the Election by 10 Points—A Talk Radio Perspective . . .

By Ellen Ratner
Talkers Magazine
Washington Bureau Chief

5. **They forgot that talk show hosts are as influential as are print and television.** One-third of Americans have listened to a talk show in the last 36 hours, but when invited to address *Talkers'* New Media Seminar, Bush showed up and Gore did not even respond to a letter or to phone calls. Bush was super friendly to the Democratic talk show hosts at the *Talkers* convention.

6. **They treated their friends in the media miserably.** Republicans made sure their talk show host friends on radio and television got the high profile interviews. They gave floor passes at the conventions, invitations to the chairman's box, and other perks to the Republican hosts and also to many of the hosts identified as Democratic. Democrats ignored their own. After much pushing, Alan Colmes was finally granted an interview with the vice president. Audio only. He waited in the studio one hour for the interview. Needing to get on the air for his television show he called gatekeeper Matis Goldman. He was told they were not doing the interview. Three days later it occurred. It was six minutes. Late in the game and not enough. They should have given Colmes anything he asked for.

9. **They listened to the polls, the focus groups, and forgot that those of us in the talk media are the keepers of the water cooler buzz.** If they had listened they might have realized what some of the undercurrents were and could have addressed them. Instead of these great campaign consultants, they could have saved themselves millions by listening to what people are talking about and asking for some advice from those of us that talk to those people every day.

"Radio is the most nuanced and niche-driven of all the major entertainment mediums," Hartmann explains. "Programmers are beginning to realize that conservative talk and liberal talk are really two separate market niches, just as are other established talk niches like sports talk, psychology talk, car talk, shock talk, and morning drive talk. Every PD [program director] knows that rock listeners don't want an hour of Beethoven in the middle of their listening day, sports fans are put off by psychology talk, and conservative listeners don't want to hear liberals (unless they're getting massacred)."

As Hartmann sees it:

> Most listeners are primarily tuning in to have their worldview reinforced and to learn the latest news from their perspective. They want to win the water cooler wars. They want to feel part of the team, a member of the tribe. They want to know they're right, and need factoids and evidence to prove it to others. And, like music listeners, they want to hear consistent programming. That being the case, formatic purity—all conservative talk all day, or all liberal talk all day—is key to programming success.

Hartmann continues: "The big difference today between conservative and liberal talk is that conservative talk is well distributed and market saturated, while liberal talk is virgin territory brimming with possibilities and profits for any station or network willing to invest the time it takes to build an audience base."

In other words, in Hartmann's view, it's time for a liberal radio network. While his niche-driven framework sounds reasonable, the problem, as we see it, is the apparent lack of exceptional liberal talent for that network to employ if it did exist. Hartmann insists, "There's a substantial pool of liberal talk talent already working across the United States," but he's short on names, giving us only one. And we wonder exactly how much patience liberal investors would show— how long they'd be "willing to invest the time it takes to build an audience base." Radio executives, acting on behalf of the investors, seem to be exceptionally shortsighted in their expectations and demands. Rush Limbaugh managed to rise fast enough in ratings to escape the sharks. Is there really another Rush Limbaugh lurking in the liberal shadows, someone who can overcome the challenges we've recounted above?

Which brings us to the most ambitious liberal plan so far to get a niche on radio—Air America Radio, a "progressive" network formed by Progress Media.

Air America Radio debuted on March 31, 2004, over stations in New York City, Chicago, Los Angeles, and San Francisco. It has ambitious plans for expansion, including a satellite partnership that would allow listeners to tune in anywhere in the country. Programming is also available online at www.airamericaradio.com.

Air America's top star is comedian and author Al Franken, whose show airs weekdays from noon to 3 PM in direct competition with Rush Limbaugh. Comedienne and actress Janeane Garofalo has an 8 PM to 11 PM show. In the afternoon drive slot, 3 PM to 7 PM, is veteran local radio host Randi Rhodes. Her West Palm Beach, Florida show was the highest-rated program in that region's afternoon drive-time slot, drawing more listeners locally than even Rush did. (For a more complete analysis of Air America's chances of success, see our Conclusion, pp. 339–342.)

Another liberal radio project, Democracy Radio, seems to have been upstaged by Air America. Tom Athans, who heads Democracy Radio, hopes to find local liberal radio hosts who are capturing their home market, and syndicate them nationally. He has raised $1.8 million from private donors to get the first syndication started—featuring Big Eddie "the Redhead" Schultz of Fargo, North Dakota. Schultz has also been brought to Washington, D.C., where he secured interviews with Sen. Hillary Clinton, Senate Minority Leader Tom Daschle of South Dakota, Sen. Dianne Feinstein of California, and a dozen other liberal legislators. But Athans had next hoped to syndicate Randi Rhodes, who has instead gone with Air America.

Meanwhile, none other than Rupert Murdoch's News Corp. has launched the Fox News Radio Service. One of its first stars is Alan Colmes, the liberal foil to Sean Hannity on Fox News' *Hannity and Colmes.* Colmes is already carried by 55 stations, which seems to make Fox and Colmes the most successful liberal radio talk effort in the nation. Isn't *that* a hoot!

Progress Media's Jon Sinton was asked by *Talkers,* "In your opinion as a programmer, is there *anything* inherent in liberalism versus conservatism that lends itself generically to being successful in talk radio or not?"

"Yes, I actually think there is," Sinton replied:

> We have tended as progressives to sort of dominate the film industry. We've tended to kind of dominate the television writing and production industry. We've tended to at least hold our own in the book publishing industry. And I certainly think we dominate the recording industry from a political perspective. In other words, my experience with liberals, real people, real Americans, not politicians, but real people liberals, is that they are very creative, very funny, very engaging, intriguing people, intriguing personalities, with really cool ideas. We make great movies. We make great television. And there's no reason why we shouldn't make great radio.

Maybe. But the talk radio host doesn't have rewrite editors to take out all of those wishy-washy liberal qualifications in the one second before he responds to the listener's question. Just look again at Sinton's response above: "*sort of* dominate," "*tended* to *kind of* dominate." A conservative host would have automatically replied, without reflection:

"Hell, we dominate the film industry! We dominate television writing and production! We can even beat your butt in the book-publishing world. And we'll show you we can do that in radio."

So, we'll see. As Paul Harvey would say, stay tuned for the rest of the story.

11

The TV Revolution in News and Talk

Put a dozen conservatives in a room and you'll get 12 different opinions about the state of the movement, what it *should* stand for, President Bush, the Republicans in Congress, which issues are most important—indeed, almost any political topic up for discussion.

On one topic, though, you will find unanimity—the three old-line television networks, NBC, CBS, and ABC. *They're liberal! They're biased! Tar and feather their anchors!*

Ah, unity.

This unanimity of opinion is no accident, nor is it misplaced. Since the 1950s—when the eldest of us became active in politics (give or take a few *really* old codgers)—network television news has been the voice of the liberal establishment. Now that Walter Cronkite has retired, he is open and outspoken about his liberal views. While he was on the little screen, he held the same political and cultural perspective but disguised it as "objective" journalism. And we're not singling out only Cronkite—all the network news anchors were the same, without exception. It was their pretense of objectivity that made their bias an even more bitter pill for conservatives to swallow.

That's a half century of TV broadcast network bias—a long period of time, which explains the intensity of conservative feelings on this subject. Those anchors and their apologists will deny that they've been biased, of course, and many of them will be sincere in their denial. In their rarefied and elitist social circles it isn't seen as anything but exemplary journalism, and to prove it they can point to the countless awards they've given each other.

For conservatives, the hardest part of those years was watching the election returns through the filter of these liberal anchors and their staffs, with no place to turn for relief on the small screen. Then things started to change. First came C-SPAN, which gave us a direct line to Congress without that liberal filter. Next came the proliferation of TV talk shows, with a conservative—John McLaughlin—once again leading the revolution. But the biggest break of all was the proliferation and growth of cable television networks in the 1990s, giving conservatives outlets they could watch without getting ulcers. Fox News led the way, of course, but Fox has also changed how the other two cable news networks approach the news. Now it's the liberals who get ulcers thinking about TV news.

C-SPAN (formally the National Cable Satellite Corporation) began in 1979. *The McLaughlin Group* debuted in 1982. The talk-radio explosion began in 1987, with the repeal of the so-called Fairness Doctrine, as discussed in Chapter 10. And the Fox News Network was launched in 1996. Together they created a revolution in how Americans get their news over television.

The revolution starts with C-SPAN

C-SPAN at first glance is an unlikely vehicle for political revolution. It was created by the cable industry in 1979 as a not-for-profit corporation that would air public service programming. President and CEO Brian Lamb is an easygoing, easy-to-watch on-air personality who can leave you wondering what *his* political views are after decades of his appearing in your living room.

What is known is that this unlikely revolutionary truly believes in grassroots democracy. Without commercialization and refusing to play the ratings game, Lamb has fashioned C-SPAN to bring gavel-to-gavel coverage of the House and Senate—plus much more—to the American people, so they can see what is happening without going through the filters of gatekeepers of any persuasion. No prior screening takes place even on call-in shows, which admittedly can lead to some far-fetched commentary.

"We're better off listening to everyone, no matter what they say, rather than us being the gatekeeper," Lamb told the *Washington Post*'s Howard Kurtz. "Politicians say things every day that aren't true. People who write columns say things that aren't necessarily true, make a lot of accusations. This is probably naïve, but I have an enormous faith in the system to work over time. There are plenty of checks and balances. Although someone on a call-in show can say things that are unfair, that's one of the prices you pay in public life."

People who watch hours of C-SPAN's programming are by self-definition a pretty serious lot, so it's not surprising that 98 percent of them vote, and they're twice as likely as non-viewers to contact Congress, donate to campaigns, and volunteer in campaigns. That's no doubt why Congress puts up with C-SPAN cameras in its chambers: You don't want to get these people angry at you, and they'd be *furious* if Congress revoked C-SPAN's coverage.

Brian Lamb created a nonideological vehicle, but it was a group of conservative Republicans in the House of Representatives who first realized how that vehicle could work to the advantage of people *with* an ideological mission. House rules allow "special orders" at the end of each day, when members can take turns speaking on any topic. Of course, by then the chambers are usually empty except for the handful who have something they want to say for the record. In early 1984, Rep. Newt Gingrich (R–GA) and his merry band of conservatives began using these "special orders" to talk methodically about conservative issues.

Only about 17 million Americans had access to C-SPAN in 1984, but, as we've noted, those who did watch tended to be hard-core activists. Word quickly spread around the nation, conservative to conservative, that there was some great viewing on C-SPAN, and soon Gingrich and company were celebrities whenever they appeared in public—outside of Washington, D.C., that is. (The District of Columbia's residents couldn't get C-SPAN until much later in the decade, so the ruling establishment in D.C. had no idea what was going on out in the boonies.) This was pretty heady and unprecedented stuff for members of the House, accustomed to taking a backseat to the president and much-more-visible senators.

C-SPAN's audience continued to grow, as cable spread across America and transformed television viewing. Gingrich had a truly revolutionary vision of how to use the media (most notably C-SPAN) to push for his group's Contract with America, in the process leading to the GOP takeover of the House of Representatives. In an interview with C-SPAN Executive Vice President Susan Swain, Gingrich admitted (or was it boasted?) that "we are to some extent manipulating you. You've provided us a vehicle to reach out to every neighborhood in America . . . "

Sometimes Gingrich wasn't aiming for Mr. John Q. Public in Podunk, Wisconsin, but for a very special citizen—President Ronald Reagan, sitting in the White House. As always seems to happen, Reagan's staff erected barriers to shield him from all the people, important and unimportant, who wanted a word with the chief executive. And as always seems to be the case with Republican presidents, that staff was more "practical" than conservative in its ideology, so conservatives who wanted a word with the president were more likely to get shut out. C-SPAN gave Gingrich a way to sometimes bypass *those* gatekeepers.

In his book *Hot Air: All Talk, All the Time*, Howard Kurtz relays what he calls "the ultimate in narrowcasting" with this quote from Newt Gingrich: "Ronald Reagan was a creature of the electronic media. Reagan would literally, particularly when Nancy was out of town, sit upstairs and watch C-SPAN. Sometimes, when we wanted to get messages to him that the staff didn't want to get through, we'd simply do special orders. And then he'd call us. He'd say, 'That was really good stuff.' We got more time with Reagan on C-SPAN than we did with Reagan in his office. That's a very important reality."

Network talk: Equal time for conservatives

Talk shows have always been part of network television but treated more or less as public-service tokens, sandwiched into time slots lacking better commercial potential—such as Sunday mornings. And, in the early years at least, conservatives (with one exception; see below) were not invited to the party. Over the years, though, TV talk shows began showcasing print journalists, and as the number of conservative columnists and writers multiplied, those with some stage presence appeared on TV talk shows in ever-larger numbers. George Will, Bob Novak, Pat Buchanan, and Bill Safire initially made their reputations as newspaper editorialists and syndicated columnists, then piggybacked onto TV for additional exposure—and, often, for lucrative lecture-circuit fees as celebrity worship spread in America.

To be fair, conservatives did have one early triumph in TV talk, but ironically it appeared not on the commercial networks but on the Public Broadcasting System (PBS), not normally considered a stronghold of conservative opinion. Bill Buckley's *The Firing Line* was a highly successful, widely seen program in the 1960s and '70s, with no equivalent on the Left. The erudite editor of *National Review* brought words such as "oxymoron" into public discourse, but an hour of that stuff was far too much for the commercial networks to even consider. Even PBS cut it down to a half hour later on.

The "modern era" of TV talk began with another *National Review* conservative in 1982. Just as Bill Buckley was the master of polysyllabic discourse, *National Review* Washington Editor John McLaughlin was the master of bombastic sound-bite political repartee. With the creation of *The McLaughlin Group* in 1982, TV talk became theater, and the decibel level went through the roof. Nobody learned very much, and probably very few viewers changed their opinions on any topic as a result of watching *The McLaughlin Group*, but it sure was—and is—fun. President

Reagan even showed up at its third-anniversary party, and declared the show to be "the most tasteful programming alternative to professional wrestling." Soon other TV talk shows copycatted the trail blazed by McLaughlin, and later cable television would follow suit.

The McLaughlin Group was a trailblazer in another way as well: Both sides—conservative and liberal—were represented, but there was no doubt the FCC had done away with the equal time regulation. McLaughlin himself (as the autocratic moderator) and either two or three of the four panelists would be conservatives to one degree or another, while liberals were represented by two panelists at most, and often only by *Newsweek*'s Eleanor Clift. For liberals watching the show, she was the heroic liberal maiden tied to the railroad tracks as the conservative train came roaring down the tracks and the villainous McLaughlin smirked with glee from within the locomotive's conductor booth. It was an example of fair and balanced commentary to be imitated later by one of the new cable news networks. Conservatives were beginning to stick it to the liberals, just as the liberals had stuck it to the conservatives in earlier years.

With that said, the network talk shows were an evolutionary rather than revolutionary phenomenon in our tale of the impact of alternative media on American politics. The growing presence of conservatives on talk shows was a reflection of growing conservative dominance in print journalism, not the result of a revolutionary jump in technology. The shows were valuable for giving the more verbally gifted conservatives an opportunity to hone their skills (and collect tidy lecture-circuit fees), but grassroots conservatives didn't turn to them as an alternative *news* outlet. Both the journalists and the politicians on these shows were Washington insiders, debating with each other rather than speaking directly to the viewers. What you got, then, were catfights staged within the parameters of the Washington establishment, albeit a Washington establishment that was increasingly conservative in its complexion. The truly revolutionary changes were taking place simultaneously with the growth of cable television (for news) and the Internet (for outsiders networking with outsiders, totally apart from the Washington establishment).

The Fox in the news house

Conservatives owe a great debt of gratitude to Ted Turner. Yes, the very same Ted Turner who calls Christianity "a religion for losers" and who became the fourth man to rescue Jane Fonda from spinsterhood (for a while at least). For it was Ted Turner the entrepreneur who took the financial risk to prove that 24/7 cable news was not only possible, but the wave of the future. And yes, he created the Cable News Network (CNN, aka the Clinton News Network) in his image, but that only opened the way for another entrepreneur, Rupert Murdoch, to beat Turner at his own game.

Turner started CNN in 1980, and in October 1996 he became vice chairman of Time Warner with the merger of Time Warner and his Turner Broadcasting System. CNN's subsequent problems can be traced to that fateful month. With the end of Ted Turner's personal direction of the network, CNN became a bureaucratic mess. The timing could not have been worse, for also in October 1996 the other entrepreneur, Murdoch, started the Fox News Channel. At the time, almost nobody gave Fox News a chance to compete with CNN, but you should never place your bet on a corporate bureaucracy in a battle with a brilliant entrepreneur. In less than seven years, Fox News not only managed to compete with CNN, it overtook CNN to become the foremost cable news channel.

Rupert Murdoch's News Corp. is the nation's seventh largest media group, following AOL Time Warner, Walt Disney, Viacom, Comcast, Sony, and Vivendi Universal. Worldwide his empire includes more than 100 newspapers, including the *Times of London* and the *New York Post*. He also owns HarperCollins, the second largest book publisher in the United States.

With six larger media empires around, News Corp. is hardly the "monopoly" threat portrayed by the Left. The combined impact of *all* those conglomerates may pose a problem of sorts, but that discussion is beyond the scope of this book. What makes the Left single out Murdoch as a threat to civilization is the fact that he's so much more visible, being an entrepreneur totally in control of his empire rather than one of the relatively faceless bureaucrats heading the other empires. That, and the fact that he aligned himself with media conservatives in the United States.

There's scant indication that Murdoch himself is an ideologue. He prefers to describe himself as a "moderate libertarian," and he talks about how "we started as a small newspaper company and grew by providing competition and innovation in stale, near monopolistic markets." His alliance with conservatives in the United States was a strategic decision. He saw a nation where conservatives vastly outnumbered liberals in the population at large, but where the media was overwhelmingly liberal. If you're an entrepreneur rather than an ideologue, that spells *opportunity.* And he ran with it.

Give the man credit, too, for picking smart people to run his various properties—and *allowing* them to work without undue interference. In the case of the Fox News Network, the man at the helm was and is Roger Ailes. Before heading Fox News, Ailes was better known as a top Republican operative than as a media executive, though he had served as a producer of the *Mike Douglas Show* and as president of CNBC. *Broadcasting & Cable* magazine says,

> Fox succeeds because it has personality, and it's all Ailes: combative, blustering, straightforward, conservative and thoroughly Middle American. . . . Rupert Murdoch's genius was not only in hiring Ailes but also in allowing him to impose his personality on the network. Americans have a choice about where to go for national TV news: General Electric, Time Warner, Disney, Viacom or some overweight guy from Youngstown, Ohio, who seems to think and talk like them. We are not surprised that a growing number are choosing the last.

Broadcasting & Cable was so impressed with Ailes that it named him its first "Television Journalist of the Year," in 2003. One reader complained that this decision "makes about as much sense as awarding the Emmy for best news anchor to Ted Baxter," but most readers probably enjoyed the magazine's lengthy interview with Ailes as much as the editors did. Who wouldn't, with repartee such as this:

> B&C: You didn't grow up as a journalist . . .
>
> Ailes: I've had a broad life experience that doesn't translate into going to the Columbia journalism school. That makes me a lot better journalist than some guys who had to listen to some pathetic professor who has been on the public dole all his life and really doesn't like this country much and hates the government and hates everybody and is angry because he's not making enough money.
>
> B&C: So if Fox News is fair and balanced, then why do so many other people not believe it?
>
> Ailes: Because they're getting their ass beaten.
>
> B&C: Why do you get your back up if somebody says you run a right-wing, Republican network?
>
> Ailes: The more they call us that, the more viewers watch us, because the American people think the rest of the media is too liberal. . . . *Most injuries in journalism are caused by journalists falling off their egos onto their IQs.* [Emphasis added.] The concept that journalism knows and the public knows nothing and they're idiots is wrong.

Critics might question Ailes's own ego and say that this exchange amounts to nothing more than breast-beating. Explain, then, why Fox News got such hearty praise in October 2003 from CBS News President Andrew Hayward, as he accepted the Edward R. Murrow Award for overall excellence from the Radio-Television News Directors Association. Hayward told his audience:

> The ability to offer something more to the viewer is, in my view, one explanation for the Fox News Channel's

> success, which has confounded so many news tradi-
> tionalists. . . . What Roger Ailes and his team have
> done so effectively is identify a niche in the market
> and patiently build a channel around a consistent,
> well-articulated vision. . . . The real lesson of Fox's suc-
> cess in my view is that, in order to stand out, you need
> to stand for something, something you believe in and
> can deliver on.

The irony, of course, was that at the time Hayward gave this tribute to Fox News—while accepting an award named for the top liberal TV icon of all time, Edward R. Murrow—Hayward's own *CBS Evening News* was losing even more viewers than the other broadcast networks. And where were their audiences headed? To the cable news networks, of course, headed by Fox. Perhaps Hayward *did* note the irony that he was getting the award while his ratings opponent was getting his audience (see Chart 2).

Cable news vs. network news

The chronology and unfolding of Fox News' rise ahead of CNN and MSNBC is fascinating, but too long for us to go into here. Suffice it to say that all of the cable news networks gained vast new audiences as a result of the most portentous events of this century thus far—the terrorist attacks of September 11, 2001, and the Iraq war in 2003. There were dips in audience size after those events, of course, but the overall trend keeps going up, with Fox News gaining more rapidly than either of its two rivals.

Both CNN and MSNBC tried to counter Fox News' rise by adding more commentators—including more conservatives—to their rosters. CNN's then-chairman Walter Isaacson even met with Republican leaders in Washington in 2001 to assure them that CNN no longer stood for the "Clinton News Network." (As the *Wall Street Journal* put it, "Mr. Isaacson's outreach to Beltway conservatives . . . had about it the aura

Chart 2
The Evening News Audience, All Networks

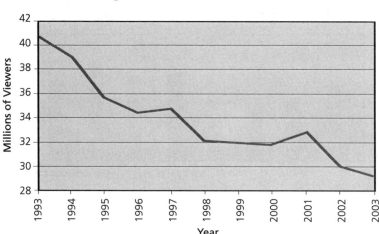

SOURCE: Nielsen Media Research unpublished data, www.nielsenmedia.com. This chart is taken from *The State of the News Media 2004*, a report by the Project for Excellence in Journalism, an institution affiliated with Columbia University Graduate School of Journalism. Ratings were measured in the month of November.

of a 19th-century Princeton anthropologist studying the Navajo. But he knew enough to try.")

It was a case of too little, too late, however. Fox had already "branded" itself as the first choice for conservatives, and in marketing, there's nothing more important than being the first to lock in a brand identification. By 2003 Fox News' Bill O'Reilly was king of the prime-time mountain with *The O'Reilly Factor*, becoming the most watched person in cable news. And there were weeks when Fox claimed 46 of the top 50 cable shows. The only major cable show not on Fox News was CNN's *Larry King Live*.

The even more significant story was the bigger picture: Cable news was replacing the TV broadcast networks as America's prime source of news (see Chart 3).

It should be noted that news channels were part of the *overall* shift from the broadcast networks to cable. The turning point came in 2002. In 2001, according to Nielsen Media Research, broadcast cornered 49

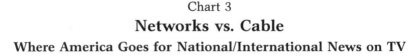

Chart 3
Networks vs. Cable
Where America Goes for National/International News on TV

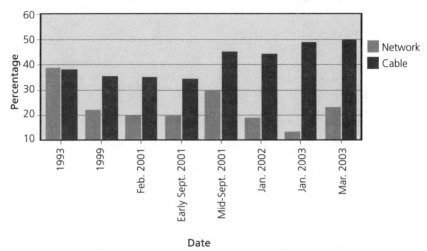

Date

SOURCE: Pew Research Center for the People and the Press, unpublished data, www.people-press.org. This chart is taken from *The State of the News Media 2004*, a report by the Project for Excellence in Journalism, an institute affiliated with Columbia University Graduate School of Journalism. Respondents were asked, "Do you get most of your news about national and international issues from network TV news, from local TV news, or from cable news networks such as CNN, MSNBC, and the Fox News Channel?"

percent of prime-time viewing; cable, 45 percent. By 2002, it was cable, 48 percent, broadcast, 45 percent. In 2003, with at least 86 percent of the nation's homes served by cable or satellite services, the figures were 51 percent for cable, 49 percent for broadcasting.

As for news, the 2003 war in Iraq marked a turning point in the shift from broadcast to cable. During the first days of the war, everyone's audience size jumped (see Chart 4), but after the first couple of days, CBS and ABC together lost nearly 2 million viewers, with NBC (which has a cable news operation) posting a slight gain. Cable, on the other hand, continued to gain viewers in the first three weeks of the war—with 300-percent gains each for Fox and CNN, and a 350-percent gain for the much smaller MSNBC.

The *New York Times* quoted Andrew Tyndall, founder of the *Tyndall Report*, which monitors network newscasts: "Going back the 15 years that I have researched it, the networks always show an increase of

Chart 4
The First Night of the War in Iraq
Where Did America Tune In?

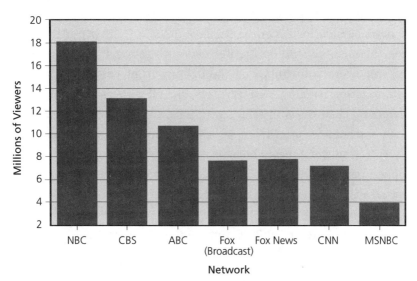

According to *The State of the News Media 2004* report, "Traditionally in times of national crisis, like the war in Iraq, viewers have turned to the networks for coverage, if not the first night, then within a day or two. That did not happen in 2003 with the war in Iraq. The total number of viewers tuned to nightly [network] news actually dropped during the war."

However: "On the first night of the war, from 9:30 to 11 PM, 42.2 million people turned to the three networks and their nightly anchors, according to estimates made by Nielsen. Less than half as many (19.2 million viewers) turned to the three cable networks and 7.7 million more turned to Fox News on broadcast. Combining Fox broadcast and Fox cable would put Rupert Murdoch's two channels in second place among the networks (at 15.6 million), well behind the combined NBC and MSNBC (at 22.2 million). But that would be ahead of CBS (at 13 million) and ABC (at 11 million), neither of which has a news cable sibling."

SOURCE: Jesse Hamlin, "NBC declares victory in war's TV ratings battle," *San Francisco Chronicle,* quoting Nielsen Media Research data. The chart presents viewership between 9:30 PM and 11:00 PM on the night of March 19, 2003. This chart is taken from *The State of the News Media 2004,* a report by the Project for Excellence in Journalism, an institute affiliated with Columbia University Graduate School of Journalism.

about 10 percent in viewing during heavy news periods. This would be an unprecedented event."

Granted, the three broadcast networks were still much larger, with some 28 million viewers compared to an average 7.3 million viewers for the three cable news networks. But when you factor in the around-the-clock coverage on cable compared to an hour or less on the broadcast networks, and the much greater dedication of cable viewers to current affairs and politics, it becomes clear that cable was now setting the news agenda for America. Andrew Heyward, the president of CBS News, blamed the shift on the Bush administration's policy of "embedding" reporters with troops on the fighting front, which made the reporting more riveting and favored the all-news-all-the-time cable networks. "This was a reporter's war, not an anchor war," he lamented.

By the summer after the war, in 2003, Americans were understandably suffering from "news burnout," and the figures for news viewing dropped considerably, even below the levels of summer 2002. But the drop-off was far greater for the broadcast networks than it was for the cable networks. And only Fox News bucked the trend, getting *more* viewers in the summer of 2003 than in the summer of 2002.

Cable vs. broadcast for campaign news

In assessing the impact of the alternative media on American politics, the vortex of the clash between the establishmentarian broadcast networks and the alternative cable news networks is the political campaign. Where do Americans get their campaign news? In a later chapter we'll consider all news sources; here we will confine ourselves primarily to the cable-versus-broadcast question.

Fortunately, the Pew Research Center for the People & the Press has conducted in-depth polling on this topic for the last three presidential election cycles. Unfortunately, their methodology has changed during that time, allowing us to compare 2000 with 1996 but forcing us to use different 2000 figures to compare with 2004. Nevertheless, despite the problems in comparing raw numbers, the *trend* moves in the same direction for all three election cycles.

Television accounts for the lion's share among all media when Americans are asked where they get their campaign news. Here is how it breaks down among cable, local, and network TV (figures do not round out to 100 percent because people could give two answers, and other types of media were included in the polling):

Where Do Americans Get Their Campaign News? (%)

	1996	2000	Change
Cable TV	23%	31%	+8%
Local TV	34	25	−9
Network TV	39	24	−15

And here is the change since 2000:

	2000	2004	Change
Cable TV	34%	38%	+4%
Local TV	48	42	−6
Network TV	45	35	−10

Despite the different base numbers for the year 2000, the trend is unmistakable. Cable news has gained in each of the past three election cycles. Local TV news has lost a considerable number of viewers, but network TV news has had a precipitous falloff.

The bottom line: Since around the year 2000, more Americans get their campaign news from the three cable news networks than from the four broadcast networks. In TV news, at least, the alternative media has become the establishment media!

If you have any doubt about where we're headed in the future, look at where the 18–29 generation gets its TV campaign news:

Where Do Americans Aged 18 to 29 Get Their Campaign News?

Cable TV	37%
Local TV	29
Network TV	23

Indeed, 20 percent of the 18–29 cohort say they get their campaign news from the Internet, and 21 percent cite comedy TV shows. In each instance, that's roughly equal to the number who cite network TV news. When Peter Jennings and Dan Rather finally retire, will the networks retire their news shows as well?

Young people aren't the only ones who prefer cable to network TV news. So do college graduates and wealthier Americans. These are coveted demographic groups for advertisers, which explains why it often seems you get more ads than news on your cable news channels.

Also helping to explain the greater *impact* of cable TV news today is the breakdown for the roughly 7 percent of the population that is heavily engaged in following and participating in the campaigns. These people, after all, are the "movers and shakers" of the political world. Here is their breakdown:

Where Do Politically Engaged Citizens Get Their Campaign News?

Cable TV	64%
Local TV	34
Network TV	46

Finally, there is one breakdown that should come as no surprise: Republicans favor cable TV, especially Fox News, while Democrats favor the liberal networks. But there is a surprise, perhaps, in the revelation that Republicans watch a broader array of TV news outlets than do Democrats, who heavily favor their tried-and-truly-liberal TV broadcast networks. Here's the breakdown:

News Audiences by Political Affiliation (%)

	Republicans	Democrats	Independents
ABC/CBS/NBC	24%	40%	30%
CNN	20	27	20
Fox News	29	14	17

Taking into account all these figures, it is tempting to agree with the observation made by Alex S. Jones in the *New York Times* that "Fox—the self-described maverick outsider—finds itself in the peculiar position of being, arguably, the most powerful television news organization in the country, playing a major role in defining what is important and what is not. Like it or not, Fox has become the establishment, with critics now bemoaning not just what they say is its bias but its dominating influence."

Okay, Fox is king—but is it really fair and balanced?

When you get down to it, "fair and balanced"—like "objectivity"—is in the eye of the beholder.

Conservatives will almost always defend Fox's claim to be "fair and balanced," but they find it hard to do so without a smirk or smile on their face. Indeed, they find it hard to suppress a giggle when they do so. They proudly *want* to claim Fox as one of their own—it's one of the movement's great success stories—but at the same time they don't want to enable the liberal enemy to cavalierly dismiss Fox as biased. For decades they've been fighting the *hidden* bias behind liberal claims of objectivity.

The bottom line is that there *is* no such creature as objective reporting. Reporting, after all, starts as an act of discrimination. Out of a bloated mass of data and raw information, you the reporter (or anchor or commentator) decide what's important. And all your criteria for selection will reflect your biases. More acts of discrimination and internal bias follow, as you connect the dots—the pieces of raw information you've selected—to create a story. About the best you can do, to still be honest about it, is to be *fair* and admit that other possibilities exist, even as you present your own "take" on the news. Oops, there's that word "fair," just two words short of the phrase "fair and balanced."

What it comes down to, then, is that (most) liberal newscasters claim to be objective—but you'll notice they don't have someone across the desk from them contesting their take on the news. You have to take their word for it. While in contrast, Fox claims to be "fair and balanced"—but the very word "balanced" admits that there is more than one viewpoint. And, of course, one of Fox's hallmarks is that it *does* have people of differing viewpoints on most of its programs. There will always be different takes on whether a particular program episode—say, Bill O'Reilly interviewing one of his many liberal guests—is "fair"; after all, O'Reilly is in the driver's seat. But at least there's an admission that different viewpoints are possible, which is a step far above the pretense of "objective" liberal reporting.

Judging by the numbers, Americans seem to be saying they like the step toward honesty represented in Fox's trademarked term, "fair and balanced."

As Roger Ailes put it in his *Broadcasting & Cable* interview: "Bias has to do with the elimination of points of view, not presenting a point of view." Brent Bozell, president of the conservative Media Research Center, says on that point: "Pick an issue—global warming, taxes, homosexuality—and Fox demonstrates the temerity to allow both sides to debate, whereas other networks still pretend that only one reasonable, quotable side exists." Of course, as Brian C. Anderson notes in the Manhattan Institute's *City Journal*, "Not only does the Fox approach make clear that there is always more than one point of view, but it also puts the network's liberal guests in the position of having to defend their views—something that almost never happens on other networks."

Bozell follows with an amusing and telling story. When the National Press Foundation gave Fox's Brit Hume its Broadcaster of the Year award, Geneva Overholser, a former ombudsman at the *Washington Post*, resigned from the foundation in protest: Hume and Fox practice "ideologically committed journalism," she complained. And who were some of the previous winners of that award? Dan Rather, Howell Raines (later fired as the *New York Times'* editor), PBS's Ken Burns, and NPR's Nina Totenberg—liberals all. Overholser had not resigned in protest over any of their awards. And so it goes.

"I had the same conception a lot of people did about Fox News, that they have a right-wing agenda," said Chris Wallace to the *Washington Post* when he left ABC to become the host for *Fox News Sunday.* But, he says, he watched Fox News Channel for months before deciding to make the switch, and he decided the network gets "an unfair rap. Its reporting is serious, thoughtful, and evenhanded. . . . If they wanted someone to push a political agenda, they wouldn't have hired me." And he added that the only remotely political question Roger Ailes asked him was, "Can you wake up in the morning without assuming the United States is in the wrong?"

That was too much for Charlie Reina, a former Fox News producer—and a liberal. He fired off a missive against Fox to Poynteronline (poynter.org), a blog that professes to present "everything you need to be a better journalist."

The heart of Reina's case was this paragraph in Poynteronline:

> The roots of FNC's day-to-day on-air bias are actual and direct. They come in the form of an executive memo distributed electronically each morning, addressing what stories will be covered and, often, suggesting how they should be covered. To the newsroom personnel responsible for the channel's daytime programming, The Memo is the bible. If, on any given day, you notice that the Fox anchors seem to be trying to drive a particular point home, you can bet The Memo is behind it.

That sounds pretty damning. Liberals thought they had their smoking gun proving bias at Fox News. The only problem: It was all smoke, with no bullet.

When Salon.com, a liberal online magazine, asked Reina, "Can you remember a specific instance in which one of your superiors told you to approach a story with a particular ideological slant?" the best he could come up with was a pollution story. His boss said: "You can obviously give both sides, but just make sure that the pro-environmentalists don't get the last word." When Reina thought about it overnight and the next morning told his boss he couldn't do the story with a predetermined outcome, the boss "was wise enough to know that what he had done was wrong, and he left it alone."

Such injustice! Conservative media critic Reed Irvine, of Accuracy in Media, noted that pro-environmentalist bias is so prevalent in mainstream liberal media that *Time* magazine Senior Editor Charles

Alexander admitted way back in 1989 that in covering the environment, "We have crossed the boundary from news reporting to advocacy." Adds Irvine, "Telling Reina to not let an environmentalist have the last word can be seen as a subtle reminder that Fox did not want him to cross the boundary from news reporting to advocacy."

And then Salon.com asked Reina, "Are you aware of times where the reverse happened—that is, where things were happening on the air and someone in management sent a message saying, 'I want this to slant more Republican?'"

Reina's answer: "No, I can't say that I've ever known them to do that."

Here's another interesting question-and-answer set:

> Salon: Are the employees at Fox ideologically aligned with Ailes?
>
> Reina: I don't think that's the case. There are probably more people there who tend to be conservative or Republican than I have encountered at other places. And I have to say that they're right when they say that people in journalism tend to be liberal or Democrat. . . . There are many people who work at Fox, as there are elsewhere, that are much more liberal and Democrat-leaning than management is.

The problem, as Reina sees it, is that "it's such a young staff of workers" at Fox, and they are "very easy to mold." Then there's the "middle management that is all too willing to just play ball." But when Reina, who was 55 when this story broke in October 2003, stood up to his boss on the pollution story, the boss let him do it his way. And Reina admitted to the *Los Angeles Times* that he left Fox over a salary and workload dispute, not politics.

So, what do we have here? We have a disgruntled former employee who thinks everyone else was a sellout and who didn't like his boss's politics. His case against Fox is more based on anger than damning evidence ("Once more we ask you, Mr. Reina, where are Roger Ailes's hidden weapons of mass deception?"). But let's assume, for a moment, that Reina is right about his former coworkers. The young are easy to mold and want to please the boss, while middle management just goes along. That can be seen as lamentable, but how would that be different from any other news organization, corporation, labor union, or non-profit organization in the land? That's not just politics; that's life.

Are young conservative reporters at the networks and major newspapers molded by their liberal editors? No doubt they are—if you can find any. The most striking revelation in the Reina story is how many liberals Fox employs. To all the other networks, we say: Show us your conservatives!

As for the daily news memo, we don't know what the policies are at the other cable news networks or the broadcast networks, but if used properly The Memo sounds like a sensible management tool. After all, don't the managing editors at the *Washington Post* and the *New York Times* assign stories to reporters, especially the younger ones? The alternative would be for every staffer to decide on his own what is news and what he wants to cover, which would result in unfocused and idiosyncratic coverage. As we've seen, focus is one of Fox's reasons for success. If you want to "do your own thing," you can now start your own blog on the Internet. But you'll have to figure out how you're going to pay the bills.

The question, of course, is how far those daily memos go beyond suggesting news topics and into directing how to slant them. Here we find it interesting that these memos are transmitted electronically, and Fox has a largely liberal staff, yet so far nobody has leaked any examples of damning bias to the outside world. Maybe such evidence is as weak as that presented by Charlie Reina.

Then there's conservative columnist Cal Thomas's take on the daily memos:

> Reina . . . says Fox executives suggest story angles. That isn't necessarily bad, because reporters, editors, and producers must be reminded that Fox News is often the "other side," giving perspectives ignored by the other networks. Fox employs many liberals, whose numbers probably are greater than the number of conservatives employed by CNN and the other networks.

> A liberal producer of one of Fox's top-rated shows told
> me last week that at another network where she
> worked, no memo from management on story coverage
> was necessary "because we all thought alike."

The final irony of this liberal "scoop" on Fox is how his Fox experience apparently changed Charlie Reina himself—perhaps because for the first time he was presented with more than one view on issues. "Part of what Fox's message is," he told Salon.com, "and I have to say that to a certain extent I agree with it, is that political correctness is a terrible thing. There are a lot of assumptions that are simply made and not questioned, and a lot of that, liberals like me have perpetrated. And I have to agree that there's too much of that."

Will the liberals get their own cable news network?

They already have NBC, ABC, and CBS, of course, but that's not enough for liberal whiners like Al Gore. He wants his own cable news network.

Gore has never kept his dislike for Fox News a secret, of course. Back in the year 2000, with the Florida recount going on, he pressed his case in interviews with NBC, ABC, CBS, and CNN—but turned down Fox's interview offer. His campaign spokesman, Mark Fabiani, told the *New York Observer* why: "I think Fox's coverage during the campaign has been decidedly one-sided."

In December 2002, Fox headed Gore's list of Really Bad Media when he told the *Observer*, during a book tour: "The media is kind of weird these days on politics, and there are some major institutional voices that are, truthfully speaking, part and parcel of the Republican Party." In case you assumed he was just suggesting that they all think the same way, he got more specific about how the conspiracy operates: "Something will start at the Republican National Committee, inside the building, and it will explode the next day on the right-wing talk-show network and on Fox News and in the newspapers that play this game, the *Washington Times* and the others." ("We understand that Gore is frustrated," replied a spokesman for the Republican National Committee. "He's the leader of a party without a message. But if he thinks that the Republican National Committee can control the American media, then perhaps he needs a break from the book tour.")

Gore's New Year's resolution must have been to stop complaining and *do* something about it, because in 2003 he began serious efforts to start his own cable news channel. After a year, the deal was announced in May 2004: Al Gore and a group of investors have bought Newsworld International from Vivendi Universal SA for an undisclosed price (trade rumors put it in the $70 million range). Gore is chairman of the board of the new network, and the CEO is Joel Hyatt, founder of a nationwide chain of low-cost legal clinics. Hyatt has served as finance chairman for the Democratic National Committee, and lost his campaign for the U.S. Senate in Ohio in 1994.

Despite their Democratic Party backgrounds, Gore insists, "This will not be a political network." He expanded this later to, "This is not going to be a liberal network, a Democratic network, or a political network." Skeptics remember another prominent Democrat who insisted, "I did not have sexual relations with that woman."

Newsworld presently reaches a mere 17 million subscribers, mostly through satellites, the rest through cable. Its present content will be gutted as soon as the Gore team gets its act together, but the new focus is still somewhat speculative. Al Gore says that the reborn network will target viewers in the 18-to-34 age bracket. Hyatt says, "It's going to be programming in the subjects that young people care about, whether that is the issues of the day, careers, relationships, the culture in which they live. We are going to be funny, irreverent, and bold." Which suggests Hyatt plans to keep Gore away from the content. Whatever, the new youth network has a daunting task: The Pew survey figures quoted in this chapter reveal that the kids are currently picking up their campaign news through one-liners on the late-night comedy shows. In a contest between Al Gore and Jay Leno, you *know* where we're placing our money.

The deal is ironic in other ways as well. *Broadcasting & Cable* noted that "Gore drove the 1992 Cable Act into law, derailed two giant mergers, chopped the valuation of cable systems by billions, and plagued operators for years." The result is that he "does not have many—if any—fans at the senior ranks of cable operators whose favor he must curry to secure additional distribution." The trade journal quotes "a top executive at one major cable operator" saying, "It's hysterical. This is a man despised by most of the people he needs."

Even more hysterical: Most Newsworld International viewers receive the channel through DirecTV, a satellite service that is controlled by Rupert Murdoch. Moreover, Newsworld's contract with DirecTV is about to expire, and needs to be renewed. Welcome to the hardball world of big business, Al.

Fox News' Brit Hume doesn't seem worried about the possibility of competition from Al Gore. "It's a little unclear what he's trying to do if he wants to start a kind of talk channel that he believes would counterprogram Fox," Hume told the *New York Observer*. "He clearly doesn't know what we're really doing. If he's trying to start a serious news organization with worldwide reach, then he immediately becomes a competitor, in my view, to CNN and MSNBC, so he does us good. It doesn't seem like it would affect us very much."

Then there's the nitty-gritty details, like cameras and mobile trucks—"I wonder if they've even *thought* about those things." And money. Gobs of money. "It is estimated that there were losses amounting to a billion dollars before Fox News turned a profit," Hume says.

Even if they get a spare billion from, say, George Soros, they'll have to find TV talent—talent that hasn't surfaced with any force so far. The liberals at Fox News, like Alan Colmes and Greta Van Susteren, aren't too likely to leave the nation's top news channel for a chance to sink with Al Gore's "Titanic Channel." And Phil Donahue, hired by MSNBC to draw an audience opposite Fox News' Bill O'Reilly, was cancelled by MSNBC in six months. After a strong opening, reported *Broadcasting & Cable*, "the Nielsen ratings fell sharply, barely registering at all."

Our bold prediction: It's quite likely that the liberals are going to have to be content with NBC, ABC, and CBS.

Wayne LaPierre and the NRA Prevail on the Gun Issue

Gun control has become a political "third rail" for the Democrats—an issue that can kill them at the polls. It did that to Al Gore in 2000, when the presidential candidate said he wanted to license all new handguns bought by Americans. Pretty much everyone, including most Democrats, agrees that the resulting gun-owner revolt cost the Democrats Tennessee (Gore's home state), Arkansas (former president Clinton's home state), and West Virginia—more than enough to lose the election for Gore. No need to blame Ralph Nader and dangling chads.

President George W. Bush's brother, Gov. Jeb Bush of Florida, was the keynote speaker at the 2003 annual convention of the National Rifle Association (NRA), the Big Bertha in the pro-gun, pro–Second Amendment lobby. In his speech, he noted that 48 percent of the voters in the 2000 presidential election were gun owners. "Were it not for your active involvement," he told them, "it's safe to say my brother would not be president of the United States." Then the line that brought down the house: "The sound of our guns is the sound of freedom."

Look at what's happened in the Democratic Party since 2000. Former president Clinton said on *60 Minutes* that he thought the NRA probably made the difference in the election. Senator Hillary Clinton told us she hunted as a youngster. Senator John Kerry even arranged a pheasant hunt for reporters during his 2003–2004 primary campaign. The centrist Democratic Leadership Council warned Democrats that it's not enough to stay silent on the issue—if you don't talk proactively about respect for the Second Amendment, Democratic pollster Mark Penn told them, voters will presume you are anti-gun: "It is very clear that silence is not golden for Democrats on the gun issue." And during the Democratic primary debates, only the Rev. Al Sharpton supported Al Gore's position on handgun licensing. The others waffled. Most hilarious of all was Senator Joseph Lieberman's assertion that "I have never supported such a proposal." When someone reminded him that he was Al Gore's running mate, Lieberman responded: "Gore came out with that position before I came onto the ticket. The issue never really came up." And, finally, none other than Senate Minority Leader Tom Daschle is sponsoring a bill to shield gun manufacturers from punitive lawsuits.

Time magazine, that establishment voice we love to hate, got this one right when it assessed Washington's hypocrisy on the gun issue in its May 26, 2003, article, "Why No One Shoots Straight on Guns":

> When it comes to guns, politicians are figuring out what clay pigeons have known for a long time: it's safer to be a moving target. So it is that President Bush can win points with gun-control groups by sticking to his campaign promise to sign an extension on the assault-weapons ban when it expires next year, while House majority leader Tom DeLay can make the gun lobby happy by suggesting, as he did last week, that no such bill will ever reach Bush's desk. And Democrats can fuss and fume over how Bush and the Republicans are trying to have it both ways—while quietly breathing a sigh of relief at being spared a vote that would expose the party's own divisions on the issue.
>
> The pantomime will continue, for behind it lies a new reality: two years into the Bush Administration, the gun lobby is on a winning streak.

Ah, yes, hypocrisy as usual in the nation's capital. But for supporters of the Second Amendment, that's far better than the anti-gun crusades of yesteryear. To learn how the National Rifle Association accomplished this turn of direction—using, incidentally, an array of alternative media—we interviewed the NRA's hard-driving executive director, Wayne LaPierre, who told us:

> The NRA's biggest problem is the bias of the big media conglomerates. There's no doubt about that. They are the single most dominant political player in our political system today, and they spew out misleading and false propaganda on the gun issue and on the NRA in general. To get around that, the NRA has been one of the pioneers in using every new and alternative media technology out there.
>
> In states like Tennessee, Arkansas, and West Virginia, gun ownership runs 60, 70, 80 percent. And the polls showed that up to 50 percent of union households that had a gun in it voted for President Bush as opposed to Al Gore *based on the gun issue.* But in order to create that level of activism, you've got to get the word out past the filter of ABC, NBC, and CBS. You have to go directly *to* the people.

Here's how they did it.

Paid-for TV news documentaries

"Starting in 1999," LaPierre told us,

> we put half-hour news documentaries on the air wherever we could buy time. They were moderated by Ginny Simone, our former NBC news anchor out of Albuquerque and Colorado Springs. Our own journalists, on the spot, reported on the gun ban in England, the gun ban in Australia, the gun ban in Canada, misleading Clinton propaganda.
>
> Where on NBC, ABC, and CBS did you hear how the politicians in Great Britain broke their promise when they said, "If you register your guns we'll never ban

them"? That's a big story—a huge story. Or how, since that gun ban, there's been a 50 percent increase in gun crime on the streets of London. Yet somehow the so-called mainstream media didn't see fit to report that *at all*.

The only way we can get this news out is to buy time and put it in our own news documentaries. And we spent $25 million on these half-hour documentaries, going straight to the American people. I don't know of any other organization that has bought $25 million in airtime like this. And I believe that was one of the major factors in the election.

Confrontational TV spots

The Clinton administration was using all of the major media conglomerates against us. They basically ran the "Million Mom March" out of the White House, with the willing collaboration of the major media.

We had to buy airtime to present our side against the Clinton administration. Charlton Heston would go on and say, "Mr. Clinton, when you know it's not the truth, it's a lie"—about whether he was prosecuting violent criminals or not, and whether he was using this issue politically. And President Clinton—remember?—ran down to the Rose Garden and badmouthed me, shaking his finger and everything else. That was when the debate was joined, and the American public got a fair debate between the NRA and the Clinton administration. But that debate would not have happened without the NRA buying media time.

Talk radio

I would spend entire days totally committed to talk radio all over the country, ranging from small towns to big cities, local and syndicated. We did hundreds of talk radio shows; in fact, some days I would do 25 shows, starting at 5:00 in the morning and running through ten o'clock at night. It was just back to back. Media consultants Craig Shirley and Diana Banister spent weeks doing nothing but lining up talk radio for us—because it *reaches* people.

Reaching NASCAR dads—and moms

NRA Sports is one of the organization's newer vehicles for bypassing the mainstream media and carrying the organization's message directly to the American people. "NASCAR Nation is NRA Nation," LaPierre proclaims. "This is a way for us to get around the negativity of NBC, ABC, and CBS as we race to meet our next goal of 5 million members. With 5 million members, we'll have the political firepower we need to win the elections and keep your freedoms safe and secure."

Through the NRA's arrangement with Speedway Motorsports, Inc., LaPierre says, "every time America's 70 million racing fans flip on the TV to watch Winston Cup races, we'll be there with the drivers, in the pits, on racetrack billboards, in programs, at hospitality suites, and on the PA system. Most important, NRA will be heard on the Performance Racing Network's 765-plus affiliate stations with more than 300 features for almost 230,000 minutes. That's the equivalent of 3,800 hours—or 159 days—on the air!"

Guns, crime, and freedom

"The other thing we did," says LaPierre, "is to put out a book. When I wrote *Guns, Crime and Freedom* in 1994, that was seen as another way to bypass the major media."

> Initially the only major bookstore chain that would even touch our book was Crown. So we went to some independent bookstores with the publisher, Regnery— and Regnery was great on this—and said, "Look, Wayne will come out there to do a booksigning. Will

you take several hundred copies of his book if he
comes out?" And we went to Nickelby's in Columbus,
Ohio; then to the Tattered Cover in Denver. Well, suddenly, there were 600 people lined up in the streets of
Denver to buy that book, 400 at Nickelby's. Then we
got Barnes & Noble to do it in a couple of their mall
stores, and you would have 400 or 500 people lined up
all the way down the mall. Well, you don't have to do
that too many times before you've got Books-a-Million,
Walden, all of them on the phone saying "Give me that
gun book!" Because ultimately those stores were making their entire month's rent on one night—by selling
that book. And it got on the *New York Times* best-seller
list without a single national TV interview. Once again,
we bypassed the filter of the major media, going
straight to the people.

"How did those hundreds of people in line learn you were going to
be there?" we asked. LaPierre responded, "They learned through publicity generated by press releases from our people and from our consultants, Craig Shirley and Diana Banister. And we let our members in
each area know through our magazines and special mailings to them."

Mobilizing the Second Amendment militia

Ten years ago the membership of the NRA was about 2.4 million.
Under Wayne LaPierre's aggressive leadership it has grown to more
than 4 million. Ask him how they did it, and you get a typical LaPierre
response:

I think the NRA proves that if you plant your flag and
fight on principle, people will follow you. You don't
have to "go along." You don't have to compromise. We
knew where the American public was—they were with
us!—so we used every communication technique out
there to reach the public. When we could get the mainstream media, we did it; when we could use alternative

media, we did it; when we had to bypass the mass media, we did it.

Of course, there's nothing like a good enemy to energize your troops, and President Clinton was perfect for that position. Rush Limbaugh, in an extensive interview with Wayne LaPierre in July 2002 (reprinted in LaPierre's new book, *Guns, Freedom, and Terrorism*), asked:

> I spoke to you soon after the so-called Million Mom March in the spring of 2000. At that time you said that you had gained over a million members in the previous 12 months, and you were the fastest growing association in the country at that time. Now we've got a Republican in the White House, and with that I think the threat to the Second Amendment is perceived, anyway, to be lessened. Has your membership growth kept up or has it slowed down a bit now with a Republican in power?

LaPierre replied:

> Our membership is hanging right around 4 million members. I consider that a tremendous accomplishment. I was worried about a big drop-off because of apathy. I thank people all over the country for realizing it's important to remain vigilant. Meanwhile, the last Million Mom March missed the mark by about 999,800 marchers. They've laid off 30 of their 35 employees. But the NRA is thriving because ultimately people in this country believe they have a right to own a firearm.

An army of 4.3 million concerned citizens is impressive in itself, but that figure represents only the core of the NRA universe—the people who pay individual membership dues to the NRA. The NRA offers *only* individual memberships, but it is also affiliated with some 30,000 clubs. Many people consider themselves to be "NRA" because they're active with one of those clubs or because they join in activities with their buddies who are NRA members. "Some 28 million people tell the pollsters they're affiliated with the NRA in some way," LaPierre told us. "I mean, that's a *huge* base! It's as large as the Democratic Party or Republican Party in terms of sheer numbers that say they're affiliated in some way."

To reach this huge membership and keep it engaged and active, the NRA uses every tool it can think of. We asked: "How many pieces of direct mail will an average NRA member receive in the course of a year?"

LaPierre's reply: "Probably 55 to 60—fax alerts on legislative issues, membership mailings, marketing solicitations, legislative updates, the magazines . . . all of that."

Multiply those 55 to 60 pieces of direct mail by 4,300,000 members and you have somewhere in the range of 236 million to 258 million mailings to members in a year's time.

"Our own magazines are probably as large as *Time* or *Newsweek*," LaPierre told us. "I don't know whether they have 3 million circulation, but we pump out about 3.5 million magazines each month. And they're *news* magazines, as legitimate as *Time* or *Newsweek*. In fact, I think they're *more* legitimate because they tell the truth."

(We checked the numbers. *Time* has a circulation of about 4.1 million. But the NRA's magazine circulation is higher than those of *Newsweek*, *Playboy*, *Prevention*, *Sports Illustrated*, and *Cosmopolitan*. And the NRA magazines operate entirely under the radar of the Washington-New York media establishment.)

"We're pumping out the truth on the gun issue every day," LaPierre continued, "over the Internet, through fax alerts, through our own Web site newscasts. *NRA Live* is our Webcast, and it gets between 50,000 and 125,000 hits a day."

We asked: "How much time do you spend personally on something related to alternative media?"

His reply: "At least 35, 40 percent of my time is spent coordinating all of that. I mean, these days you're dead if you're running an organization and you can't communicate. You're going to be overrun, swamped, and defeated. A big challenge to an organization like the NRA is to keep out there, keep on the cutting edge, and keep the message out there in front of people."

12

Conservatives in Print
Newspapers, Magazines, Books

Back in the not-so-good old days—the late 1950s and early 1960s, when the conservative movement was just getting started—the print media were king.

In the nation at large, the network TV evening news shows were growing in importance as the average Joe's or Jane's source of news, but they hadn't yet overthrown newspapers for that role. That would come shortly, with the dramatic events of the later '60s—the leftist antiwar demonstrations, the civil rights protests, and the assassinations of the two Kennedys and Martin Luther King, Jr.—events so graphic and stirring that Americans began turning to the tube first for their news. But if you could transport yourself back to, say, 1960, you would note that virtually everyone read a newspaper every day. And not just for the TV listings.

If you were a political junkie in 1960, the print media were even more firmly ensconced as your primary source of news. In addition to at least one newspaper, you probably subscribed to at least one of the news weeklies (*Time, Newsweek, U.S. News*), as well as several of the general content magazines that also interpreted current events (*Life,*

Look, Reader's Digest, the *Saturday Evening Post, Collier's,* and others)
and perhaps one of the smaller ideological journals (such as *The Nation*
and *The New Republic*).

No one was distracted from these print media by talk radio as we
know it today (didn't exist), cable television (didn't exist), or the Internet (*really* didn't exist).

Conservatives, being shut out of any representation on TV, were almost entirely dependent on print media as our sources of news. And
there we were on the margins. As we recounted in Chapters 4 and 5 on
the formative years of the conservative movement, we were pretty
much shut out of the mass-circulation magazines, and newspaper
reporting—even then—was dominated by the liberals. All we had were
some newspaper editorial pages (among the least-read pages of the
newspaper) and *our* tiny alternative media, *Human Events* and then *National Review,* plus a few even tinier publications.

What has happened in the decades since then, of course, is the
explosion in new and alternative media, as documented in this book,
giving conservatives (finally!) a seat at the mass-media table. The
print media haven't disappeared as news sources, they just have lots
of competition today, and each year that competition gets more of the
spoils.

Within the world of the print media during the past four decades,
liberals continued to dominate the ranks of newspaper reporters—
every survey of the political beliefs of newspaper reporters shows that
to be the case. (Of course, they *say* it doesn't affect their reporting.)
Newspaper editorials have lost their importance as they've become increasingly bland, but the op-ed (opposite the editorial) page—once it
was invented in the '60s—has become an important source of political
interpretation. Steadily, conservatives have come to dominate the ranks
of op-ed columnists. So while newspapers are not a new or alternative
medium, op-ed newspaper columns could be considered an alternative
medium for conservatives, offsetting the liberal tone of the rest of the
newspaper. The newsmagazines continue to be establishment liberal in
orientation, but few people read them cover to cover as they once did—

you're more likely to skip through them while waiting for your dentist's or chiropractor's appointment. The mass-circulation general content magazines have disappeared, replaced by hundreds of special-interest niche magazines—no political revolution there. The small-circulation ideological magazines have expanded in numbers if not in overall importance, and conservatives now have a fair representation among them. And one of the most noticeable changes has come in the world of book publishing. Books have not disappeared, as it once was the fashion to predict. They have maintained their importance as transmitters of political and cultural ideas, and conservatives now have far more representation in this medium than before.

These are the trends in the print media we will consider and document in this chapter.

Who reads a newspaper, anymore?

Surveys taken by the Pew Research Center for the People & the Press show a steady decline in newspaper readership by the American public, and it's going to get worse (see Chart 5). The younger generations are the least likely to read a newspaper and don't pick up the habit as they get older. There's a similar decline in the use of newspapers as a source specifically of campaign news. Political *activists*, however, still can't do without their newspaper fix.

General news readership. When the Pew survey asked if people read a newspaper "yesterday," this downward trend was revealed:

Americans Who Read Newspapers (%)				
1993	1996	1998	2000	2002
58%	50%	48%	47%	41%

The 2002 figures show the differences between the generations, too, regarding newspaper readership:

Chart 5

U.S. Daily Newspaper Household Penetration
(The Percentage of Households Buying a Newspaper)

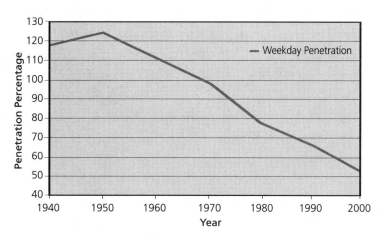

Before 1970, many households bought more than one newspaper, resulting in an *average* household penetration of more than 100 percent.

SOURCES: Editor and Publisher Yearbook data; U.S. Census Bureau. This chart is customized from a chart appearing in *The State of the News Media 2004*, by the Project for Excellence in Journalism, an institute affiliated with Columbia University Graduate School of Journalism.

Percentage of Newspaper Readers in Specific Age Groups

18–29	30–49	50–64	65+
26%	37%	52%	59%

This trend in age groups has been remarkably consistent in all surveys since 1991. "People in their twenties today (born between 1972 and 1981)," says Pew, "have never been avid newspaper readers, and there is little evidence they are getting the newspaper habit. . . . Equally problematic, there has been a decline in readership among those in their 30s." However, "Newspapers have seen far less falloff among older generations."

Since the newspaper audience is an older audience, and people tend to become more conservative with age, it's not too surprising that twice as many newspaper readers describe themselves as conservative as compared to liberal. Specifically, 35 percent say they are conservatives; 18 percent, liberals; and 41 percent, moderates. Rounding out the newspaper-reader profile, readership consists of more men (45 percent) than women (38 percent), and readership rises with education and family income—no surprises there.

Newspapers as a source of campaign news. Just as the overall use of newspapers is consistently declining, the use of newspapers as a source of campaign news is consistently declining, too. Here we face the methodological problem that Pew asked one question in 1992, 1996, and 2000, then used new wording in another survey in 2000 and again in 2004. The raw numbers from the two questions don't jibe, but the downward *trend* is consistent.

Using the first question, here's the percentage of Americans who said they went to newspapers as a source of campaign news:

Americans Who Get Their Campaign News from Newspapers (%)		
June, 1992	**April, 1996**	**January, 2000**
55%	48%	31%

Using the second question, here are the results:

2002	**2004**
40%	31%

As you can see, the trend moves consistently *downward*, whichever question is used.

For a moment, we'd like to depart from the Pew figures to do a bit of informed speculation. We think it's fair to guess that back in 1960 something like 70 percent to 80 percent of the American people used newspapers as a source of campaign news—there was so little competition, after all. Today that figure is somewhere in the range of 30 percent. *This means that newspapers have lost way more than half of their audience for campaign news. That's a tremendous loss of their power as a campaign news filter. And given that the overwhelming majority of news reporters are liberals, that's a tremendous loss of power for liberals. Liberal newspaper reporters are selling horseshoes while the nation is buying automobiles.*

Back to Pew.

As with general newspaper readership, Pew's 2004 survey shows that things in the campaign news department are only going to get worse in the future. Here's the age breakdown on who was using newspapers for campaign news in January 2004:

**Americans Who Get Their Campaign News
from Newspapers, by Age Group, 2004**

18–29	30–49	50+
23%	27%	40%

"The survey shows that young people, in particular, are turning away from traditional media sources for information about the campaign," Pew says. Moreover: "The decline in the percent saying they regularly learn about the campaign from newspapers has been just as pronounced among those over 30 as among those in their teens and their twenties."

But, political activists still use newspapers. The general public may be turned off, but political activists and political news junkies still need to get their newspaper fix while gulping down their caffeine fix. Pew's 2000 report finds that "Most people who are active in politics regularly learn about the campaign from newspapers (63 percent)." Of course, activists are more likely to use *every* news source, but that 63 percent was greater than the number of activists who regularly used any of the other campaign news sources.

In its January 2004 report, Pew paid special attention to politically engaged Americans. "While the majority of Americans are at most marginally engaged in the Democratic [Party] primary process," it said, "a small number keep close tabs on campaign news and events. These people have been following the campaign closely, enjoy keeping up with election politics, and are familiar with all of the election events and facts asked about on the survey. Overall, they represent roughly 7 percent of the population." And among these citizens with "very high campaign engagement," 59 percent regularly get campaign news from newspapers. Only cable news scored higher, with 64 percent. So, even where it's still popular, the newspaper is losing ground to cable TV news.

A few newspapers swim against the tide. The newspaper industry is painfully well aware of these trends. Free dailies have been started in a number of major metropolitan regions and even some smaller markets, in an attempt to capture younger readers by emphasizing short articles over in-depth ones, and entertainment over "hard" news. The real newspapers financing these freebie ventures hope that once they get the young adults reading these freebies, they will get hooked on newspapers and graduate to the real thing. Meanwhile, they hope to get enough advertising to keep the freebie ventures in the black.

It all sounds desperate and dubious to us. These parent newspapers are already *giving away* their content on the Internet, and haven't quite figured how to make *that* profitable. This looks like just another way to throw away gobs of money.

The State of the News Media 2004, a report by the Project for Excellence in Journalism, an institute affiliated with the Columbia University Graduate School of Journalism, puts the problem in historical perspective: "The root problems go back to the late 1940s, when the percentage of Americans reading newspapers began to drop. But for years the U.S. population was growing so much that circulation kept rising and then, after 1970, remained stable. That changed in 1990 when circulation began to decline in absolute numbers."

Most recently, circulation figures from the Audit Bureau of Circulations (ABC) for 813 newspapers found a miniscule gain of 0.2 percent in 2003 over the previous year. Putting the best face on this situation, the president of the Newspaper Association of America declared: "Flat is better than down."

Of the 20 largest newspapers in the United States, only two, the *Wall Street Journal* and the *New York Post*—both of them editorially conservative, coincidentally—posted substantial gains in circulation in 2003 over the previous year. *The Wall Street Journal*'s gains, however, all came from the 290,412 paying online subscribers that qualified under the ABC's rules. The other winner, posting a 10.6 percent gain in circulation, is none other than Rupert Murdoch's *New York Post*. The *Post* is engaged in a heated "battle of the tabloids" with the *New York Daily News*, and is well on its way to overtaking the *Daily News*.

The raw figures showing newspaper circulation losses over the past 10 years are bad enough, *but when you also factor in the growth in population, the picture is dismal.* To see just how bad the situation is, we took five liberal flagships from around the nation and got their circulation figures for 1993 and 2003. Then we got the Census figures for their metropolitan regions from 1990 and 2000. We determined what their circulation would have been in 2003 if they had just maintained the same penetration of their metropolitan market they enjoyed in 1993. We compared that with their actual circulation in 2003 to determine what we call their *effective loss of circulation penetration in their metropolitan region.* Here's what we found:

- The *New York Times* had a 5.5 percent decrease in circulation between 1993 and 2003, while its metropolitan market increased in population by 8.4 percent. On the surface, this suggests that it had an effective *loss* of circulation penetration during those 10 years of 13.5 percent. Actually the loss in its metropolitan region was probably double that, because the *Times* has been transforming itself into a national newspaper and now has nearly half its circulation outside the New York City area.
- The *Los Angeles Times* had a 16.4 percent decrease in circulation between 1993 and 2003, while its metropolitan market

increased in population by 12.7 percent. Its effective *loss* of circulation penetration during those 10 years was 26.2 percent.

- The *Washington Post* had an 11.9 percent decrease in circulation between 1993 and 2003, while its metropolitan market increased in population by 16.6 percent. Its effective *loss* of circulation penetration during those 10 years was 24.4 percent.

- The *Boston Globe* had an 11.1 percent decrease in circulation between 1993 and 2003, while its metropolitan market increased in population by 6.7 percent. Its effective *loss* of circulation penetration during those 10 years was 16.7 percent.

- And the *Atlanta Journal-Constitution* had a 15.6 percent decrease in circulation between 1993 and 2003, while its metropolitan market increased in population by 38.9 percent. Its effective *loss* of circulation penetration during those 10 years was an astounding 39.2 percent.

One caveat: While these newspapers are bleeding from circulation losses and even bigger population-adjusted losses, these losses in themselves have not diminished the newspapers' impact on the political and ideological fronts. This is particularly true of the *New York Times*, the *Washington Post*, and the Associated Press, because they still determine, to a great extent, what is news in America by the articles they publish (and therefore the topics discussed). Television networks and stations simply have not made a similar investment in thousands of reporters around the nation and the globe, so they rely on the *New York Times* and the *Washington Post*, plus their syndication services, and the wire services (primarily AP), to dig up most of the news stories that get reported. Talk radio, cable TV, and the Internet have helped by providing a wider range of *interpretation* of those news stories, but this has only dented the liberal domination of the news media, not eliminated it.

Conservative columnists come to the fore

When the conservative movement first started, the two most influential columnists in the United States were Drew Pearson and Walter Lippmann. Pearson was a dependably leftist muckraker. Lippmann was a classically liberal (i.e., conservative) intellectual on some topics during some periods of his life, but by the time we're talking about he had shed those convictions and was a modern welfare-state liberal.

Conservatives had no national counterparts to Pearson and Lippmann. We had some excellent Washington correspondents, for papers such as the *Chicago Tribune* and *Baltimore Sun*, but they appeared only in their local papers. And we had nationally syndicated columnist David Lawrence, who was also editor of *U.S. News.* Lawrence had an excellent commonsense business approach to issues, but he had neither the intellectual firepower of a Lippmann nor the muckraking power of a Drew Pearson.

Then, as in so many other areas, came Bill Buckley. In addition to *National Review* and his PBS show, *The Firing Line,* and countless speeches, WFB Jr. found time to write a three-times-a-week syndicated column that spared no liberal and quickly became one of the top columns in America.

Buckley was the first new conservative columnist with nationwide impact in the Sixties. As the conservative movement grew, the number of conservative columnists grew. Go today to Townhall.com and you'll find 67 conservative columnists; go to ConservativeChronicle.com and you'll find 35 columnists and 27 cartoonists. And that's just part of the picture.

Christian Rightist Cal Thomas may be the most widely distributed conservative writer in the nation, with more than 550 newspapers printing his column. Pulitzer Prize–winning columnist George Will appears in more than 460 newspapers. William F. Buckley Jr. is still going strong with more than 300 newspapers; Robert Novak and Mona Charen each appear in more than 200; Phyllis Schlafly, in more than 100. Go through the roster and you'll find a variety of right-wingers

ranging from Joseph Sobran to *Washington Times* chief political correspondent Donald Lambro, to libertarians such as Thomas Sowell, Alan
Reynolds, Charley Reese, Doug Bandow, and Bruce Bartlett.

Celebrating the 40th anniversary of his career as a columnist,
Robert Novak noted that he had been called a "redbaiter, Arabist, Communist China (and U.S. corporate) apologist, labor baiter, homophobe,
warmonger, isolationist—and, most recently, unpatriotic conservative.
All these are base canards, but they reflect the tensions of our era. . . .
The Washington of the '60s was neither as polarized nor as partisan as
the Washington of today."

Training new journalists

As bad as the imbalance toward liberals is in the ranks of journalists, it
would be worse were it not for one of the relatively unsung heroes of
the conservative movement, M. Stanton Evans. Stan was associated for
years with *Human Events*, served a stint as editorial page editor of the
Indianapolis News, and is the author of a number of books. But the role
in which he's had his most lasting impact is as a teacher of young budding journalists of the conservative persuasion.

Evans's initiation in that role came in 1957, when he was the managing editor of *Human Events* and he supervised the first three
work/scholarship students in the *Human Events* Journalism School—
David Franke, coauthor of this book; William Schulz, who later became
Washington editor of *Reader's Digest*; and Douglas Caddy, who rounded
out his career as a lawyer with political activism and the writing of a
number of books. Twenty years later Evans created the National Journalism Center in Washington, D.C., training more than 1,400 students
before his recent retirement. Of those trainees, an estimated 900 have
taken media and media-related positions.

And they don't just write for tiny right-wing rags—not that there's
anything wrong with writing for tiny right-wing rags. Take a look at na-
tionaljournalismcenter.org and you'll find articles written by alumni
that have appeared in the *New Yorker,* the *New York Times, Time,*

Newsweek, the *Washington Post, Wired*—even *The New Republic.* Every week in the *Wall Street Journal* you'll find the column of John Fund (NJC summer '81), and elsewhere you'll find a column by bestselling author Ann Coulter (NJC spring '85). The National Journalism Center has indeed made a difference by teaching young conservatives: Don't just complain about the media—join and help make it right.

Since Evans's retirement the National Journalism Center has been run by Young America's Foundation (which also owns Ronald Reagan's ranch in California), under the direction of libertarian newsman Kenneth E. Grubbs Jr. The group's financial resources should assure the continued expansion of this valuable link in the conservative movement's penetration of the media. (See also "Conservative Success Story: Morton Blackwell Trains Tomorrow's Cadre," starting on page 167, for another notable conservative effort at training future journalists.)

About those tiny right-wing rags

Given our personal backgrounds writing for and publishing a number of ideological magazines, we trust you'll understand we're referring to them as "right-wing rags" only in the most affectionate sense of self-mockery. We're hooked on them, and every movement needs them. Their subscription numbers may be miniscule compared to those of the media giants, but they have an importance far beyond those numbers. These publications are the laboratories where a movement tests out new ideas and strategies, and where the different factions duke it out. They serve as advance warning systems that give you a peek at the issues you'll hear about on TV next, and then out of the mouths of political candidates.

Of course, time is more and more compressed in modern society. The same people serving as editors and writers for these ideological magazines now also appear as "talking heads" on TV and radio talk shows, and sometimes even as speechwriters for candidates. So it doesn't take as long as it once did for ideas to make this transition into general currency, but the ideological magazines still serve a useful function as incubators.

No magazine had a greater impact—as an incubator of ideas, as a political petri dish creating the recipe for a new political culture—than *National Review*, of course, and we described its critical role in the formation of the conservative movement in Chapter 5. In the 1970s, The Viguerie Company's *Conservative Digest* served as the transmission belt for New Right ideas and programs, as that faction transformed the conservative movement. Because of its forthright leadership, *Conservative Digest* received more publicity than any other opinion magazine in America between 1975 and 1985.

Then conservative opinion journals really took off during the Clinton years—ideological magazines thrive in an adversarial climate. During the Clinton era, the *American Spectator* became the largest opinion magazine in America—reaching a peak circulation of around 280,000—with its exposés of the many sins of the Clinton administration and its entourage. That bubble burst for a number of reasons, among them the eviction of the Democrats from the White House. The magazine underwent changes in ownership and editorial direction that mystified its dwindled band of followers. While it's now back in the hands of its founding editor, R. Emmett Tyrrell, its financial future is shaky, and it's hard to find a copy of the *Spectator* on a newsstand.

Just as *National Review* played a key role in shaping the original conservative movement and *Conservative Digest* was the organ of the New Right, so, today, the *Weekly Standard* serves as the ideological flagship of the "neoconservatives" in their takeover of the intellectual division of the conservative movement. This is the faction that called for war in Iraq and for forcefully exporting American-style democracy around the world. William Kristol started the *Weekly Standard* in 1995 with $3 million in start-up money from Rupert Murdoch, and while it has never achieved a large circulation it probably is the most influential ideological magazine in Bush-era Washington.

National Review is still in business, but Bill Buckley has turned over the reins to Rich Lowry and his band of—yes—neoconservatives. While

National Review now shares the conservative spotlight with a number of competitors, it still has the highest circulation among them. That's probably because of its "branding" as the first intellectual organ of the conservative movement.

The neoconservative takeover has been massive but not complete. Many traditional conservatives find neoconservatives agnostic about free market economics and dangerous failures in foreign policy (see Iraq), so a reaction has set in. Donald Devine has given focus to this reaction as editor of *Conservative Battleline Online,* the new e-magazine of the American Conservative Union.

Also, in October 2002, Pat Buchanan and Taki Theodoracopulos started the *American Conservative* to promote Buchanan's brand of Old Right views, including opposition to the war in Iraq. Scott McConnell, formerly editorial page editor of the *New York Post,* is executive editor of the *American Conservative,* and Ronald Burr—who had brought the *American Spectator* to its peak circulation of 280,000 during the Clinton years—is handling the new magazine's circulation. In addition, from out in the boonies (Rockford, Illinois), *Chronicles* gives a voice to Old Right writers and academicians on political and cultural issues.

Then there are the libertarians—an important part of the Right, but not conservatives. The libertarian flagship is *Reason* magazine, based in Los Angeles, which promotes "free minds and free markets." And out in Port Townsend, Washington (the state), you'll find the offices of the small-circulation but lively *Liberty* magazine. Of course, we're only considering print publications in this chapter, and libertarians are much more active and prominent on the Internet, as we'll see in our next chapter.

And throughout the ups and downs of the conservative movement, from the very beginning, there's been *Human Events.* Originally a newsletter, this tabloid serves as both a journal of opinion and a source of news on what's happening in the movement. Tom Winter (editor in chief) and Terence Jeffrey (editor) oversee its invaluable function as "the national conservative weekly."

Yet another hybrid publication—part newsmagazine, part opinion

journal—is *Insight on the News,* a national biweekly published by the
Washington Times. "You won't have to guess about what is authentic
news and what is opinion," says managing editor Paul Rodriguez. "We
tell you each and every issue what's what *and* we label it."

When we look at circulation figures for the larger, established ideological magazines, this is what we find on the Right (see also Chart 6):

Circulations of Right-Wing Ideological Magazines

National Review	160,000
Human Events	65,000
The Weekly Standard	60,000
Reason	52,000
Insight	40,000

And this is what we find on the Left:

Circulations of Left-Wing Ideological Magazines

Mother Jones	228,000
The Nation	160,000
The New Republic	61,000

Then there are the magazines that deal with a broad array of cultural
topics, but whose politics overall are in the liberal camp. They're not,
strictly speaking, "opinion magazines," but they certainly have an impact on the political conversation of the nation, and in particular the intellectual class. To appreciate the great advantage held by the liberals
in this realm, look at these circulation figures:

Circulations of Liberal "Cultural" Magazines

Vanity Fair	1,183,000
The New Yorker	987,000
Atlantic Monthly	494,000
Utne Reader	240,000
Harper's Magazine	229,000

Chart 6
Circulations of Selected Opinion Magazines

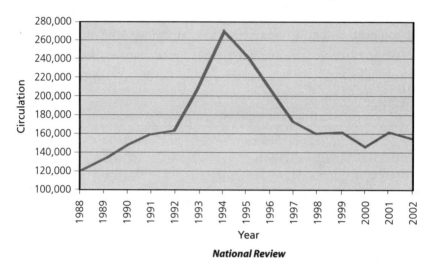

National Review

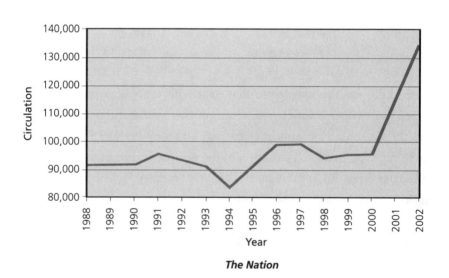

The Nation

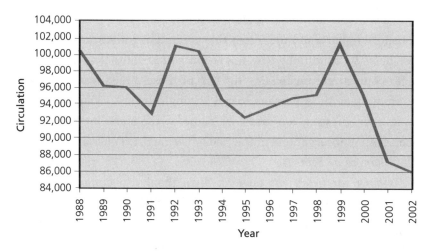

The New Republic

Ideological opinion journals thrive on adverse political environments—if they play the game and unequivocally denounce the other side. *National Review*, a conservative journal, spiked in circulation during the Clinton administration. *The Nation*, a liberal journal, spiked in circulation during the George W. Bush administration. *The New Republic* is a liberal journal that was more favorable to Bush and supported the Iraq War—positions not popular with most liberals—and paid for these deviations from liberal orthodoxy with circulation that plummeted during the Bush years.

SOURCE: Audit Bureau of Circulation, annual audit reports. These charts are customized from *The State of the News Media 2004*, a report by the Project for Excellence in Journalism, an institute affiliated with Columbia University Graduate School of Journalism.

From these figures, it is obvious that liberals remain dominant in print-based opinion journals, though conservatives have a decent beachhead. A liberal could counter that any number of financial magazines and religious publications have editorial views that are conservative. True, but most people don't turn to them for their political views. They turn to them primarily for financial advice or religious counsel. One exception might be *World* magazine (circulation 134,000), where the conservative Republican conent is as prominent as the religious content.

Books with ideas that have consequences

Newspapers, as we've seen, have been sliding downward in circulation for decades; Americans increasingly read less (and view more) to get their news; and the news reading that does still take place is done in ever shorter spurts of time. From this you might gather that Americans have been so conditioned by television sound bites that they can no longer concentrate on reading for any purpose, much less reading for the amount of time it takes to get through a book. That's what we would have guessed, too, until we came across some interesting (and encouraging) observations in the 2002 Pew report, *Public's News Habits Little Changed by Sept. 11.*

Reading for news *has* taken a dive, thanks to competition from radio and television, plus the growing competition from other activities such as exercise and athletics. But, adds Pew: "Reading also is a popular daily activity, despite the drop in newspapers and magazine consumption. One in three (34 percent) say they read a book yesterday, not including school or work-related reading, with most saying they read for an hour or more. Twice as many Americans (18 percent) spent an hour reading yesterday as spent an hour with a newspaper (8 percent). And nonfiction outpolled fiction by a slight 19 percent to 13 percent margin."

That's not all the good news for us book lovers. Pew also reports:

> While younger generations are turning away from newspapers, this does not mean that they are not reading. Younger Americans are just as likely as their elders to read both books and magazines. In fact, Americans under age 35 are more likely to have read a book on any given day than to have picked up a newspaper. Young people read nonfiction slightly more than fiction, and they are just as likely as older people to be regular readers of news magazines, business magazines, and literary magazines.

Underground bestsellers of 1964

We can make a good case for the argument that the conservative movement was started by avid book readers who acted out the title of

Richard Weaver's 1959 classic, *Ideas Have Consequences*. In Chapter 4 we noted the important role played by conservative authors and publishers such as Henry Regnery in the formation of the conservative movement. And in Chapter 6, we noted that John Stormer's *None Dare Call It Treason*, Phyllis Schlafly's *A Choice Not an Echo*, and J. Evetts Haley's *A Texan Looks at Lyndon* mobilized grassroots conservative support for Barry Goldwater's presidential campaign. Let's take a closer look at how these books sold millions of copies without benefit of a New York publisher or even a mention in the *New York Times* bestseller list.

John Stormer tells us that having been in the magazine business, he was aware of the limited distribution possibilities for right-wing books. He decided, therefore, to market *None Dare Call It Treason* on his own. During the three years he took to write it, he collected the names and addresses of some 125 people he thought would be interested in it; some were friends, some were heads of organizations. When he finished writing the manuscript, he sent them a mimeographed letter about what he wanted to do with it and asking for advance orders. If he could get orders for 100,000 copies, his printing costs per book would be low enough to make the project feasible.

Stormer did get advance orders for 65,000 copies, and decided to take the gamble that he could sell the rest. Indeed, that first printing sold out in a couple of weeks. Word of mouth multiplied the demand, and at one point he had a new printing of 800,000 copies. At that time only two printing presses in the U.S. could handle runs that large. Stormer ended up selling 7 million copies.

"I tried to interest the [John] Birchers," Stormer told us, "but they had their own publishing program. Many of their local leaders bought [his book], however, and the John Birch Society had so many demands for it from their members that they joined me in selling it. They ended up selling 500,000 copies. Fred Schwarz's Christian Anti-Communism Crusade was also very helpful in selling the book."

"I had been telling Phyllis Schlafly that she should expand her 'Choice, Not an Echo' speech into a book," he continued. "She replied,

'Oh, nobody reads any more.' When she saw what my sales were, though, she wrote the book in a week and started selling it herself, using the same methods as I had used."

Schlafly confirmed Stormer's account to us—except that the writing took slightly longer than a week: "Yes, John really had the idea of putting out a paperback. I got the idea and the price structure from him. I wrote *A Choice Not an Echo* in the first two months of 1964, and the first printing of 25,000 copies arrived at my house and went into my garage around the first of April."

"I typed out a one-page letter on my old Royal standard typewriter onto a stencil, the old stencils," she recalled, "and I used a mimeograph machine I had in the basement to grind out a hundred letters. I sent them to a hundred friends I had around the country whom I had met through various channels. The letter said, 'Please read this book today, and then buy copies to send to your delegates to the Republican national convention.' I got a very good response, and that was my only advertising—ever."

One friend in Glendale, California, owned a door business and ordered 5,000 copies to distribute at a United Republicans of California statewide meeting. That led to one of the most telling effects of the Schlafly book: "The California primary was in early June, and in April and May we sold over half a million copies in California," she told us. "The California primary was absolutely crucial that year, and the national committeeman, Gardiner Johnson, credited *A Choice Not an Echo* with turning the state for Goldwater." Conservative precinct captains had already canvassed their precincts, and they knew who was for Goldwater, who was for Nelson Rockefeller, and who was for Lyndon Johnson. They targeted the Rockefeller and Johnson supporters with copies of *A Choice Not an Echo*, and when they went back to them a week later, many had switched their support to Goldwater.

"Morton Blackwell was, I believe, the youngest elected Goldwater delegate at the GOP's San Francisco convention," Schlafly continued, "and he said on a video that I produced several years ago that *A Choice Not an Echo* made him believe that he, Morton Blackwell, *could* make a difference. The book absolutely empowered conservatives to believe that they could win."

"Ultimately we sold over 3 million copies—all out of my garage," Schlafly said. As with the Stormer book, there was no space advertising, and no benefit of mentions on any bestseller list. This was all under the radar of the liberal establishment. The alternative media used by Stormer and Schlafly were the mimeograph machine, a list of friends, and a self-promoted paperback. And the third conservative bestseller of 1964, J. Evetts Haley's *A Texan Looks at Lyndon*, was promoted the same way and sold millions. Tom Paine was alive and well in 1964.

Turning 1964 into a continuing book revolution

Neil McCaffrey was an ardent Catholic, an ardent conservative, and a skilled practitioner of direct mail. He had gained editorial experience at Doubleday & Co., then was mail order manager for the Macmillan Company, so he had both editorial and marketing experience as the conservative movement geared up for the 1964 Goldwater campaign.

McCaffrey saw millions of conservatives mobilizing, yet the few small book publishers that were conservative could barely get their titles into bookstores. That spelled opportunity to him. He founded the Conservative Book Club to promote wider distribution of conservative books; he founded Arlington House to publish many of those books; and he founded the Nostalgia Book Club to serve as an outlet for his other great interest—the music and films of the 1920s through the '40s.

Marty Gross, who ran the Nostalgia Book Club and helped McCaffrey on the conservative side as well, recalled that "at its peak, in the 1970s, the Conservative Book Club had some 75,000 members. We had traditional conservatives, libertarians, Republicans, Southern Democrats, anti-communists, family values people, your hard-money people, or 'gold bugs,' and members who weren't at home in any other established political faction so they felt most at home in conservatism and the CBC. We supplied books for all of them."

"At a time when other, broader book clubs and publishing ventures foundered or were apt to get into trouble," Gross continues, "we prospered. Today McCaffrey would be called a niche publisher. In a way his vision was precocious, because that's the direction the book club business later took. We probably could have grown even larger, but he resisted any attempt to grow the company beyond what he could manage himself."

Arlington House published notable political books, such as Kevin Phillips's first book, *The Emerging Republican Majority*, which served as a blueprint to election victory for the Nixon camp. And Arlington House was the nation's foremost publisher of hard-money books during the dismal Carter years of long lines in front of gas stations, when gold and silver were riding high.

Arlington House and the Conservative Book Club were also pioneers in conservative religious ecumenicalism. McCaffrey knew how to appeal to his home base—conservative Catholics like himself—but he took special pride later when he figured out how to appeal to Protestant Evangelicals as well. Arlington House also published the first books for politically conservative Jews, and even got the U.S. rights to publish the official 25th anniversary commemoration of the State of Israel, with an introduction by Israel's Prime Minister Golda Meir.

Later the company faced a series of ownership changes (at one point Walt Disney's nephew Roy Disney bought into the parent company). It sank into oblivion after Neil McCaffrey's death under management that didn't know how to appeal to the conservative movement, only to be resuscitated years later when Tom Phillips bought the Conservative Book Club and added it to his Eagle Publishing stable (more on that below). Neil McCaffrey had proven that a market existed for conservative books, but he could never have imagined just how huge that market would someday become.

Once again, thank you, Mr. Clinton

Well into the 1990s, most New York book-publishing houses treated conservative authors as inhabitants of *terra incognita*, those uncharted wild areas on the edge of the map filled with strange beasts. It wasn't where they sold books. Oh, sure, if you became president of the United States you could get your memoirs published, but ordinary conservative authors found it tough going, hawking their wares on the streets of Manhattan. Every so often there'd be a match between a friendly editor willing to try something new and convince the publisher to take a chance with a conservative, and every so often an imprint such as the Free Press or Basic Books would come under the control of management friendly to some brand of conservatism or anti-communism—that is, until new management came along. But the general feeling along Book Row was that conservatives, whatever they do, don't read books; and if by perchance they do, they certainly don't buy the kinds of books *we'd* want our friends to catch us publishing.

To get an idea of the insularity of New York publishers, consider that in 1990 Rush Limbaugh was already a nationwide talk radio sensation, broadcasting out of his home station in New York City. Raymond Jay certainly knew who he was, because Jay spent a lot of time in his car listening to the radio in between sales stops in Minnesota and Wisconsin for his publisher, Simon & Schuster. Jay was so impressed by the "Rush effect" everywhere he drove, he pitched Rush as a possible author to his big boss, Irwyn Applebaum, president and publisher of Pocket Books, a division of Simon & Schuster. *Applebaum didn't know who he was talking about.*

It was still a couple of months before the *New York Times Magazine* did a major article on the Rush phenomenon out in the boonies, which was how most book people in Manhattan learned that Rush even existed. *Publishers Weekly,* the book industry trade journal, tells what happened at Pocket Books:

> Judith Regan was an editor at Pocket Books in the early
> '90s when she first suggested publishing a book by talk
> radio host Rush Limbaugh. "The editorial director said,
> 'Judith has reached a new low,' and people booed," she
> recalled. "People left nasty notes around the office and

even in the bathroom." Still, she was able to sign up
the book, which became a national bestseller.

Hawking his "upcoming bestseller," *The Way Things Ought to Be*, on
his own program, Rush became Pocket Books' fastest seller in the four
years it had been publishing hardcovers. Rush particularly delighted in
the fact that his book was number one on the *New York Times* bestseller list for *several months* before the *Times* finally conceded it was
part of "all the news fit to print" in the form of a review.

Rush's first book contract was signed with a $150,000 advance
against royalties—a pittance for someone with his drawing power.
Rush's second book—*See, I Told You So*—cost Pocket Books a little more
pocket change: $2.5 million in its advance against royalties.

The lesson: If you weren't a Rush Limbaugh (and who else was?),
don't waste your time trying to get New York publishers interested in
your conservative book. Even if you *were* Rush Limbaugh, you first had
to convince them you existed. But then someone came along who gave
conservative authors a big, *big* step up. Their dear friend was none
other than President Bill Clinton.

Rush's second book, after all, was the book he had threatened to
write if Clinton were ever elected president. And after just a short time
in the White House, it became obvious that co-presidents Bill and
Hillary Clinton were the ticket out of terra incognita for conservative
authors.

The publishing house that led the way was none other than the
granddaddy of conservative booksellers, Regnery Publishing (see Chapter 4). When its founder, Henry Regnery, died, his son Alfred Regnery
became the new publisher and moved operations from Chicago to
Washington, D.C. Later, conservative newsletter publisher Tom Phillips
(formerly a vice president at The Viguerie Company) bought Regnery,
the Washington newsweekly *Human Events*, and the Conservative Book
Club, placing them all under his Eagle Publishing umbrella. Regnery is
now headed by long-time Phillips executive Marji Ross.

As the 1990s unfolded, conservatives were outraged by the Clinton scandals, both political and domestic. All those conservative columnists and writers we've talked about in this chapter had a perfect target for that bestseller they *knew* they could write, but New York houses weren't interested, of course. Regnery became the conservatives' publisher at least partly by default—no other publisher was interested in conservative books—and Regnery cleaned up. This tiny operation (by New York book conglomerate standards) publishes only 25 or so titles a year, and in 2002 seven of them landed on *The New York Times* bestseller list. That had to be a book industry record for the percentage of one publisher's titles making it onto the nation's most prestigious bestseller list. Moreover, Regnery followed up with more *Times* bestsellers in 2003.

Not only was Regnery an "alternative" book publisher, it sold its books largely through alternative channels. Regnery authors are often given intensive training on how to be effective on radio and TV, then placed on a barrage of national and local talk shows. Author interviews on talk radio are an especially effective medium for selling books. The goal is not so much to get the book *reviewed* (very few people read book reviews) as to get it treated as *news*—controversial or breaking news. A sizzling appearance on a good talk show can get a book on Amazon.com's bestselling chart overnight.

Which brings up another arrow in the new conservative arsenal. Amazon.com is a gift to anyone shut out of establishment review and sales outlets. So, too, are most of the big bookselling chains, such as Wal-Mart and Barnes & Noble, and price clubs such as Costco. There's no noticeable ideological bias in any of their operations, unlike the leftist bias of so many independent bookstores and the leftist bias among establishment reviewers.

Regnery's success in marketing conservative books through alternative channels caught the attention of major New York publishers and other alternative publishing ventures. The results are a lot of new competition for Regnery, and more opportunities for conservative authors.

In New York, the largest book conglomerate, Random House, now has a conservative imprint, Crown Forum. The second largest book publisher, Rupert Murdoch's HarperCollins, is actively seeking conservative titles. Penguin is yet another New York publisher starting a conservative imprint. Then there's the independent Spence Publishing out of Texas. Also, the conservative Internet newspapers *WorldNetDaily* and *NewsMax* are now each involved in publishing books as well. *WorldNetDaily* has created the WND Books imprint with Thomas Nelson, and *NewsMax* has a joint venture agreement with Random House.

Even more astounding is the entry of a second conservative book club into the market. The American Compass book club is a venture of Bookspan, which operates over 30 book clubs including the Book-of-the-Month Club, the Literary Guild, the Quality Paperback Book Club, and the History Book Club. In other words, American Compass has parents with deep pockets.

Brad Miner, formerly of *National Review*, is American Compass's editor in chief. Its marketing strategy, as he outlined it to us, is pure alternative media: direct mail, and space ads in those conservative and libertarian journals we refer to as "right-wing rags." Marketing launched in January 2004 with direct mail totaling 800,000 pieces, representing 15 percent of the lists being tested. The second wave came in March with space ads in various publications, and in July Miner planned (as we were going to press with this book) a big direct mail rollout to the lists that tested well in January. Numbers such as 800,000 in a single month point to the advantage of having rich parents, and the stable of Bookspan book clubs confers another great advantage: Plenty of books offered in those clubs can also be offered as alternates to members of American Compass. Miner explained that the club understands conservatives have other interests besides politics, so history books, self-improvement titles, even cookbooks will supplement the political main selections.

Having *two* book clubs bidding for their titles is a luxury few conservative authors previously enjoyed. But conservatives of a more scholarly bent are also being courted today as never before. ISI Books (of the conservative Intercollegiate Studies Institute), *City Journal* Books, Encounter Books, and the Free Press publish conservative tomes, not to mention major university presses such as the University of Chicago Press and Yale University Press.

Beyond the *Times* bestseller list

Yet another long-time bone of contention for conservatives has been the elitist bias of most bestseller lists. By carefully selecting the bookstores you use as sources for sales figures, you can make sure your list weeds out "unsuitable" books—such as religious books. You end up with a list not of what America is reading, but a list of what cosmopolitan liberals are reading.

Enter Nielsen BookScan. BookScan produces the most comprehensive data of what books Americans *really* are buying, utilizing those electronic sales scans right at the point of sale, the checkout counter. As the *Washington* Post noted when it adopted this system, "Every time a barcode on a book is scanned as a sale is being made, the information is recorded, collected, and passed along to BookScan."

BookScan revolutionizes the bestseller data in two ways. First, it offers the most comprehensive collection of data available. Second, it cuts out the "filter" of the bookstore manager or clerk who may want to report only politically correct titles. "The independent bookstores are all controlled by leftists, and they're totalitarians," Regnery's Marji Ross told the Manhattan Institute's *City Journal*. "They will not display conservative books, or if they do, they'll hide them in the back. We have experienced our books being buried or kept in the back room when a store manager or owner opposed their message."

In the *Washington Post's* *Book World*, Clive Thompson decried how elitist bestseller lists are "antiseptically cleansed of the reading that's done outside the traditional range of the nation's cultural capitals." For example, he wrote:

> For years, these lists thus ignored the seismic popularity of books such as the Christian apocalyptic Left Behind series, as numerous critics of bestseller-compiling

have noted. These books will hit the bestseller list for a few weeks, then quickly vanish, even though they continue to enjoy brisk sales in Christian bookstores nationwide. "The book industry is like the only industry where you can't get definitive numbers on what's selling. You can massage the numbers any way you want," complains Dan Balow, director of business development for the Left Behind series at Tyndale House Publishers. That a single series has its own designated business director is itself testimony to its market power. By the end of 2001, Tyndale had sold more than 50 million copies in the series.

Incredibly, Thompson got this response from Chip McGrath, editor of the *New York Times Book Review*: "We're missing the boat, calculatedly so, on things like religious books. I don't think we have to apologize for that." So much for the *New York Times'* promise to give us "all the news that's fit to print."

That's where things stood when we decided to check for ourselves and directly compare the BookScan bestseller list with the *New York Times* bestseller list. Would the first lean heavily conservative, the second heavily liberal? Quite frankly, we were surprised at what we found, and the results made us reassess the environment faced today by conservative authors.

First of all, though, it's hard to compare the two lists face to face. BookScan's clients are primarily publishers and distributors, and it doesn't (so far) have a *nationwide* bestseller list that it releases to the public. When the *Washington Post* prints its bestseller list each week, for example, that list is customized to reflect what's selling in the Washington, D.C., area, not nationally. However, BookScan did make available to us one week's nationwide listings (the week ending February 22, 2004), so we could compare those with the listings on the *New York Times* bestseller list for the same week.

Even with this help, a problem remains: The *New York Times* separates out advice and self-help books into their own list; BookScan doesn't—those kinds of books appear on the same list with political books. So we couldn't directly compare "number one" on one list with "number one" on the other list, and so on. What we could do was look at the *order* of the political books among the top 20 titles on both lists, and this is what we found.

Hardcover Political Books

(Conservative titles are listed in roman type; liberal and anti-Bush titles, in **bold**.)

New York Times	*BookScan*
Sean Hannity, *Deliver Us From Evil*	Sean Hannity, *Deliver Us From Evil*
Kevin Phillips, *American Dynasty*	**Kevin Phillips, *American Dynasty***
Ron Suskind, *The Price of Loyalty*	**Ron Suskind, *The Price of Loyalty***
John Stossel, *Give Me a Break*	John Stossel, *Give Me a Break*
Al Franken, *Lies* . . .	Michael Savage, *The Enemy Within*
Michael Moore, *Dude* . . .	**Al Franken, *Lies* . . .**
Bill O'Reilly, *Who's Looking out for You?*	**Michael Moore, *Dude* . . .**
Michael Savage, *The Enemy Within*	

You can see the reason for our surprise: There is no measurable difference between the two lists. In fact, the *New York Times* list may be a tad more favorable to conservatives because it lists four conservative titles, BookScan only three, among the top 20 or so books. For some inexplicable reason, Bill O'Reilly was way down in the number 34 slot on the BookScan list.

When it comes to the top-selling books, therefore, we could find no discernible elitist bias to the *Times* list. One explanation could be that, having broken the bestseller barrier and become visible, conservative books now sell as well in New York City and Borders as in Oshkosh, Wisconsin, and Wal-Mart; therefore they show up on the *New York Times* list in roughly the same order as they do on the BookScan list.

Another factor could be the demise of those politicized independent bookstores that shun conservative books. The *New York Times* says its "rankings reflect sales . . . at almost 4,000 bookstores plus wholesalers serving 50,000 other retailers (gift shops, department stores, newsstands, supermarkets), statistically weighted to represent all such outlets nationwide." John Wright of the *Times Book Review* told us their reporting base hasn't expanded significantly over the past 10–15 years, but what *has* changed is the book industry—fewer independent booksellers and increasing dominance by the chains.

"We get input from lots of independent stores that don't report electronically" [as with BookScan], Wright told us. And, as we noted above, the *Times* admits some of its sales reports are "statistically weighted." But when we checked BookScan's sources for sales reports, we noted that "general independents" are "weighted" there, too. Susan Pavliscak, BookScan's sales manager, explained that "weighted means that we have used the data we have to project the sales for these retailers." So both lists use weighting and projection for those troublesome independent bookstores. Since the details of how they accomplish this are, of course, proprietary information, we couldn't dig much deeper to assess the possibility of fudging sales at the local-store level. The bottom line, at any rate, was the lack of any significant difference between the two lists.

One final matter: We didn't notice any religious bookstore chains on the list of BookScan's sales sources. "I do not believe that any independent Christian retailers are included in the data," Susan Pavliscak confirmed to us. "We include some religious bookstores—not a lot, but a representative sample," the *Times Book Review's* John Wright told us. They do the same with other specialized types of booksellers, he added, such as New Age bookstores. So here, too, there is no discernible difference between the two bestseller lists.

We have a suggestion for these bestseller lists: Perhaps it's time they consider adding a religious/spiritual bestseller list. This is an era, after all, when bookstores bought up the entire initial print run of 1.9 million for the final volume in the Left Behind series of religious novels by Tim LaHaye and Jerry B. Jenkins—three weeks before it went on sale! Go ahead and include New Age spirituality books, Zen and other Buddhist books, just don't overlook the Christian books either—and let the sales chips fall where they may. It would be interesting and significant to see what Americans *really* are reading for their spiritual education each week, and it might help keep trendy fads in perspective.

A caveat, and a warning to conservatives

We noted earlier how the conservative resurgence of bestselling book titles came in response to the Clinton administration and its policies. As we've seen with other alternative media, conservatives thrive in "attack mode"—particularly when the "other side" is in power.

That fact begs the question: How long will the conservative book Renaissance last, now that the Republicans—"conservative" Republicans, supposedly—are the political establishment in Washington? Can "conservative" books continue to sell when they defend the biggest-spending administration since Franklin Delano Roosevelt? It would be one thing if these conservative authors stuck to principle and attacked Big Government policies no matter which party was in power, but regrettably they too often fail to make the distinction between conservative and Republican.

The warning signs are already in the air. As we went to press with this book, *USA Today* noted that "former president Bill Clinton used to be fodder for best-selling conservative authors. Now, the only two political books on *USA Today*'s best-selling books list are critical of Bush." Those same two anti-Bush titles appeared in the number five and number nine slots on the *Washington Post*'s bestseller list—a BookScan-generated list, remember. But the *Washington Post*/BookScan list also included conservative Sean Hannity's *Deliver Us From Evil* (number three), as well as two culturally conservative titles, Rick Warren's *The Purpose Driven Life* (number two) and Laura Schlessinger's *The Proper Care & Feeding of Husbands* (number nine). Thus, even as we can see the value of the more inclusive BookScan list, there is also a warning: Two anti-Bush political books are on the list, and only one conservative political book. And when we look at the *New York Times'* hardcover nonfiction list for the comparable period, only two of the top 10 books are conservative (numbers one and four), while four anti-Bush and liberal books make the top 10 (at numbers two, three, seven, and 10). To recap, here's the score:

Ideological Breakdown of Hardcover Nonfiction Lists		
	Anti-Bush	Conservative
USA Today	2	0
Washington Post/BookScan	2	1
The New York Times	4	2

In 2002 and early 2003, conservative titles dominated the political bestsellers. By late 2003 the tide seemed to be shifting, with both sides roughly equal. Today, anti-Bush and liberal books seem to be in ascendancy. As for the future, there's this warning from *USA Today*: "In the first half of 2004, major commercial publishers will publish at least 25 books critical of Bush."

Such are the perils of being the defender of the establishment when your natural mode is to be on the attack.

13

The Internet Empowers the Individual

On January 17, 1998, the Internet made its debut as a world-shaking tool of political communication. That was the day Matt Drudge used his Web site to introduce Monica Lewinsky to the world as the White House lover of President Bill Clinton. Drudge's expose started a chain of events that culminated in the president's impeachment, and in the process, he placed the spotlight on an irrevocable change in the balance of power between the ordinary citizen and the political establishment.

Monica wasn't the beginning of the Internet's involvement in politics, by any means. Drudge himself had been covering all the Clinton scandals for four years. Jim Robinson's FreeRepublic.com was the leading right-wing political site on the Web, and in 1997 Joseph and Elizabeth Farah started *WorldNetDaily*, the first independent newspaper on the Web. But in 1998 the Internet was just beginning to penetrate mainstream America, and print media—notably *The American Spectator*—had been getting most of the spotlight for Clinton exposes. Monica changed all that.

Drudge grew up in Takoma Park, Maryland, a politically far-Left suburb of Washington, D.C., also known as "the People's Republic of

Takoma Park." He graduated 325th in his high school class of 350, but loved current events and was hooked on talk radio. "What a great place, Washington, D.C., to grow up in," he later reminisced. "I used to walk these streets as an aimless teen, young adult, walk by ABC News over on DeSales, daydream; stare up at the *Washington Post* newsroom over on 15th Street, look up longingly, knowing I'd never get in . . . "

Instead he headed west to Hollywood and became manager of the gift shop at CBS Studios. He volunteered in the mail room from time to time. "I hit pay dirt when I discovered that the trash cans in the Xerox room at Television City were stuffed each morning with overnight Neilsen ratings, information gold." He sensed the thrill of a scoop, but didn't know what to do with his inside knowledge.

Then his father bought him a computer, hoping it might spark a desire for a more promising career. Matt was a quick learn, and within two months he was posting his gossipy scoops on Usenet and AOL and doing some writing for *Wired* magazine. "I collected a few e-mail addresses of interest," he later recalled. "People had suggested I start a mailing list, so I collected the e-mails and set up a list called 'The Drudge Report.' One reader turned into five, then turned into 100. And faster than you could say 'I never had sex with that woman' it was 1,000—5,000—100,000 people. The ensuing Web site practically launched itself."

"Lewinsky almost fell through the cracks," says Drudge. "It was a stray e-mail that came in. You just go for it." The results were far beyond anything he expected. "I had something like 400,000 visits that Saturday when that thing broke." For three days he had the story to himself, and the whole world was clicking in. "I barricaded myself in the apartment. I was terrified, because from my Hollywood apartment a story of this magnitude was being born. I remember I teared up when I hit the 'Enter' button on that one that night, because I said, 'My life won't be the same after this.' And it turned out to be right." Then Rush Limbaugh read his entire reports over the air; then finally the establishment media acknowledged the story, which they had known about for weeks but had hushed up.

Speaking at the National Press Club a few months later, Drudge asked both himself and all those *credentialed* reporters listening to him: "How did a story like Monica Lewinsky break out of a Hollywood apartment? What does that say about the Washington press corps? It just baffles me. I haven't come up with answers on that."

Drudge vs. the media establishment

Throughout this book we have shown how the new and alternative media empower the individual citizen by bypassing the gatekeepers of the media establishment, those editors and news anchors who want to decide exactly what news you should be allowed to read or hear or see. Direct mail, the fax machine, talk radio, cable television—each has given you stories and viewpoints you never would have gotten from Dan Rather or the *New York Times.*

These new and alternative media have also given you new ways to communicate *your* wishes directly to other citizens and the politicians who are supposed to represent you, again by bypassing the gatekeepers. In this case the gatekeeper may be a union chief who wants Congress to believe all union members think alike on a piece of legislation, when you know it isn't true. Or a Republican lobbyist who wants the Congress to cave in on an issue *you* consider critical. Thanks to the new and alternative media, you now have ways to be heard.

None of these new and alternative media, however, empower you *directly,* as an *individual,* quite as effectively and forcefully as the Internet does. Your modem is your equalizer, your cyber-Colt .45. You have a direct line, with *no* intermediaries or filters, to any publication or Web site around the world, to other citizens who share your interests and viewpoints, to government bureaucrats, to your political representatives, to the stores you want to do business with, to people who want to buy something you're trying to unload—you name it.

It is to Matt Drudge's credit that he fully understands all this—the Big Picture beyond his own Web site. He probably sensed it from the moment he sat down in front of that keyboard and monitor his dad bought him. To see how fully he comprehends this, take a look (www.frontpagemag.com/archives/miscellaneous/drudge.htm) at his address before the National Press Club on June 2, 1998, and his sharp answers to the contemptuous questions presented to him afterward.

"What's going on here?" he asked rhetorically. "Well, clearly there is a hunger for unedited information, absent corporate considerations." Zap! Right off the top he slams the ball back at all those reporters facing him, who, with all their credentials and college degrees and corporate conglomerate bosses, let this gift shop clerk in Hollywood scoop them on the biggest story of the decade.

"We have entered an era vibrating with the din of small voices," he continued. "Every citizen can be a reporter, can take on the powers that be. The difference between the Internet [and] television and radio, magazines, newspapers is the two-way communication. The Net gives as much voice to a 31-year-old computer geek like me as to a CEO or Speaker of the House. We all become equal."

"And you would be amazed what the ordinary guy knows," he added.

Then he rubbed their noses in it, citing major stories *other* than Monica that he broke in *The Drudge Report*. And all the links on his Web site—another great innovation of the Internet era: "This marks the first time that an individual has access to the news wires outside of the newsroom. You get to read all the news from the Associated Press, UPI, Reuters, to the more arcane Agence France-Presse and the Xinhua. I'm a personal fan of the Xinhua."

Drudge continued:

> And time was only newsrooms had access to the full pictures of the day's events, but now any citizen does. *We get to see the kinds of cuts that are made for all kinds of reasons, endless layers of editors with endless agendas* changing bits and pieces, so by the time the newspaper hits your welcome mat, it had no meaning. *Now, with a modem, anyone can follow the world and report on the world—no middle man, no big brother.* [Emphasis added.]

(Later interviewed by *WorldNetDaily*'s Geoff Metcalf, Drudge asserted, "We don't need the gatekeepers: the Ted Koppels, the Peter Jennings, the Dan Rathers, Tom Brokaw. They're all the same anyway. . . . You don't need these gatekeepers in Washington who are basically just feeding off each other and bouncing things off of each other.")

Drudge acknowledges that each new medium scares the devil out of the old media. But, he assured his National Press Club audience, "The Internet is going to *save* the news business. I envision a future where there'll be 300 million reporters, where anyone from anywhere can report for any reason. It's freedom of participation absolutely realized."

Drudge (and the future) vs. Hillary (and the past)

It's not just the media-establishment types who worry about the lack of gatekeepers in the new media. That worries members of the political establishment, too. The new media jeopardize their cozy arrangement with reporters who know their place.

Speaking to the Wednesday Morning Club in Los Angeles, a series of talks arranged by David Horowitz, Drudge told how he tried to remain civil with First Lady Hillary Clinton, to no avail: "I tipped my hat to her at the White House Correspondents' Dinner a couple of months ago and got quite a dirty look."

One of Hillary Clinton's functions as co-president was to handle the White House Millennium Project. At a press briefing on the Millennium Project, she was asked her opinions about the Internet, and she came across as far less enthusiastic than, say, the vice president at that time.

Stumbling for words at times, she rambled on about how "we are all going to have to rethink how we deal with this," whatever that means. "As exciting as these new developments [the Internet] are . . . there are a number of serious issues without any kind of editing function or gatekeeping function . . . . ["I wonder who she was referring to," Drudge quipped about this.] I mean, it is just beyond imagination what can be disseminated. So I think we're going to have to really worry about this . . . "

"Sounds like you favor regulation," someone asked.

"I don't know what I'm in favor of," she replied. (Actually, her actions as First Lady tell us a lot about what she'd like to do with the Internet. See below.)

The First Lady continued: "I don't have any idea what we're going to do legally, regulatorily, technologically—I don't have a clue. But I do think we always have to keep competing interests in balance. . . . Anytime an individual or an institution or an invention leaps so far out ahead of that balance and throws a system, whatever it might be—political, economic, technological—out of balance, you've got a problem . . . [and] it can lead to all kinds of bad outcomes . . . "

To this amazing example of Ludditeism, Matt Drudge responded: "Would she have said the same thing about Ben Franklin or Thomas Edison or Henry Ford or Einstein? They all leapt so far ahead out that they shook the balance. No, I say to these people, faster, not slower. Create. Let your mind flow. Let the imagination take over. And if technology has finally caught up with individual liberty, why would anyone who loves freedom want to rethink that?"

Summing up their opposite reactions to the Internet, Drudge avowed: "The First Lady says we need to rethink it. I say we need to embrace it."

Why Hillary doesn't like the Internet

Hillary doesn't like the Internet because she (and her leftist co-conspirators) can't control it. It's that simple.

Think back about the exact nature of Matt Drudge's Monica scoop. He wasn't the first journalist to learn about Monica—he was just the first to *report* it. Specifically, his scoop was that *Newsweek* had spiked the story. The establishment press had been intimidated, just as the establishment press of an earlier era had been intimidated into not reporting Jack Kennedy's sexual escapades. Bill and Hillary had no such power, however, over that wild weed called the Internet. Moreover, with like-minded sites linking to each other, a story can spread faster than wildfire—for a really hot story, we're talking instantaneous combustion around the globe.

Ten days after the Monica story broke, and with the White House under siege, Hillary told NBC's Matt Lauer what she thought was behind it all: "I do believe that this is a battle. I mean, look at the very people who are involved in this . . . this vast right-wing conspiracy that has been conspiring against my husband since the day he announced for president." And if most of NBC's audience was puzzled over what she was referring to, *she* knew. Several of her staffers at the White House had put it all together into a 331-page "enemies list" and report called *The Communications Stream of Conspiracy Commerce*. (You can still get excerpts on the Web today; use your search engine.) And the report made it clear that it was the Internet that made this conspiracy work:

> The Internet has become one of the major and most dynamic modes of communication. The Internet can link people, groups and organizations together instantly. Moreover, it allows an extraordinary amount of unregulated data and information to be located in one area and available to all. The right wing has seized upon the Internet as a means of communicating its ideas to people. Moreover, evidence exists that Republican staffers surf the Internet, interacting with extremists in order to exchange ideas and information.

You can get this story in detail in the new book by Richard Poe, *Hillary's Secret War: The Clinton Conspiracy to Muzzle Internet Journalists.* As the subtitle indicates, Hillary wasn't about to surrender to her enemies without a fight—and she had some powerful friends.

Case in point: Joseph Farah's Western Journalism Center (precursor to *WorldNetDaily*) supports the investigative reporting of Christopher Ruddy on the Vincent Foster "suicide." Suddenly it's the subject of an IRS audit. IRS Field Agent Thomas Cederquist demands "copies of all documents relating to the selection of Christopher Ruddy as an investigative reporter and how the topic was selected. Who was on the review committee?" When Farah protests, Cederquist tells him: "Look, this is a political case and the decision is going to be made at the national level."

Case in point: The day after he joins the Clinton White House, Sidney Blumenthal starts action to sue Matt Drudge for $30 million in damages over a story. He also sues America Online, which carried columns by Drudge at that time. "Had Blumenfeld succeeded in holding AOL liable for Drudge's writings," says Poe, "crusaders for Internet censorship—such as Hillary Clinton—would certainly have used the ruling as a steppingstone for more ambitious actions."

Case in point: Drudge has no lawyer or money, so David Horowitz of FrontPage.com sets up a Drudge Legal Defense Fund. The *Wall Street Journal* gives it national publicity. "Within five days, I was being audited by the IRS," says Horowitz.

Many other conservatives were on Hillary's IRS hit list, among them Bill O'Reilly (audited three years in a row), *The American Spectator*, *National Review*, and the Heritage Foundation. The joke in conservative circles was that you must not be very important if you aren't being audited.

Of course these actions are reprehensible, and the three cases we cite here were eventually dismissed. But the point of an IRS political audit is as much to harass as to convict, and often for years. We have a pretty good idea of what conservatives can expect if the Clintons return to the White House.

Hillary's Secret War also recounts the early conservative days on the Web, primarily through portraits of the work of Jim Robinson (Free Republic.com), Chris Ruddy (*NewsMax*), Joe Farah (*WorldNetDaily*), David Horowitz (FrontPage.com), and, of course, Matt Drudge (*The Drudge Report*).

As with all wars, Hillary's war had unintended consequences. One occurred when Joe Farah read Section IX, "The Internet Influence," of

The Communications Stream of Conspiracy Commerce, the Hillary-commissioned report on the vast right-wing conspiracy. As Farah told author Poe:

> The ironic part is that we weren't utilizing the Internet very well back then. We did have a Web site called etruth.com, and it did get a high level of traffic. I was always surprised that there were more people reading our stuff on the Internet than were reading our newsletter. But it still never occurred to me that it had all that much potential until the Clintons connected the dots for me.
>
> When I saw that report, I became convinced that the Internet was the vehicle for keeping government under control, because if these guys were so scared of it, I felt we could do much more as journalists to utilize it. That report really was the genesis for WorldNetDaily.com.

Conservatives embrace the Internet

Most of the world sees Matt Drudge as a conservative. In his 1998 *Playboy* interview, Drudge talked about liberal and conservative political leaders and affirmed: "I am a libertarian, not trusting any of them." Whatever. He certainly isn't a *liberal*.

Matt Drudge showed us the future, and both conservatives and libertarians followed in his footsteps without hesitation. Web sites are so pervasive today—every organization, every candidate, every big ego needs one—that it's hard to remember what a recent development this all is, less than a decade old. Matt Drudge introduced us to what we now call a "blog," or personal Web page, in 1995; the *Washington Times* inaugurated its Web site in 1996; and Joseph and Elizabeth Farah started *WorldNetDaily*, the first independent Net newspaper, in 1997. All of that is just yesterday, yet the world has changed so much.

Liberals have joined in the act, too, but not nearly as forcefully as libertarians and conservatives. In some ways, however, today they are ahead of the Right. As we go into the 2004 election year, we see a general pattern taking shape: The Right has been better at utilizing the Internet as a news and opinion medium, while the Left has been better at utilizing it as a medium for political organization. (We're not talking here about the two major political parties, but rather the independent groups that constitute the Right and the Left in America.)

Take a look at our list of ideological and news Web sites (see table, p. 287). Of the million-plus sites on the Internet, covering an endless variety of topics, these are some of the most heavily trafficked ideological sites.

First, to keep things in perspective, compare the sizes of the ideological sites with the sizes of the news sites (remember: the smaller the ranking number given to a site, the bigger its readership). The ideological sites, in general, pale in comparison with the news sites, which basically are online extensions of their establishment print parents. For all its complaining, the liberal establishment still reigns—not *supreme* anymore, but *foremost*.

That's not to denigrate the accomplishments of the ideological warriors on the Right. Think of the hundreds, even thousands of employees on the payroll of each of those big establishment media sites. Then consider that Joe and Elizabeth Farah, with a staff of about 25 at *World-NetDaily*, and Chris Ruddy, with a staff of about 50 at *NewsMax*, each publish a newspaper whose Internet viewership is somewhere between the *Wall Street Journal* and CBS News. Then consider that Matt Drudge, essentially all by himself, is able to get more of an audience on the Web than MSNBC or Reuters, and Lew Rockwell, with the assistance of just one-third of his webmaster's time, is giving the *Los Angeles Times* and the prestigious *Financial Times* of London a run for their considerable money. Incredible! Matt Drudge wasn't so wacky after all when he proclaimed this the age where "every citizen can be a reporter."

Next, look at the composition of the top ideological sites. Let's draw a line, say, at the top 10,000 Web sites among the more than a million total. In this top-pulling group, we find 24 right-of-center sites, 11 left-of-center sites. Indeed, at the top of the list we pass four

Rankings of Ideological and News Web Sites

This table represents traffic as of March 22, 2004, measured by Alexa.com, a division of Amazon.com.

Alexa.com ranks all Web sites—over a million of them, commercial and noncommercial—by the amount of traffic they get from visitors. *The lower the ranking number, the greater the traffic* (Yahoo.com is no. 1, for example). These rankings will not tell you the *number* of visitors a site has, only where it stands in relation to other sites. *The Drudge Report,* for example, has well over 2 billion visits a year, but we learn from this table that as of March 22, 2004, it was the 264th largest Web site in cyberworld.

NOTE: **Right-of-center sites are listed in boldface;** left-of-center sites are listed in roman type.

Ideological Sites

Rank	Site
No. 264	**The Drudge Report** (drudgereport.com)
766	**WorldNetDaily** (worldnetdaily.com)
944	**NewsMax** (newsmax.com)
971	**LewRockwell.com** (lewrockwell.com)
1014	Salon.com (salon.com)
1351	**Town Hall** (townhall.com)
1369	**Free Republic** (freerepublic.com)
2320	**National Review Online** (nationalreview.com)
2346	**The White House** (whitehouse.gov)
2469	**The Economist** (economist.com)
2660	**Antiwar.com** (antiwar.com)
2798	**Rush Limbaugh** (rushlimbaugh.com)
3138	**Wall Street Joural editorial page** (opinionjournal.com)
3178	**Ludwig von Mises Institute** (mises.org)
3360	John Kerry for President (johnkerry.com)
3551	Howard Dean for America (deanforamerica.com)
3688	Common Dreams (commondreams.org)
3731	Bush in 30 Seconds (bushin30seconds.org)
3763	**Washington Times** (washingtontimes.com)
4176	Democratic Underground (democraticunderground.com)
4483	Moveon.org (moveon.org)
4566	Village Voice (villagevoice.com)
5128	**Lucianne Goldberg** (Lucianne.com)

Ideological Sites (continued)

Rank	Site
5860	**Front Page Magazine** (frontpagemag.com)
6794	**The Weekly Standard** (weeklystandard.com)
7033	**Bush Cheney '04** (georgewbush.com)
8032	CounterPunch (counterpunch.com)
8496	**Reason** (reason.com)
8662	daily KOS (Markos Moulitsas Zuniga) (dailykos.com)
8685	The Nation (thenation.com)
8941	**Jewish World Review** (jewishworldreview.com)
9140	**Andrew Sullivan – The Dish** (andrewsullivan.com)
9187	**InstaPundit.com** (Glenn Reynolds) (instapundit.com)
9582	**Focus on the Family with James Dobson** (family.org)
9778	**Sean Hannity** (hannity.com)
10447	Buzzflash Report (buzzflash.com)
11649	The New Republic (tnr.com)
12222	Talking Points Memo (Joshua Micah Marshall) (talkingpointsmemo.com)
12488	**Cato Institute** (cato.org)
12677	World Socialist Web Site (wsws.org)
12708	**Cybercast News Service** (Media Research Center) (CNSNews.com)
13390	**Tech Central Station** (techcentralstation.com)
13593	**Sobran's** (sobran.com)
13647	**Heritage Foundation** (heritage.org)
14004	Democratic National Committee (democrats.org)
15350	**WorldTribune.com** (worldtribune.com)
15636	**Bill O'Reilly** (billoreilly.com)
15711	**Anti-State.com** (anti-state.com)
16161	**Future of Freedom Foundation** (fff.org)
17053	**The American Conservative** (amconmag.com)
17180	Z Magazine (zmag.org)
18155	**The American Spectator** (spectator.org)
18968	Mother Jones (motherjones.com)
19613	**American Family Association** (afa.net)
20493	TomPaine.com (tompaine.com)
20508	**Etherzone** (etherzone.com)
20819	**Libertarian Party** (lp.org)
21597	The American Prospect (prospect.org)

Ideological Sites (continued)

Rank	Site
21618	**Human Events** (humaneventsonline.com)
22388	**Insight Magazine** (insightmag.com)
23226	Greenpeace International (greenpeace.org)
23530	**American Enterprise Institute** (aei.org)
25077	American Civil Liberties Union (aclu.org)
25156	New York Review of Books (nybooks.com)
25380	Sierra Club (sierraclub.org)
26365	**Free-Market.net** (free-market.net)
28392	**Republican National Committee** (rnc.org)
29339	**The Washington Dispatch** (washingtondispatch.com)
31349	**The World & I** (worldandi.com)
32383	**Sierra Times** (sierratimes.com)
32858	Planned Parenthood (plannedparenthood.org)
34215	Adbusters (adbusters.org)
35679	**GOPUSA** (gopusa.com)
36239	**Karen De Coster: Queen of Political Incorrectness** (karendecoster.com)
39071	**Harry Browne** (harrybrowne.org)
39968	**Right Wing News** (rightwingnews.com)
40809	**Laura Schlessinger** (drlaura.com)
41502	Democrats.com (democrats.com)
43799	**The Independent Review** (Independent Institute) (independent.org/review.html)
45467	**Foundation for Economic Education** (fee.org)
46181	**Home School Legal Defense Association** (hslda.org)
49706	Ralph Nader (votenader.org)
50833	**World Magazine** (worldmag.com)
51774	The Progressive (progressive.org)
52587	**Grassfire.org** (grassfire.org)
52909	**Family Research Council** (Gary Bauer) (frc.org)
59103	Public Citizen (citizen.org)
59672	Natural Resources Defense Council (nrdc.org)
61137	**National Rifle Association** (nra.org)
63492	**Center for Strategic & International Studies** (csis.org)
65083	**New York Observer** (nyobserver.com)
71342	**City Journal** (Manhattan Institute) (city-journal.org)

Ideological Sites (continued)

Rank	Site
71410	**The New American** (John Birch Society) (thenewamerican.com)
72314	National Organization for Women (NOW) (now.org)
75206	Kausfiles.com (Mickey Kaus) (kausfiles.com)
76967	**Opinion*Editorials*.com** (Frontiers of Freedom Institute) (opinioneditorials.com)
78117	**Judicial Watch** (judicialwatch.org)
78474	Progressive Review (prorev.com)
85423	Essential.org (Ralph Nader) (essential.org)
86925	**Gay Marriage: Constitutional Amendment Petition** (nogaymarriage.com)
88614	Southern Poverty Law Center (splcenter.org)
90150	**Virginia Postrel** (dynamist.com)
90152	**The American Enterprise** (taemag.com)
90155	**Institute for Humane Studies** (theihs.org)
92604	**TheRealityCheck** (therealitycheck.org)
93870	Corporate Watch (corpwatch.org)
97781	Union of Concerned Scientists (ucsusa.org)

News Sites

Rank	Site
21	ABC News (abcnews.com)
28	CNN (cnn.com)
29	BBC News (news.bbc.co.uk)
74	New York Times (nytimes.com)
103	Xinhua (xinhuanet.com)
196	Washington Post (washingtonpost.com)
248	USA Today (usatoday.com)
251	Fox News Channel (foxnews.com)
403	MSNBC (msnbc.com)
468	Reuters News Online (reuters.com)
552	Boston Globe (boston.com/news/globe)
617	New York Post (nypost.com)
635	Wall Street Journal (wsj.com)
647	San Francisco Chronicle (sfgate.com)
857	Los Angeles Times (latimes.com)
939	Seattle Times (seattletimes.nwsource.com)

News Sites (continued)

Rank	Site
945	CBS News (cbsnews.com)
1024	FT–Financial Times (ft.com)
1046	Chicago Tribune (chicagotribune.com)
1095	PBS Online (pbs.org)
1219	Newsday (newsday.com)
1285	New York Daily News (nydailynews.com)
1347	Miami Herald (miami.com/mld/miamiherald)
1358	Time Magazine (time.com)
1442	Atlanta Journal-Constitution (ajc.com)
1729	Chicago Sun Times (suntimes.com)
1774	Houston Chronicle (chron.com)
2118	Minneapolis Star Tribune (startribune.com)
2246	Philadelphia Inquirer (philly.com)
2321	NPR News Now (news.npr.org)
2682	Dallas Morning News (dallasnews.com)
2793	PR Newswire (prnewswire.com)
2860	Newark Star-Ledger (nj.com/news/ledger)
3162	Detroit News (detnews.com)
3415	International Herald Tribune (iht.com)
3856	St. Louis Post-Dispatch (stltoday.com)
4392	Cleveland Plain Dealer (cleveland.com/plaindealer)
4413	U.S. News & World Report (usnews.com)
4610	South China Morning Post (scmp.com)
6159	Denver Post (denverpost.com)

conservative and libertarian sites before we come to the first liberal site, Salon.com. Then we pass another nine conservative and libertarian sites (plus the White House site) before coming to the next liberal sites, those of the Kerry and (now-defunct) Dean campaigns.

Before conservatives get too confident, though, try and find the conservative equivalents of the Dean Internet campaign and Moveon.org. Political organization is the one area where liberals outshine conservatives on the Web.

Bear in mind, we've tried to be as inclusive as possible in

compiling this list. We didn't set out to find more conservative sites than liberal ones—this was a process of discovery for us, as it is for you. We even went to our local Barnes & Noble and Borders bookstores to check their extensive displays of political and ideological publications, to make sure we weren't inadvertently leaving out some important publication. It's probably inevitable that we've forgotten *someone*, but that wouldn't change the overall picture. If you don't find one of your favorite ideological publications here, it's probably because their Web presence is so minimal that it hardly registers. Remember, there's no necessary correlation between a publication's print impact and its Web impact, and here we are looking at only their Web presence.

Off we go into the wild blogosphere

Given how the Internet empowers the individual, the lightning-like growth of personal Web logs—"blogs"—should come as no surprise. Software packages are now available that make designing the www.you.com Web site possible even for those of us who are decidedly not geeks. If you just want a family blog, or something simple, you may choose to pay a "hosted site" that does the work for you and gives you an account for a fee. And from the University of California at Berkeley to your local community college, courses are now being offered for those who prefer the classroom approach (and if you're a full-time student it eats up a few credits).

The National Institute for Technology and Liberal Education (NITLE), in its latest blog census, estimates that active Web logs number something like 1,200,000. Nearly all are hosted sites, however. There are only about 50,000 standalone individual Web logs—the kind you'd use for serious political discourse, with updates every week or day. Of course, people create blogs covering all kinds of topics, not just politics.

So far blogging is mostly an American phenomenon, with about 75 percent of the world's blogs using English as their language. That will change, of course—another imperialist American cultural export. For whatever reason, Portuguese is the second most common language, Farsi the third.

In the United States, blogs are becoming an alternative news and editorial medium of their own. They may share the Internet with the huge corporate news sites, but the cyber-conglomerates constitute the meat and potatoes of the resulting stew, while the blogs provide the spices. The most popular ones (you'll find them on our listing of ideological Web sites) have *personality*, with lively exchanges between the blogger and the audience, and among the active visitors themselves. Peter Jennings and George Will deliver lectures, insulated from their viewers or readers; most bloggers and their visitors have real conversations, and those conversations sometimes get a little heated. But that's why people keep coming back to them.

As the Internet becomes more complex to navigate, with its myriad sources of information, Web users who have a life outside the Internet often choose a couple of blogs they trust and bookmark them, letting those bloggers do the job of surfing hundreds of sources for them. And sometimes bloggers will come together to serve as a one-site shopping mall giving you everything you could want to know about a single topic. Blogger Mike Krempasky tells us that during the Iraq war, for example, something like "150 bloggers 'blogged the war' with posts every minute or two on www.command-post.org, covering television, Internet, radio, eyewitness reports—the works."

Academics are taking to the blogosphere in greater numbers, and the ones who have something interesting to say can get quite successful. *InstaPundit*'s Glenn Reynolds, for example, is a law professor at the University of Tennessee, and his blog usually makes any listing of the most influential. Lots of economists seem to be getting into the act, including the "classical liberals" over at Mises.org.

Newspaper reporters are one category you'd think would take to the Web, but they've been stopped in many instances by their overcautious editors. *Editor & Publisher*'s Steve Outing took a look at newspaper policies about letting their staffers write blogs on their own time. Most tried to discourage the practice, even for family blogs, afraid that something might be written that could harm the newspaper's reputation in some way. The "most restrictive, by far," says Outing, was our old friend, the king of gatekeepers, the *New York Times*. "I don't like the concept of the personal blog in terms of the *New York Times*," said editor-in-chief Len Apcar. This visceral fear of the ungated Internet is ironic, to say the least, given the revelations of fabricated articles by Jayson Blair in the *Times* itself.

L'Affair Blair led to the forced resignations of *Times* executive editor Howell Raines, a committed liberal, and managing editor Gerald Boyd on June 5, 2003. It was perhaps the biggest scandal ever to hit the *New York Times* (if you don't count their propagandizing for Stalin and Castro). Many people think, however, that *Times* publisher Arthur Ochs Sulzberger, Jr. never would have required their resignations had it not been for the Internet blogosphere, where critics posted a steady stream of exposes of the *Times'* mistakes and ideological slanting of the news. "If this had happened 10 years ago, when the Internet didn't exist, Raines would still be running the place," suggested Mickey Kaus on his blog. And Andrew Sullivan said on his blog:

> Only, say, five years ago, the editors of the *New York Times* had much more power than they have today. If they screwed up, no one would notice much. . . . But the Internet changed all that. Suddenly, criticism could be voiced in a way that the editors of the *Times* simply couldn't ignore. Blogs—originally smartertimes.com, then this blog [AndrewSullivan.com], kausfiles.com and then Timeswatch.com and dozens and dozens of others—began noting errors and bias on a daily, even hourly basis. The blogosphere in general created a growing chorus of criticism that helped create public awareness of exactly what Raines was up to.

Editor & Publisher's article describing newspaper editor antipathy to blogging got one retired newsman angry enough to write a testy letter to the editor. Describing himself as a daily reporter for 20 years at the *Los Angeles Times*, some time ago, Evan Maxwell lambasted the pretense of "objectivity" as "a kind of pablum that seems high-minded and worthy but is, in actuality, a scam, a sham, or a quasi-religion."

Turning to the matter of blogs, Maxwell added:

> The Web, with its ability to publish all kinds of opinion at the cost of a few electrons, is ultimately threatening to the institutions and corporations which rely on their monopoly of the means of publishing. I can put together a Web log and distribute it even more cheaply than the old broadsides [that] used to be published and distributed. It is completely revolutionizing communication, and the establishment is very, very uneasy with that revolution.

Dramatic increase in the use of the Internet for alternative campaign news

There is a big gulf between people who use the Internet as a source of news, and those who don't, when asked about the *reliability* of Internet news. As you'll see from our chart 7, "Do You Trust Internet News?" more than 80 percent of Internet users trust the news they get there, while less than 15 percent of non-Internet users say they would expect such news to be reliable. Obviously this is a matter of *perception* for them, since they're not using the Internet. At any rate, each year fewer and fewer Americans remain offline.

The Internet today is an important source of campaign news for Americans. While it is still overshadowed by television (both broadcast and cable), newspapers, and talk radio, use of the Internet is increasing dramatically while broadcast TV and newspapers are losing their audience even more rapidly. To get an idea of just how recent a phenomenon the Internet is as an *overall* news source, take a look at Chart 8, "Internet News Audience."

According to the Pew Research Center for the People & the Press, 13 percent of the American people were regularly getting campaign and candidate information through the Internet as we entered 2004—a

Chart 7

Do You Trust Internet News?

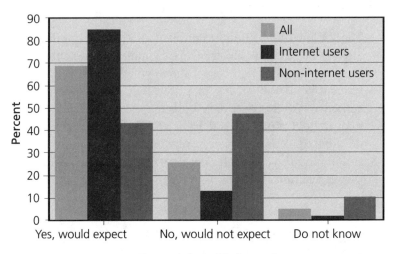

SOURCE: Pew Internet and American Life Project, "Counting on the Internet," December 29, 2002. The survey question was: "If you need reliable, up-to-date news, would you expect to be able to find this online?" Taken from *The State of the News Media 2004*, a report by the Project for Excellence in Journalism, an institute affiliated with Columbia University Graduate School of Journalism.

jump from 9 percent in 2000. The future growth of the Internet can be seen when we break down the 2004 responses by age groups.

Individuals Who Regularly Get Campaign, Candidate Information Online (%)	
Ages 18–29	20 %
Ages 30–49	16
Ages 50 and over	7

As more and more Americans use the Internet, the reasons why they go there change. After all, a few years back Internet users were mostly geeks and hardcore political activists. Today it's a much broader

Chart 8
Internet News Audience

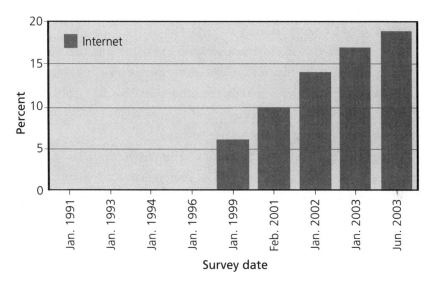

Survey date

SOURCE: Pew Research Center for the People and the Press unpublished data, www.people-press.org, based on survey responses (respondents were allowed to give two answers) to this question: "How have you been getting most of your news about national and international issues? From television, from newspapers, from radio, from magazines, or from the Internet?" This chart is taken from *The State of the News Media 2004*, a report by the Project for Excellence in Journalism, an institute affiliated with Columbia University Graduate School of Journalism.

cross-section of the American people. You would expect that as the Internet audience grows more inclusive, the percentage going there for "mainstream" sources would increase. And that's what Pew has found—but the way this information is presented masks an important fact about ideological politics on the Web, as we'll see.

Pew asks people who use the Internet for campaign and election news: *Why* do you go there? These are the categories Pew gives us for their responses:

- "Information is more convenient"
- "Other media don't provide enough news"
- "To get information not available elsewhere"
- "Internet news sources reflect my personal interests"

As we see it, the first two answers reflect nonideological reasons for use of the Internet—you can click on your computer at any time to get the news, and from many sources, rather than wait for the evening TV broadcast or the next morning's newspaper.

Also, as we see it, the last two answers are reasons to use the Internet that are probably driven by ideological conviction—you want news and views that you don't get in the traditional media. This is true whether you're a liberal or a conservative who's dissatisfied with the traditional news media.

Now, Pew compares answers in 2000 with answers in 1996, and says the Internet "has gone mainstream in its preferences and pursuits. A majority now cites convenience, not a desire to tap new or different information sources, as the main reason they go online for election news."

Yes, *but* . . . Pew's statement is true when you look at the *percentage* of Internet users giving at least one of the two ideologically motivated replies, but it tells us nothing about the *raw numbers* of people who turn to the Internet for alternative campaign news. The size of the pie is as important as the percentage of that pie, when you're experiencing a 450-percent growth in your market in just four years.

We've done the math. We've taken into account that 450 percent increase in the size of the pie *plus* the U.S. population growth of around 15 million between 1996 and 2000. The result? *Between 1996 and 2000 the number of people using the Internet to get alternative campaign and election news more than doubled.* That's why both conservative and liberal political sites have grown so much in recent years, a trend we're confident will continue when 2004 data is available.

The Internet as a haven for dissent from both the Left's *and* the Right's establishments

Way back in 1999, *Talkers Magazine* asked Newt Gingrich about the political role he foresaw for the Internet—after all, as Speaker of the House he was the person most responsible for initiating the

Thomas.loc.gov Web site, which puts congressional and legislative information on the Internet.

"I believe the Internet will have an even bigger long-term impact than talk radio or than television commercials," Gingrich replied. One of the impacts he mentioned was the "underlying ability for people to sort of segment themselves into their own niches" through chat rooms and other interactive devices—a process that has expanded far beyond what most people could have imagined in 1999.

The irony today, five years later, is that most conservatives have accepted a role as defenders of the Washington establishment (in the form of the Bush/Republican administration and Congress) while retaining the rhetoric and mindset of the days when they were the political underdogs. We hope to explore this tension in a future book. Here, we'd like to note a critical difference between organizational politics and Internet politics.

As our basis for comparison, let's take the most dramatic political event since 9/11—the U.S. war against Iraq. Our purpose here is not to stake out a position for or against going to war, but to contrast the differences on the Right between the world of organizational politics and the world of Internet politics.

Organizational politics: The political decks are stacked against third parties in the United States, making it extremely difficult to mount a successful third-party campaign. The result is the two-party "duopoly" and the ascendancy of my-party-right-or-wrong partisanship, in both the Democrat/liberal and Republican/conservative camps, rather than factions based on political principles. Whether you're a Democrat or a Republican, you face enormous pressure to tow the party line rather than consider issues on the basis of their merits—especially when the issue is as important as war.

Thus, on the Right, there has been virtually no political opposition to the war against Iraq. This was a war conducted by a Republican administration, therefore all Republicans (and, by extension, all conservatives) were expected to support it. And indeed, almost all did. A mere handful voted against giving President Bush the green light to go to war, and out of 51 Republican senators and 229 Republican representatives, *only one*—Rep. Ron Paul of Texas—has consistently and vocally taken an anti-interventionist stand.

Internet politics: Go to the liberal establishment's media—the influential newspapers, big magazines, and TV networks—and you would never guess that anyone on the Right has been opposed to the war. Indeed, go to the new conservative establishment's media—talk radio and Fox News—and you get pretty much the same picture. Only on the Internet do you find a dramatic difference. Antiwar voices are probably still a minority, but there's a rough parity between the prowar and antiwar sides. *The Internet has made a break—on the most important issue of our day—with all the other media: both the liberal establishment's media and the new conservative establishment's media.*

Go back to our list of the top ideological sites on the Internet. Of the top 25 right-of-center sites, from *The Drudge Report* to the Cato Institute, five (LewRockwell.com, Antiwar.com, Mises.org, Reason.com, and Cato.org) are non-interventionist, and antiwar voices can be found on some of the other right-of-center sites. LewRockwell.com outdraws *National Review Online*, and Antiwar.com has a larger audience than Rush Limbaugh (on the Internet, remember), the *Wall Street Journal* editorial page, and the *Weekly Standard*.

This is very interesting, but what in the world is going on here? What does it mean? The answer, we think, goes back to what we said above—how "none of these new and alternative media . . . empower you *directly*, as an *individual*, quite as effectively and forcefully as the Internet." And the implication, as the Internet grows in political influence, is that both Democrats and Republicans, both liberals and conservatives, are going to have a continually more difficult job keeping the troops in line. On the Internet, every individual is his or her own political party.

Take a look at Chart 9, "Why People Went Online during the Iraq War." Three of the reasons that people went online during the war have no relationship to any ideological perspective. But more than 45

Chart 9

Why People Went Online during the Iraq War

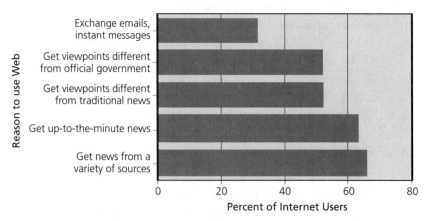

SOURCE: Pew Internet and American Life Project, "The Internet and the Iraq War, April 1, 2003." Internet users during the beginning of the Iraq War were asked: "When you are online for news, information, and opinion about the war in Iraq, how important is it that you can get [the following] online?" Taken from *The State of the News Media 2004*, a report by the Project for Excellence in Journalism, an institute affiliated with Columbia University Graduate School of Journalism.

percent answered that they wanted to get "viewpoints different from official government" positions, and more than 45 percent also said they sought "viewpoints different from traditional news." Of the people who gave those two answers, we can't tell how many are on the Left and how many are on the Right. But we can tell that, together, nearly half the people who went online during the Iraq War were looking for alternative news and views. The Internet is a natural haven for dissidents.

Will the Internet help us transcend government?

Historian and economist Gary North writes:

> It is my firmly held belief (this week) that what brought down the Soviet Union was the photocopier. It replaced carbon paper as the technology of *samizdat*: underground writing. Surely, the fax machine was a key tool in Yeltsin's ability to resist the Communist

Party's coup. There were other technological factors besides the photocopier, but it was surely not people's access to guns that brought down the USSR. It was access to forbidden ideas.

Every political establishment rests on a specific view of the way the world works—or at least should work. To maintain their power, men must control the public's access to ideas. Those ideas that run counter to an establishment's paradigm are a threat to the system. . . .

Part of every political establishment's means of control, North goes on to argue, "has been the printing press"—controlling the flow of information. Enter the Internet: "For the first time in the history of man, there are no longer gatekeepers who can control the flow of information to the public. No longer can the Powers That Be control ideas by controlling printing presses, paper, and ink."

Lew Rockwell has this to say:

In one sense, the Web is a lot like the world: filled with good and evil, dumb and smart. . . . In another sense, the Web is not at all like the world because the government does not dominate it. Yes, there are .gov Web sites, but they exist in a cooperative relationship among all the others, and not as master of them. For the most part, people go where they want, read what they want, and do what they want. The order we witness—from the massive reference sources and free offerings to the immense commercial apparatus that knows no borders—is a product of voluntary cooperation.

Or, as Gary North puts it, referring to one of the foremost free-market economists and philosophers, "an international digital revolution—no other word suffices—is today verifying Hayek's theory of the spontaneous order."

Could Adam Smith ever have imagined that his "invisible hand" might end up being cyberspace?

The Internet has empowered Lew Rockwell as surely as it empowered Matt Drudge. Lew tells how:

> I started, during the war on Serbia, to share interesting links with friends. But then my own personal e-mail list became too long. It occurred to me that perhaps people I don't know might be interested in these links. Thus was born my public site, just an interface to display things I saw (this was pre-blog). Then I started publishing people's thoughts, my own thoughts, and the next thing I know, I'm the editor of one of the most trafficked centers of political and economic opinion in the world.

We received an e-mail recently from our good friend Jon Utley, with a typically Utleyish subject heading: "News from behind the Neoconservative Curtain."

"Governments can't lie anymore," he started out, "or rather get away with it. That's the real lesson of the Second Iraq War. No wonder dictatorships as in China and Saudi Arabia, Syria, etc., do everything they can to prevent unfettered Internet access."

"But there's another great result of the Internet," Jon continued: "Governments can't hide information for long. Searching with some thoughtfulness brings up all sorts of information barely reported in America, if at all."

There it is again: that Internet information explosion. Look on Antiwar.com and you'll find links to articles from around the world. Jon himself has created www.againstbombing.com as a conduit for three of his virtual communities—Americans Against Bombing, Americans Against World Empire, and Conservatives for Peace. Look on that Web site and you'll find hundreds and hundreds of links to articles from around the world.

That's the way it is on the issue of war and peace, and, thanks to the Internet, that's the way it is with *any* issue. If you're not satisfied with the range of viewpoints you find in the print media and on TV, you can go to talk radio and Fox News. If they don't satisfy you, you can go to the Internet. And if the American sources on the Internet don't please you, there's a whole world of information (metaphorically *and* geographically) awaiting you. There are no boundaries on the Internet.

14

Liberals in Cyberspace

Ideological talk and news on the Internet is dominated by conservatives and libertarians, as we saw in the last chapter. When it comes to political organization on the Internet, however, liberals have been the trailblazers and have far outshone the Right.

Some conservative groups have stressed activism through the Internet from the beginning—Free Republic, for example. Many other conservative groups have an online presence that supplements their base in direct mail activism, but none of these has the innovation or clout of MoveOn.org.

For conservative politicians, too, their Internet operations are merely a supplement to the real action taking place elsewhere. Independent politicians—Jesse Ventura and John McCain, for example—do better on the Internet. But again, none of them came close to the Internet revolution that was the Howard Dean campaign, although California conservatives scored a spectacular victory using the Internet and talk radio to recall their Democratic governor.

Internet politicos come from both the Left and the Right, and some express themselves as wordsmiths, others as online activists. They all, however, are testimony to the Internet's capacity for empowering the individual, or a small group of individuals.

Moving on past the impeachment

It was September 1998, and one word was in the air, over the airwaves, and on everybody's minds in Washington: impeachment. Republicans smelled blood; liberals smelled a plot to bring down their entire program because of a sex scandal. After it became impossible to deny or defend President Clinton's actions in regard to a certain intern, a common liberal line was to say: Okay, let's censure him, but a sex scandal doesn't rise to the level of an impeachable offense.

Out in Berkeley, California, Joan Blades and her husband Wes Boyd shared in the liberal pain. Even though they had no experience in politics, they were tech-savvy Silicon Valley entrepreneurs and they decided to do something about it. They posted an online petition at www.moveon.org to "Censure President Clinton and Move On to Pressing Issues Facing the Nation," and issued a press release on September 22 with the headline "Disgusted citizens organize on the Internet . . . " The press release advised: "The email campaign began at 9 AM PST today, with the first dozen signatories each sending their email notices out to several dozen friends."

Like Matt Drudge in his Hollywood apartment, Joan Blades and Wes Boyd could hardly have expected the deluge that followed. Within days they had hundreds of thousands of signatures, and realized they must seize this opportunity to give these people more to do than just circulate the petition. By June 1999 their petitioners had also generated 250,000 telephone calls and a million e-mails to Congress.

It was to no avail. The Republican House impeached President Clinton for lying under oath in the Monica Lewinsky affair, giving MoveOn its next crusade: revenge at the polls against Republicans in swing districts who had voted for impeachment. Rep. James Rogan

(R–CA) was the only member of the impeachment team itself to go down to defeat, but MoveOn and its liberal allies had some successes elsewhere. All told, MoveOn raised over $2 million to help elect four new senators and five new House members in 2000.

Since then, MoveOn has found other causes for mobilization, most notably opposition to the war in Iraq and support for the Howard Dean presidential campaign, and each time it comes out bigger and stronger. Today it has over 2 million members (membership is free), who are involved in "electronic advocacy groups" based on topics such as campaign finance, environmental and energy issues, media consolidation, and the continuing Iraq war. And MoveOn's political action committee (PAC) contributed more than $3.5 million in the 2002 election.

In the current 2004 election cycle, MoveOn is the fourth largest "527" political organization (named for the section of the IRS code that applies to them) in the nation, with expenditures of more than $4.8 million as we go to press. Most of that money is being spent on TV ads in 17 presidential battleground states urging defeat of President Bush. Billionaires George Soros and Peter Lewis have pledged to give $1 for every $2 given by members, up to a cap of $5 million.

What are some of the keys to MoveOn's success?

- Hot issues, and a willingness to take an unequivocal stand on those issues. The key to winning is, Boyd told a Take Back America conference, "lead, for God's sake."
- On a potential minefield of a topic like the Iraq war, MoveOn aligned itself with the mainstream Win Without War coalition, while not wasting energy picking fights with the crazier elements in the anti-war movement. MoveOn's Eli Pariser told *Salon.com*: "The message is a very mainstream one. We're patriotic folks concerned about our country's security and concerned about the threat that Saddam Hussein poses, but we don't think this rush to war is something that serves our country well or serves the world well."
- No bureaucracy stifling creativity. The whole show is run by

just four people, with minimal support staff. This is appreci-
ated by members, too. Bob Muehlencamp told AlterNet.org
that people love the sense of "a direct line to god. There is no
big bureaucracy. You make a contribution, you sign something, and you get immediate action."

- An emphasis on grassroots support by tens of thousands of
  small contributors, rather than financial dependence that can
  also stifle creativity. (It will be interesting to see whether the
  billionaire support gained in 2004 leads to any internal tensions.)

- An easy-to-navigate Web site that involves the visitor with a
  minimum of hassle. Reading and signing a petition takes
  only a couple of minutes. Mark Rovner, senior vice president
  at Craver, Mathews, Smith & Company, says "MoveOn's Web
  site is very accessible. It has almost no graphics. It's all about
  the messages. It's a brilliantly low-tech use of high technology."

- *Involving* the member. Not only by signing petitions, giving
  money, and writing to Congress, but also in the big MoveOn
  decisions. In June 2003 MoveOn held what was widely
  hailed as the first Internet presidential primary, where members decided who should get the group's support. (Dean
  came in first, but didn't get the 50 percent support required
  for formal endorsement. This also proved to be a brilliant
  way to coax the Democratic presidential campaigns to get
  their members to join MoveOn in an effort to influence the
  vote, and thus swell its membership rolls.) Members were
  also invited to submit chapters for consideration in compiling the organization's new book, *MoveOn's 50 Ways to Love
  Your Country*.

Put all this together and you get an Internet-based activist organization
with more than 2 million members—which, as liberals love to point
out, is more than the Christian Coalition had at its peak.

But how and where are all these liberal activists going to meet?

Meetup.com calls itself "a free service that organizes local gatherings about anything, anywhere." As we went to press, the site said 1,146,000 people have already signed up for meetups concerning 4,190 topics.

Founded it 2002, Meetup.com gives you two approaches to its services for finding other people in your area who share your interests. You can look through all the groups currently meeting in your area, and sign up for the next meeting. If you don't find what you're looking for, you can suggest the topic that interests you and then see if others in your area sign up. You vote on where you want to meet, and take it from there.

If this sounds like an ideologically neutral design, that's indeed the case. But just as Newt Gingrich and his band of House conservatives were the first to realize that neutral C-SPAN gave them an opportunity to spread the conservative message, so were Howard Dean campaign operatives the first to realize that neutral Meetup.com could help them spread their candidate's message.

Even today, only a third of Meetup's gatherings are politically oriented, but the Dean campaign is what put the site on the map. Even though Dean is no longer a candidate, he continues to have twice as many supporters signed up for meetings (now under the rubric of Democracy for America) as John Kerry does.

The top topics in politics and activism, as of the end of March 2004, were:

1. Dean in 2004 (> 164,100 members)
2. Kerry in 2004 (> 84,600)
3. Wesley Clark (> 62,500)
4. Democratic Party (> 44,200)
5. Townhall (conservatives) (> 23,200)
6. Kucinich in 2004 (> 21,900)

7. John Edwards (> 12,700)
8. March for Women (> 11,600)
9. MTV and RTV (> 7,900)
10. Common Cause (> 6,700)
11. Republican Party (> 6,200)
12. Impeach Bush (> 4,500)
13. Environmental Defense (> 4,400)
14. Bush in 2004 (> 3,800)
15. Nader in 2004 (> 2,800)

The perfect liberal storm

Put together a well-oiled Internet vehicle for liberal activism (MoveOn.org), machinery that enables these online activists to meet each other and organize (Meetup.com), and a solitary Democratic politician who passionately voices the discontent of these liberals (Howard Dean), and you've got the makings of the perfect liberal storm. In the end this storm didn't destroy the Democratic establishment, but it sure changed its contours, just as a major weather storm doesn't destroy the earth but can change the way it looks.

Joe Trippi, Dean's campaign manager until after the New Hampshire primary, dismisses the analogy between the dot.com boom and crash of the past decade with the Dean campaign. "The Dean campaign was a dot-com miracle, not a dot-com crash," he insists.

For proof, go back to January 2003 and see how many political pundits, how many media outlets, how many politicians themselves, were giving any serious attention at all to the presidential campaign of the former governor of the nation's second smallest state, Vermont. If you find any, here's a tougher search: How many of those pundits gave Dean any chance at all to capture the Democratic Party's nomination? No, Dean was viewed as one of those quixotic candidates like Al Sharpton or Dennis Kucinich or Carol Moseley Braun, destined never to get beyond a couple of percentage points of support during the primary process.

What Dean ended up doing, however, was to *lead* the Democratic polls prior to the first primary in Iowa, to reset the agenda of the Democratic Party, to give the Democrats the resolve to stand up to President Bush rather than to accommodate him, to involve more campaign workers than any of the other candidates, to raise more money than any of the other Democratic candidates, and to be the first politician in either party to raise most of his money online. He accomplished most of that through the Internet, and his subsequent loss to John Kerry was a failure attributable to conventional politics, not the Internet. Joe Trippi was right: This was a dot.com miracle, not a dot.com crash.

Among serious presidential campaigns, Dean's was the third to revolt against the political establishment by utilizing alternative media as its principal modus operandi. For Barry Goldwater, the alternative media utilized were below-the-radar political journals, self-published political books, and a grassroots network of citizen activists who met each other through those outlets. George McGovern was the first to utilize direct mail as his principal modus operandi. And Howard Dean was the first to utilize the Internet as his principal organizing medium. All conventional political campaigns now include alternative media as components in their mix, but only Goldwater, McGovern, and Dean made alternative media their *major* modus operandi—so far.

And what do these three politicians have in common? Each was a natural rebel, determined to say what he thought, refusing to keep his mouth shut for "the good of the party." Each lambasted me-too politics, promising (in Phyllis Schlafly's words) "a choice, not an echo." Each captured a large, idealistic, and motivated following that would change American politics even if it didn't capture the White House. And each found himself shut out by traditional routes to power in his party.

Let's take a closer look at the Dean Internet campaign to get some idea of how he did it, and how this may now become part of our political landscape.

Trippisms

Quotations from Joe Trippi, chairman of the Dean for President campaign: .

"If television took the grass roots out of politics, the Internet will put it back in."

"The Net wasn't mature enough prior to now. You needed all those Americans to buy a book at Amazon.com, or to do an eBay auction, and to get used to using their credit card or doing something online."

(Asked by the *New York Times* about the original reception to his Internet campaign ideas.) "Well, the other campaigns laughed at us. I mean, we were the bar scene out of 'Star Wars'—that's what they thought a meetup was."

"There's finally a medium in the country that allows the American people to have control of it."

"The political press has no clue what the Internet is; they put it in their old context. The Internet community doesn't understand the hard cold realities of the political process. This is the problem/disconnect."

"Dean taught the party how to be an opposition party. Suddenly there was a debate about WMD [weapons of mass destruction], a debate that started because of the Internet, which made everyone realize the direction needed. The four remaining candidates are against the war, taking on Bush's foreign policy regardless of how they previously voted."

"The Dean campaign was a dot.com miracle, not a dot-com crash."

"The Internet is the most powerful tool put in the hands of the average American."

"This is just the beginning of real empowerment of people."

"You gotta believe." (In an e-mail message to supporters six days before the Iowa caucus.)

The first Internet-based presidential campaign

Howard Dean was not the first politician to use the Internet, only the first to use it so effectively. Back in 1992, another former governor—California's Jerry Brown—used FTP (file transfer protocol) sites to distribute his policy papers in his presidential campaign. In 1996 Bob Dole raised several hundred thousand dollars by mentioning his Web site during a debate with Bill Clinton, despite the fact that he managed to get the URL wrong. In 1998 Jesse Ventura was the first candidate to win statewide office by utilizing the Internet (and talk radio) to galvanize and organize supporters in his independent bid for the statehouse. In 2000, Steve Forbes became the first candidate to announce his presidential bid on the Internet, while Republican John McCain and Democrat Bill Bradley set records for online fundraising for their respective parties. And in 2003, Arnold Schwarzenegger became the new governor of California thanks to a recall campaign fueled by the Internet and talk radio.

Dean, however, not only broke previous Web fundraising records by far, he was the first to make the Internet the central structure of his campaign. Just as conservatives in the 1970s turned to direct mail because they were shut out of the establishment media, so Dean turned to the Internet in 2003 because he had no nationwide fundraising network and couldn't afford to hire the field staff he needed. The Internet gave him a way to break through to the two groups who supported him from the beginning—the gay community (because he signed the nation's first gay civil union law in Vermont) and the antiwar community (because of his principled opposition to the war, unlike the other Democratic candidates).

As 2003 arrived, the Dean campaign had less than $200,000 in its coffers. Turning to the Internet, it raised nearly $3 million in the first quarter, with massive jumps in each successive quarter. By the end of 2003 the Dean campaign had raised over $40 million, most of it through the Internet—more than any other Democratic candidate. Some 60 percent of Dean's contributions were for $200 or less, compared to 31 percent for Wesley Clark, 19 percent for Al Sharpton,

17 percent for John Kerry, 14 percent for Dick Gephardt, and 10 percent each for Bob Graham and Joe Lieberman. On the GOP side, President Bush got only 17 percent of his contributions in donations of $200 or less.

Another important comparison, this time with direct mail donors: Web contributors on average are 15 years younger than non-Web contributors (45 compared with 60) and they give more than twice as much money ($45 compared with $20).

Learning how to raise campaign money over the Internet was a major accomplishment of the Dean campaign. But somebody was going to be the first to do it, simply because Americans were becoming more at ease with the Internet. As Joe Trippi has said, "The Net wasn't mature enough prior to now. You needed all those Americans to buy a book at Amazon.com, or to do an eBay auction, and to get used to using their credit card or doing something online." An even greater accomplishment of the Dean campaign was demonstrating how to *communicate* with your supporters over the Internet.

As we've mentioned before, using the Internet as just another platform for preaching to your audience is underutilizing it, and possibly counterproductive. The Dean campaign used the Internet to *involve* its supporters, just as MoveOn.org had done with its members. And its deal with Meetup.com allowed the Dean campaign to sponsor its own meetups and to keep the e-mail addresses of its members who signed on through that site—provisions that were essential elements of its growth. Eventually over 600,000 people would sign up to get on the Dean mailing list, nearly half of them through Meetup.com, and well over 150,000 of these 600,000 would contribute to the campaign. As an example of the value of the Meetup tie-in, on one day alone— November 4, 2003—some 138,000 Dean supporters met at 820 locations to work for their candidate.

One of Joe Trippi's first jobs, once he signed on with Dean, was to start the first official campaign blog for a presidential candidate. It was enormously popular and successful, giving supporters a chance to vent their opinions and concerns, to communicate with each other, and to offer suggestions to the campaign—some of which were adopted, not just read. More than 100,000 messages were posted on the campaign's Blog for America.

One especially popular feature was the fundraising drive just before the end of a calendar quarter, when campaigns have to report the amount of money they've raised to the Federal Election Commission. Most campaigns keep their goals and their progress secret, to avoid negative media attention if they fail to reach their goals. Not the Dean campaign. The Dean Web site featured a baseball slugger trying to hit his fundraising goal, and showing his progress. So many supporters wrote in to urge more contributions and announce their own that at one point the blog crashed. "It got to be almost like a Jerry Lewis telethon," said Carol Darr, director of the Institute for Politics, Democracy and the Internet at George Washington University.

People who support an insurgent anti-establishment candidate are notably self-reliant, pro-active, and tend to "do their own thing" without clearing it first with headquarters. In the Goldwater campaign, grassroots volunteers would write and pass out their own literature, hold events, and talk to the press without thinking of getting some higher-up's approval. On occasion this proved embarrassing to the campaign leadership, but the overall benefits of all that spontaneous energy far outweighed the costs. With the Internet, grassroots democracy is even more firmly entrenched. "Deaniacs" could turn to the campaign's Web site for how-to advice on the mechanics of campaigning, but for the most part they were on their own, even creating their own local campaign Web sites without supervision from headquarters. Howard Dean and his campaign executives wisely understood that the Internet is not a suitable environment for micromanagement. And they actually *listened* to their supporters, learning from them, when the usual campaign process is for the candidate and his handlers to speak, while the workers listen.

It is appropriate that *Wired* magazine's Rave Award for politics in 2004 was shared by the Dean campaign's Joe Trippi and Scott Heiferman, cofounder and CEO of Meetup. Between them, they have rewired grassroots organizing for the Internet age. Having said this, what went wrong? Howard Dean may indeed be "the most consequential loser since Barry Goldwater," as the *Wall Street Journal* put it in an editorial, but the bottom line still is: He lost.

This is not the place to go into a lengthy analysis of what went wrong, but some things can be noted. Gobs of money were raised, but it was spent as fast as it was raised, often wastefully, leaving the campaign—incredibly—essentially broke on the eve of the first actual votes in Iowa and New Hampshire. There never seemed to be anything resembling a business plan, which campaigns need as much as new business ventures. And as liberal columnist E. J. Dionne, Jr. put it, "It was always more of a movement than a presidential campaign."

If liberals or conservatives want to learn how to run a successful ideological campaign—if they actually want to *win* rather than just put up a good fight—they will have to think hard about how to build the next new and improved version of the Dean campaign. Some way has to be found to harness the creativity of the next Joe Trippi but insist that he coexist within the campaign structure with a real businesslike CEO. Likewise, the Internet component may be the top growth engine for the campaign, but it cannot be *the* campaign.

Here are some of our first thoughts on how to do this.

First, Dean showed how to use the Internet to create a national campaign, raise money nationally, and increase the candidate's poll numbers nationally. That's great. Keep everyone, everywhere, working and contributing. But a major part of the money raised nationally then has to be deployed in the first states to vote, primarily Iowa and New Hampshire, and then not just with an Internet campaign. Spend the money in Iowa and New Hampshire to build a real on-the-ground field organization and a corps of *local* volunteers. Most people don't take too kindly to out-of-staters and strangers telling them how to vote, no matter how enthusiastic and well intentioned they are.

Second, the Dean campaign did a great job of listening to its grassroots supporters, not just preaching to them. But we've seen little evidence that they took the same approach when attempting to expand beyond their hard-core cadre and actually convince a majority of Iowa and New Hampshire Democrats to vote for them. It looks to us as if the Dean campaign was preaching to Iowa Democrats, not listening to them. That's the value of a vibrant local field organization. It can't (in an ideological campaign) tell you to change your key positions on key issues, but it can tell you which ones to emphasize and which to sublimate, plus give you helpful hints on how to frame the issues for voters in Iowa. You can't get that sort of feedback from your national hard-core supporters. You must be able to campaign simultaneously on both the national level, stroking your hard-core supporters, and the local level, convincing voters who have a quite different (but not necessarily antagonistic) perspective.

Third, give a hard look to the most expensive component of political campaigns: those TV ads. Ideally a good proportion of your TV ads should ask for a response—such as a contribution and/or a promise to join the campaign as a volunteer. That brings in money, names, and addresses. General "name recognition" ads are a colossal waste of money, especially at the early stage of the campaign and outside of the first primary states. The Internet and direct mail give you much cheaper means of spreading the word. And you can use the money you save to build those field organizations in Iowa and New Hampshire. You can start advertising over TV stations in those states once you get closer to primary day.

Howard Dean was leading the Democratic pack of candidates before Iowa. Taking these steps well in advance could have won Iowa for him, and that momentum would have carried him through to the Democratic nomination.

Stirrings on the Right side of the Internet

Most, but not all, of the political activism on the Internet for the 2003–2004 election cycle has been on the Left. Conservatives, for the most part, have been trying to copy what the liberals have successfully been pursuing.

Meetup officials approached Townhall.com, an online operation of the Heritage Foundation, in the fall of 2003. Howard Dean and the other Democrats were utilizing Meetup to the max because of the Democratic primaries. Meetup wanted people to understand that it is a nonpartisan, nonideological vehicle, open to conservatives and Republicans as well. Would Townhall be interested in sponsoring meetups for conservatives?

A deal was struck, and Townhall issued a "conservative alert" through its online newsletter: "Liberals such as the ACLU, Howard Dean, and the Sierra Club have already had successful meetups. Don't let conservatives remain 'the silent majority'—make the Townhall.com Conservative Meetup the most successful Meetup yet."

Conservatives responded so enthusiastically that Meetup CEO Scott Heiferman told CNN News it was the fastest takeoff in Meetup's history—11,000 participants in the first month, nearly 20,000 in over 500 cities by the end of the second month.

MoveOn.org has also sparked a reaction on the Right, appropriately called RightMarch.com. RightMarch was founded by conservative Internet entrepreneur Bill Greene. "Our motif is to counter the actions of liberal groups," Greene told CBS News in March 2004. "And so if a group like MoveOn.org does something, then RightMarch.com will usually respond to what they're doing and send out alerts."

RightMarch's Web site describes itself as "an umbrella Web site for many conservative organizations, as well as thousands of hardworking, patriotic Americans across the country." It suggests actions to take against amnesty for illegal aliens, it keeps visitors current on the activities of its own political action committee (PAC), and it announces publication of a full-page ad in *USA Today* backing Secretary of Defense Donald Rumsfeld.

And in California, conservative activists used the Internet and talk radio in 2003 to launch the recall petition that toppled Democratic Gov. Gray Davis and replaced him with Republican Arnold Schwarzenegger. While Schwarzenegger wasn't the conservatives' first choice, most of them (not all) jumped on his bandwagon when it became obvious that his Hollywood superstar status offered the best hope for getting rid of Davis.

To understand the odds against the recall petition when it was launched, consider that 31 previous recall efforts had failed to make the ballot. The state's Left-establishment media, led by the *Los Angeles Times* and the *San Francisco Chronicle*, was opposed to it. The state Republican leadership, accustomed to playing a dead man barely walking, didn't want to get involved. And President Bush's point man in California, fundraiser Gerald Parsky, was opposed to a recall because he thought it would derail momentum for Bush in 2004.

Two things turned the tide despite those odds: overwhelming public disdain for the ineffectual Governor Davis . . . and the alternative media. In this instance, talk radio was the agitator that built support for the recall petition, and the Internet was the facilitator, making it easy to contribute money and download petition forms. Former GOP state legislator Howard Kaloogian was the key organizer of the radio and Internet campaigns. Leading the charge over the airwaves were radio hosts Melanie Morgan of San Francisco's KSFO-560 ("the mother of the recall") and Roger Hedgecock of San Diego's KOGO Newsradio 600 (Hedgecock is a former mayor of San Diego). Other important hosts included Eric Hogue in Sacramento (KTKZ 1380), Rick Roberts of KFMB-760 in San Diego, and Los Angeles hosts John and Ken (KFI-640), George Putnam (KPLS-830), Mark Lawson (KRLA-870), and Al Rantel (KABC-790).

Between them, talk radio and the Internet made mincemeat of the liberal media establishment, the GOP naysayers, and of course the Democratic Party establishment in the state. It was an awesome demonstration of what can be done on the Right under the right conditions.

Where We Are Today, How We Got Here, and Where We're Going Tomorrow

When Ronald Reagan beat Jimmy Carter in 1980, there were two news cycles a day, morning papers and evening newscasts. CNN was five months old. There were no satellite phones, no *USA Today*, no Fox News Channel, no CNBC, no Comedy Central, no *Weekly Standard*, no Rush Limbaugh show, no *Slate*, no *Salon*, no Google, no *Drudge Report*. Now campaign stories change hour by hour.

Howard Kurtz, *Washington Post,* Jan. 29, 2004

Make that minute by minute. With the burgeoning growth of the Internet and embedded reporters and the blogosphere, there no longer is any compartmentalized news cycle—the news is under constant

321

revision. If you don't like the news you're getting this instant, come back in a minute.

Most of us have better things to do than watch a news streamer all day long, of course, but the important factor is that now we can *choose* when we want to get our news. As a Pew Research Center report put it: "The 24-hour availability of news on cable and the Internet has enabled many Americans to set their own schedules for getting the news. About half (48 percent) describe themselves as news grazers—people who check in on news from time to time over the course of the day. Roughly the same proportion (49 percent) get the news more habitually, watching or listening at regular times."

Just as we have unlimited choice as to *when* we get our news, in practical terms we have unlimited choices as to *where* we get our news—no one could possibly utilize all the choices out there. In this book we've drawn the distinction between traditional, mostly establishment-liberal news media, and alternative, mostly conservative, news media. For years we used the phrase "below-the-radar" to describe these alternative media, but now it's safe to say they've been outed (along with virtually everything else in our society). The major categories of establishment-liberal media are the TV broadcast networks, the wire services and newspapers (especially the major trend-setting ones like the *New York Times*), and National Public Radio (NPR). The major categories of alternative media are direct mail, talk radio, cable news TV, and the Internet.

The importance of this transformation of the news cycle and the explosion in the number of news outlets is that *an elitist clique cannot control the news today.* News today is unmanageable and uncontrollable. Those of us who have published, edited, or otherwise operated a news site recently do the best we can to bring some order to the news, but we know that our product represents the total reality in roughly the same degree that our solar system represents the universe.

U.S. News' Michael Barone caught the significance of this during the 2000 election campaign, in his article "The Death of Big Media." Barone is not easily typecast in ideological terms and is widely respected as one of the most astute observers of the American political scene (he writes the unequaled *Almanac of American Politics*). Here is part of what he said during the 2000 campaign:

> Twelve years ago, I decided that the ideal way to cover the 1988 presidential campaign would be to report on what happened in just five rooms—at the morning meetings in the candidates' headquarters in Washington and Boston, and at the late-afternoon meetings of the producers of the ABC, CBS, and NBC network newscasts, all on the West Side of Manhattan. My theory was that American voters got most of their information about the campaign from television, that the campaigns' morning meetings would show what they wanted on the evening newscasts, and that the networks' afternoon meetings would show how successful each campaign had been. . . .
>
> It was a good idea, then. From the 1960s to the 1980s the three network nightly newscasts were, in fact, the town square of American politics. . . .
>
> You can't cover the 2000 presidential election in five rooms. It would take hundreds.
>
> This is not altogether a bad thing. The old-line nets' dominance put great power in a very few—and mostly liberal—hands.

Also in the year 2000, one of your authors, Richard Viguerie, spotlighted this change on ConservativeHQ.com with his article, "Now, This Is Real Campaign Reform":

Have you wondered about the following?

> (1) The establishment media with few exceptions declared Gore the winner of the first debate. College debate professors declared Gore the clear winner. Instant overnight polls gave Gore a strong victory.

(2) In the 12 days since the first debate that "Bush lost" he's gone from about five points behind to about five points ahead.

How could Bush gain 10 points in 12 days if he lost the first debate? The answer lies in the non-establishment media. . . .

Now, for the first 24 hours after the first debate, the establishment media crowed loudly about Gore's superior knowledge and Bush's inability to defend his tax cut proposals. But by the second day after the debate, the below-the-radar media was operating in full force. Gore's expressions, misstatements, off-putting sighs, condescending looks and mannerisms when Bush was speaking—all that began to get traction on national, state, and local talk radio, on cable TV, and on the Internet.

Three days after the debate, the establishment media could no longer ignore the direction the debate discussion was going around America's water coolers and kitchen tables. The new and alternative media almost single-handedly forced the establishment media to take a second look at their analysis of the first debate.

This presidential election is the first to feel the full weight of the conservative below-the-radar media— which is where about 40 percent of the voters get most of their political/public policy news and information. . . .

All of this says American politics will never be the same.

What the liberal reformers such as Ralph Nader have been calling for, is happening in real time right in front of their eyes. But unlike the liberals who receive billions of dollars each year from America's taxpayers, the conservatives use the free market to finance their below-the-radar media.

Buckle up your political seat belt and welcome to the new reality of American politics. The establishment media monopoly has been broken for all time.

Alternative media continue to grow

That was four years ago. Since then the trend favoring alternative, mostly conservative media sources has accelerated, and, as we've already noted, those "under-the-radar" media have been outed. The role of cable news TV, talk radio, and the Internet is a hot topic everywhere politics is discussed.

There's one notable exception, however. When commentators—even most conservative ones—talk about the types of alternative media influencing the election, they tend to forget direct mail. Yet the Viguerie firm alone has mailed more than 2 billion letters over the past 40 years and will mail over 100 million pieces of direct mail in this campaign year—and that's just a small portion of what you'll find in your mailbox this year. We've surveyed the field, Right and Left, and here is our estimate of the amount of direct mail political advocacy likely to target voters this year:

- 3,100,000,000 letters will be mailed this year by the Republican and Democratic national committees, as well as national and local political and public policy organizations with an ideological point of view—everyone from the Sierra Club and the NAACP to the Heritage Foundation and the National Rifle Association.
- 1,400,000,000 magazines, newsletters, and policy papers will be mailed by these same groups.
- And 2,700,000,000 letters will be mailed by candidates for public office at every level of government—from the president to your local sheriff.

And that's just direct mail. Add in talk radio, cable news TV, and the Internet and it's clear that one-half of the American voters today get most of their political news from the alternative media.

Figures for 2004 haven't been released as we go to press, but in 2002 the Pew Research Center for the People & the Press (in its report

Public's News Habits Little Changed by Sept. 11, June 9, 2002, available at www.people-press.org) asked people where they got their news. (Direct mail wasn't given as a choice, of course.) Television and newspapers were still the major sources, but from an ideological perspective it was significant that cable TV had moved ahead of the broadcast networks' evening news programs:

Where Americans Get Their Television News (%)	
Cable TV news	33%
Nightly network news	32

Similarly, talk radio slightly bested NPR:

Where Americans Get Their Radio News (%)	
Call-in radio shows	17%
National Public Radio	16

Also, 25 percent of Americans were already citing the Internet, a huge jump from 2 percent in 1996 and 13 percent in 1998.

Where we're headed in the future can be seen by comparing the median ages of viewers of different types of TV news. The stereotype of the person addicted to the Weather Channel is a retiree who has nothing better to do, but we find that the audiences for the liberal network news programs and the liberals' favorite PBS news program, *News Hour with Jim Lehrer,* are older than the weather groupies:

Median Age of Viewers	
Program	**Age of Viewers**
News Hour with Jim Lehrer	54
Network TV evening news programs	50
Weather Channel	47
CNN	46
Fox News Channel	44
Talk radio and NPR	42

Ideological profiles of news audiences

Throughout this book we have referred to the ideological leanings of the various news media—the TV networks and major newspapers being in the liberal corner, while talk radio, cable news TV, and the Internet are mostly conservative. Now it will be extremely illuminating to look at what the Pew study we've continually cited found regarding the ideological leanings of media audiences.

Some highlights:

First, American news consumers are far more conservative than they are liberal. Indeed, twice as many say they are conservative (36 percent) than liberal (18 percent). This one factor alone reveals the uphill struggle facing the new Air America Radio network (see Chapter 10), which flaunts its liberal credentials. America may be divided 50-50 between Republicans and Democrats in presidential campaigns, but ideologically it is overwhelmingly conservative and centrist.

Second, to quote Pew: "For all the controversy over Fox News Channel's supposed ideological leanings, its audience is only slightly more conservative than the national average." The percentage of liberals (18 percent) who watch Fox is the same as the percentage of liberals found in the nation at large.

Third, because the nation is so heavily conservative, it turns out that far more conservatives than liberals watch such liberal programming as the nightly network TV news, print news magazines, and NPR. As Mickey Kaus is rumored to have said: "No wonder conservatives are so pissed off!"

Fourth, to quote Pew: "The only news-oriented media that has a decidedly liberal profile is the readership of literary magazines such as the *New Yorker, Atlantic Monthly,* and *Harper's Magazine.* Fully 45 percent of people who regularly read these magazines identify themselves as liberal, two and a half times the national average." No surprise there.

Bottom line: America has always in our time been a conservative

Ideological Self-Identifications of Audiences (%)

Regularly watched, read, or listened to	Conservative	Moderate	Liberal	Don't Know
Rush Limbaugh	72%	18%	6%	4%
Religious radio	67	22	6	5
O'Reilly Factor	56	36	5	3
Political magazines	52	24	23	1
Call-in radio shows	46	31	18	5
Business magazines	46	32	18	4
Fox News Channel	46	32	18	4
CNBC	44	33	14	9
CNN	40	38	16	6
MSNBC	40	38	16	6
Morning news	40	38	16	6
Local news	38	40	16	6
Larry King Live	38	35	19	8
Nightly network news	37	41	16	6
News magazines	37	40	20	3
Network newsmagazines	36	41	17	6
Nationwide Self-Identification	**36**	**38**	**18**	**8**
National Public Radio	36	38	20	6
Newspaper	35	41	18	6
News Hour with Lehrer	35	37	21	7
Letterman/Leno	34	41	19	6
Oprah/Rosie	32	36	19	13
Jerry/Ricki	32	37	26	5
Literary magazines	20	25	45	10

nation. As we stressed in Chapter 4, in 1955 the nation was politically and socially conservative while the media were overwhelmingly liberal. That was the impetus for conservatives to start and nurture their own alternative media. Today those alternative media are healthy and powerful, *but liberals are still overrepresented in the media as a whole compared to the American people.* All the liberal harping about the conservative alternative media is just fear and alarm over finally having some competition.

How did conservatives reach today's level of influence?

Our primary purpose in writing this book has been to tell the story—in its entirety for the first time—of how the conservative movement came to power by utilizing new and alternative media. Our secondary purpose is to use what we've learned to predict, as much as possible, the future of the ongoing conservative-versus-liberal power struggle. First, then, let's review the historical lessons we've presented in the past pages.

Our story began in 1955, in an era of liberal hegemony over America (Chapter 4). Liberal gatekeepers at the most influential newspapers and magazines, as well as the three television networks, decided what was news and what wasn't. A tone of faux objectivity disguised what was in reality elitist control of the nation's political discourse. Put together all the influential media, we concluded, and you get a score of something like liberals 95, conservatives 5. Or 97/3. That's the sort of monopoly enjoyed by Pravda in its Soviet heyday. At the same time the United States was pretty evenly divided between "conservatives" and "liberals," as we use these terms today. This chasm between the conservatism of the American people and the liberalism of America's media would fuel the resentment conservatives feel against the liberal media to this day. And because the traditional media were closed to them, conservatives had no choice but to develop their own media. We examined the effects of each of the new media as they unfolded in history.

Under-the-radar publications, books, and networks. We chose to start our story in 1955 because that's the year *National Review* was founded (Chapter 5). The editors of *National Review* taught its audience on the Right to think of themselves as a *movement* and to adopt a longterm strategic outlook. (The fact that a number of its editors were ex-communists helps to explain this proactive mindset.) And *National Review's* founder and editor in chief, William F. Buckley Jr., became the first media superstar of the new movement. It is no exaggeration to say there wouldn't be a Rush Limbaugh or Sean Hannity today without the trailblazing work of Bill Buckley.

Over the next decade the movement grew politically and in 1964 secured the nomination of Barry Goldwater as the GOP presidential candidate (Chapter 6). This was a feat made possible by alternative media—*National Review, Human Events,* and all the other under-the-radar periodicals, as well as riveting paperback tracts that sold in the millions without ever appearing on the *New York Times* bestseller list. Thanks to this underground media network ("underground" because the liberal establishment media chose to ignore it, in hopes of crushing it), grassroots political networks were formed, making the Goldwater campaign the most broadly based presidential drive to that date. At the same time, those networks were no match for the fierce public assaults mounted by the liberal political and media establishments. The result was electoral disaster—but also the beginnings of a new, improved movement, fueled by a new secret weapon.

Political direct mail. Liberals thought they had exterminated the threat from the Right, but, once again out of the spotlight, conservatives continued to organize, proselytize, and search for ways to bypass the liberal stranglehold on the mass media. When they found a way, the liberals didn't take it seriously until it was too late.

The conservatives' new secret weapon was political direct mail. Direct mail was and is the second largest type of advertising in the commercial world, but politicians had only experimented with it intermittently. Richard Viguerie, coauthor of this book, saw it, however, as a way to build a mass movement (Chapter 7), and he had the field pretty much to himself from 1965 into the 1970s. The U.S. mail quickly became the principal method of communication for conservatives.

Leading the way for the other alternative media to follow, direct mail gave conservatives these advantages:

- A way to bypass the liberal gatekeepers of the mass media by taking the conservative message directly to the individual conservative's mailbox, without distortion.
- A way to find, identify, and activate millions of concerned citizens, adding them to the conservative roster and giving conservatives a voice in setting the nation's political agenda.
- Freedom from the restrictions imposed by the Republican political hierarchy, enabling conservatives to become an independent, vibrant force.
- Freedom from dependence on the big corporations that had traditionally financed GOP and Democratic politics (and expected to be paid back with favors).
- A way to make fence-straddling Washington politicians more accountable to their conservative grassroots constituents.
- And a way to bring a conservative candidate over the top to victory, by adding or shifting a critical 5 percent of the vote based on single-issue appeals.

We mentioned that the liberals didn't take direct mail seriously until it was too late. The exact moment when liberals were jolted awake was the evening of November 4, 1980, when Ronald Reagan was elected president and the GOP captured the Senate. The right wing had captured Washington undetected, largely with direct mail as its principal weapon.

Talk radio. When the so-called Fairness Doctrine bit the dust in 1987, thanks to President Reagan, radio broadcasters no longer had to shy away from airing controversial positions. In the next six years, over 1,000 radio stations switched to a talk-radio format—*because that's what their listeners wanted.* And *who* they wanted to hear, more than anyone else, was a former DJ named Rush Limbaugh (Chapter 10).

Talk radio gave conservatives a second way to bypass the liberal gatekeepers at the *New York Times* and the TV networks—this time with a human voice. Limbaugh spurred his huge audience into action, making life miserable for co-presidents Bill and Hillary Clinton. And it wasn't just Rush. Almost all of the top radio hosts were conservatives. And on the receiving end of the dial, grassroots conservatives were thrilled to hear *their* viewpoints expressed over the air.

Talk radio was a driving force behind the defeat of Hillarycare and other key legislation sought by the Clinton administration. And it became a key factor in the Republicans' capture of the House of Representatives under Newt Gingrich. By the time we were in a new century, conservative talk radio had a bigger audience and was politically far more powerful than liberal (and taxpayer-subsidized) NPR.

Cable news television. Liberal icon Ted Turner started the Cable News Network (CNN) in 1980, and its ideological slant under his reign led conservatives to dub it the "Clinton News Network." Turner didn't realize it at the time, but he was actually doing conservatives a great favor. He took the financial risk to prove that 24/7 cable news was not only possible, it was the wave of the future. Turner's innovation opened the way for another entrepreneur, Rupert Murdoch, to beat him at his own game with the Fox News Channel (Chapter 11).

Fox is now the leading cable news network. Its number one superstar, Bill O'Reilly, is the most watched commentator on cable television. Fox's number two star, Sean Hannity, is the only person to achieve superstardom on both cable TV and talk radio. Moreover, Fox's success has prompted a noticeable shift rightward at both CNN and MSNBC.

Nothing has fed conservative resentment of the three TV broadcast networks more than the networks' treatment of conservatives in their campaign coverage. Well, conservatives now have their revenge. In each of the last three presidential campaign cycles—1996, 2000, and 2004—cable news TV has gained market share and the TV broadcast networks have lost market share. Since 1993, in fact, the nightly network news shows have seen their regular audience cut nearly in half—from 60 percent of Americans in 1993 to 32 percent in 2002. And the network news magazines (*60 Minutes, 20/20, Dateline,* etc.) have lost more than half of their audience, which has plummeted from 52 percent of Americans in 1993 to 24 percent in 2002. Since around 2000, more Americans get their campaign news from the three cable news networks than from the three original broadcast networks. In TV news, at least, the alternative media has displaced the establishment media.

Internet. The Internet, the newest of the alternative media, has been a political force since Matt Drudge outed President Clinton and Monica Lewinski in 1998 (Chapter 13). Conservatives have followed Drudge's lead in embracing the Internet, at least for news and commentary. When we looked at the Alexa ratings for the top ideological and independent news sites on the Internet, we found 24 right-of-center sites and 11 left-of-center sites. The top four conservative and libertarian sites on the Web each have a larger online audience than such print titans as the *Financial Times, Chicago Tribune, New York Daily News,* or *Time* magazine.

Put the four alternative media together—direct mail, talk radio, cable news TV, and the Internet—and you can appreciate why the liberals are on the run. They've seen the four horsemen of the conservative apocalypse.

Using the alternative media to promote God and country

Our emphasis in this book has been on how secular (if often quite religious) political organizations and causes have used alternative media to advance their programs. A consistent sidebar, though, has been the efforts of religious groups that have a political impact. This is quite common in the United States, which, it's generally agreed, is far more religious than any other advanced industrialized nation.

We started our modern story in 1955, when a liberal hegemony ruled over the nation's political life. The religious activism of that day was almost entirely liberal and leftist in its orientation, with liberal "mainstream" churches leading the way. There were few complaints

from the Left that this violated "the separation of church and state"—
religious activism was fine as long as it advanced the leftist political
cause. It was only when religious conservatives became politically active
that we started hearing fearful tales about the dangers of theocracy.

In Chapter 8, we saw (pages 131–133) how the Religious Right was
created using alternative media—direct mail, religious radio programs,
and religious television programs and networks. The Rev. Jerry Falwell
and the Rev. Pat Robertson were the key figures of the movement in
that era. It was also during the '70s and '80s that activists from various
Right-oriented denominations started working together on shared concerns. This had been common on the Left, but rare on the Right up to
this time. In our profile of the Stop ERA movement (pages 137–144),
Phyllis Schlafly gave us a lively example of what these first ecumenical
encounters were like.

In Chapter 10, we discussed the culture wars on talk radio, particularly in regard to Dr. Laura Schlessinger (pages 192–193), then looked
at the growth of religious broadcasting networks (pages 193–195),
among them the Crawford Broadcasting Company, Salem Radio Network, and American Family Radio. Catholics are also active on talk
radio, and one of the most popular hosts is Ray Flynn, former mayor of
Boston and former ambassador to the Vatican. We expect ever-increasing impact in coming years from Domino's Pizza founder Tom Mon-
aghan, founder of the new and conservative (both religiously and
politically) Ave Maria College in Florida. Already his Ave Maria Radio
Network operates two radio stations in Michigan and syndicates Al
Kresta's daily three-hour talk show throughout the United States.

Some of the most interesting religious outreach taking place today
is on the Internet. For example, every paper and press release published by the Family Research Center is available on its Web site
(www.frc.org). Focus on the Family features a subsection (www.family
.org/cforum) of its Web site where activists can get involved. And the
Traditional Values Coalition (www.traditionalvalues.org) has an e-mail
list of over 800,000 subscribers and Web site resources for activists—
including policy backgrounders and talking points. Conservative

Catholic sites include the comprehensive portal www.catholic.net, as well as sites like www.catholicanswers.com and www.priestsforlife .com. And blogging is not reserved for purely political sites—Christians are get-ting into it in a major way. You can find (at last count) 313 sites listed on St. Blog's Parish, "the ring for Catholic bloggers"—accessible at www.ringsurf.com/netring?ring = stblogs;action = list. And on the Protestant side, www.blogs4god.com has an incredible list of around 1,100 blogs, subdivided into eight categories: apologia, church polity, journals, metablogs, ministries, pundits, techBlogs, and zines.

As this book goes to press, the big story in conservative Christian circles is the imminent plunge into political activism on the part of Dr. James C. Dobson. He plays roughly the same role in the conservative Christian community as Rush Limbaugh does in the talk radio community: that of the Big Enchilada. A child psychologist, Dr. Dobson has built his Colorado Springs–based Focus on the Family into a behemoth. As noted recently by the *New York Times*, he has sold more than 7 million books and "he sends his Focus on the Family newsletter to more than 3 million donors, a number comparable to the circulation of *Newsweek*." In the past he has been largely nonpolitical—but that was before activist judges took steps to promote gay marriage. Now he has started Focus on the Family Action to campaign for socially conservative causes, with an emphasis presently on fighting same-sex marriage. Expect fireworks.

When you can't compete, kill your opponent with legislation or regulation

Sadly, there are few principled supporters of the First Amendment in America today—or, for that matter, the rest of the Bill of Rights. This is true on the Left and the Right, and most certainly true of a majority of those who sit in the Congress, the White House, and the Supreme Court. It's also true of those grand organs of liberal preachiness about civil liberties, like the *New York Times* and the *Washington Post*, who are all too ready to put an axe to their competition's rights when it's to their benefit.

The desire to use regulations, legislation, and the police power of the state to silence your opponents corrupts many politicians and government officials, Democrat and Republicans alike, at the federal, state, and local levels.

It is important that every citizen understands what is at stake here. The mail you get from your favorite political organizations, the talk shows you listen to on the radio, the news you get on TV or the Internet—all of this is the First Amendment in action, your right to have a voice in politics, your right to *choose* your sources of news. With alternative media *you do have a choice*. You can throw that piece of political mail in the trash if you don't want to read it. If you don't like a particular radio host or TV commentator, you can change the dial or channel, or shut the machine off. And if you don't like what some Web site is saying, heck, you can start your *own* blog! The alternative media are all about giving power to the people, and that's why so many politicians and lobbies and corporate conglomerates distrust the alternative media and try to legislate it out of business or regulate it to limit its effectiveness.

Take John Kerry, for instance. Apparently he doesn't really believe that Air America Radio will have what it takes to compete in the marketplace with conservative hosts, because he wants to close down the whole talk radio format. Oh, he's not honest enough to say it that forthrightly, of course; rather, he disguises his intentions by talking about bringing back the so-called Fairness Doctrine: "The loss of equal-time requirements, I think, was a blow. I was for equal-time requirements. Because I think what's happened is that we got networks that are almost providing a single point of view, and I don't think that is wise."

Somehow we doubt he was referring to NBC, ABC, CBS, or NPR— the networks that come closest to providing a single (liberal) point of view, under the guise of objectivity and, in NPR's case, a huge helping of taxpayer subsidies. No, we suspect he's talking about those nonsubsidized shows where you can actually call up and voice *your* opinion, which too often isn't all that favorable to John Kerry and his fellow politicians in Washington.

Rush knows what that means: "Liberals can't beat us in the arena of ideas . . . so what they want to do is shut us down."

Or take a powerful lobby like the National Association of Broadcasters. But, hey, they represent media, you say—wouldn't they be all the way *for* the First Amendment? Correction: They represent the established media conglomerates that want to protect their market share by regulating out competition that uses a new business plan and new technology to give consumers new choices . . . like satellite radio, for example, which wants to be able to offer localized programming.

Or take President Bush and the majority of Congress and the majority of the Supreme Court, who all conspired against the First Amendment, first by passing the McCain-Feingold campaign finance law, then by upholding its constitutionality. President Bush was especially hypocritical. He indicated that he thought the law was unconstitutional but, like a modern-day Pontius Pilate, washed his hands as he signed it and passed it on to a Supreme Court that acts more like an unelected branch of Congress than an enforcer of the Constitution.

McCain-Feingold is the gravest threat to your free speech today. The goal, said its backers, was to fight corruption by limiting the power of Big Money in our campaigns. Helllooo! Has anybody noticed how Big Money has been driven out of Washington now that we have McCain-Feingold?

The real purpose of McCain-Feingold was to silence *your* voice in the campaign process, by placing a gag order on the organizations that represent you and your views. It does this by prohibiting these groups from broadcasting any issue ads that refer to specific candidates for federal office in the 30 days before a primary, or 60 days before a general election. And why were those dates chosen? Because "that's when people are most interested in the elections!" replies Rep. Martin Meehan (D–MA), one of the law's most ardent supporters. In other words, to silence our voices—all of us ordinary citizens who contribute to these organizations—at the times when we can exert our greatest influence on the political process.

Nat Hentoff, who *is* a principled and consistent defender of the

First Amendment, notes that "George Soros—who is increasingly politically active and is determined to send George W. Bush back to Texas
[in 2005]—now has more First Amendment rights, thanks to this Mc-
Cain-Feingold 'reform' law, than those of us who contribute to the
ACLU or the National Rifle Association during those weeks and
months when our voices count."

Wouldn't you expect the giants who owe their very existence to the
First Amendment to rush to its defense and oppose McCain-Feingold—
giants like the broadcast networks, the *New York Times*, the *Washington
Post?* Not if you're at all familiar with their history. They are for the
First Amendment when it protects *their* right to free speech, but that
concern doesn't extend to *your* free speech.

The truth is that the establishment media want to preserve their
monopoly over the news you get, which is why they oppose the alternative media—their upstart competition. They want to regain that
golden era when they were the gatekeepers of the news, when politicians toadied to them and sought their approval rather than the approval of citizen groups.

And the print media conglomerates have always had an abiding
disdain for their print competition—direct mail—which, after all, is the
primary funding source for those citizen groups. (In fact, the very term
"junk mail" was coined by Scripps Howard to denigrate its principal
competitor for advertising dollars.) This disdain was never revealed
quite as blatantly as in a November 30, 1992 editorial in the *New York
Times*. Bashing Richard Viguerie and his clients who had the temerity
to suggest that the Social Security Trust Fund is a fraud, the *Times* hit
upon a solution: Have "the IRS, the Postal Service, and state officials
crack down" on these tax-exempt groups. And then the most surreal
zinger: "The IRS could also require mailings to be submitted for inspec-
tion so that fraudulent claims can be detected sooner."

Would the *New York Times* ever entertain a suggestion that its own
writers submit their editorials and articles to the IRS for approval
prior to publication? The suggestion is ludicrous, not worthy of anyone
who purports to believe in a free society. But that's how low the

establishment media will stoop in their attempts to squash their competition with the iron fist of the Gestapo.

Alternative media and the future of liberalism

Air America Radio is the most ambitious effort by liberals so far to compete with conservatives in the alternative media marketplace, rather than try to legislate or regulate the conservatives out of business. On its launch date, we took to the op-ed page of the *Los Angeles Times* to explain why we thought the odds are against Air America. The liberal network's approach reveals a lot about why liberals find it tough going almost everywhere in the alternative media, not just on the airwaves.

Let us expand on those reasons.

That liberal Y chromosome. When we interviewed the dean of liberal direct mail fundraising, Roger Craver (Chapters 9 and 10), he bemoaned the wussiness of so many liberal commentators: "Quite frankly, I think one reason liberals haven't done well in mass communication is that they have this Y chromosome that looks for balance and dignity and decency, and whatever adjective they want to come up with. And they don't know how to go for the jugular."

We all laughed, but Craver was serious: "The most effective communication on either side of the political spectrum is black and white. When you get right down to it, all this alternative media is simply professional wrestling. That's all it is. There's good and there's bad. You pick who in your audience are the good, and you vilify the bad. And the Left ought to do the same thing."

On the surface, Air America seemed to be doing one thing right at its launch. Instead of picking tired and retired politicians like Mario Cuomo as their radio hosts, they were turning to articulate entertainers with liberal political convictions (Al Franken and Janeane Garofalo) as their superstars. That is critical, because conservative stars like Limbaugh, O'Reilly, and Hannity are entertainers who just happen to be conservative, not conservatives who are trying to be entertaining. Since Air America's launch, though, a surprising number of liberals have been critical of the muddled message they get from the network, and we wonder if even Al Franken is afflicted with the Y chromosome. In Russell Shorto's profile of him in the *New York Times Magazine*, Franken comes across as a nuanced liberal, much like John F. Kerry. But on talk radio you want to sound like Howard Dean or Ralph Nader, not like Kerry. If Al Franken is going to be the John Kerry of talk radio, Air America is in trouble.

Fear of long-term commitment. Conservatives didn't build their alternative media empire overnight. It was the result of decades of hard work—mastering direct mail in the 1970s, talk radio in the late 1980s, and cable television and the Internet in the 1990s. Yet Franken reportedly has signed only a one-year contract and said, "I'm doing this because I want to use my energies to get Bush unelected. I'd be happy if the election of a Democrat ended the show."

That attitude doesn't bode well for Air America. If all they want to do is elect Kerry, their money would be better spent buying radio and TV time, not starting a new network.

We assume, though, that the network's executives have longer-term aspirations than Franken does. Then they'd better worry about what happens if Kerry *does* win in November. Will their liberal audience feel so happy and vindicated that they no longer need solace on the radio dial? Building an alternative media presence works best when the other side is in power and your audience is disgruntled and seeking power. Yes, today's conservative alternative media are closely allied with the new Republican establishment, but they were *built* when LBJ and Jimmy Carter and Bill Clinton were in power.

Inadequate capitalization. From what we've read, Air America's business plan seems optimistic, to be charitable about it. Starting a network with clout, and then running it, will cost a lot more than the $20 million to $30 million in capital they claim to have raised so far. And to expect to start making a profit in just four years is unrealistic. Ask Rupert Murdoch—or liberal Ted Turner, for that matter.

When the initial cash runs out, Air America has two paths it can take, neither of which seems too promising. It can go to someone like billionaire George Soros for the financing it really needs, along the lines of $100 million, say. But Soros, like Franken, seems to be more interested in simply defeating Bush than in building a new movement. Or Air America can seek broad public support, which brings us to our last point and the most important reason why we're skeptical of Air America's chances for success.

There's no liberal _there_ there. Ambitious ideological projects like Air America require a mass ideological movement to sustain it, and if a robust liberal movement exists today, it can teach the Air Force something about stealth. Hiding behind a pseudonym like "progressive" fools no one and is a sign of weakness. Liberals cannot build a viable movement if they are afraid to be called liberals. Conservatives for decades were called every name in the book, up to and including "fascist" and "Nazi," but we didn't disown our identity as conservatives. Also, Democrat-Republican wars shouldn't be confused with building a movement. The partisan timeframe always looks ahead four years max; building a movement, as we've said, requires decades.

Here is where the prognosis for liberal projects like Air America gets most dismal. Polls consistently show that fewer and fewer Americans consider themselves to be liberals. As we saw on page 328, only 18 percent of American news consumers consider themselves to be liberal, compared with 36 percent who identify as conservative, and 38 percent as moderate. And Hal Malchow, a leading fundraiser for the Democratic Party, told us (Chapter 9): "If we had to live off the liberal market, we'd be nothing because the size of the donor list on the liberal side has been shrinking. A lot! The basic liberal universe that's available to the DNC right now is probably around a half million to 600,000 unique names that we don't have yet as donors. Ten years ago it would have been a million, a million and a half names."

By way of comparison, the Republican Party regularly solicits new donors from conservative lists totaling 5 million or more names. And the number of those names has been holding steady, not plummeting by 50 percent or more, like the number of liberal names has.

Is that a light at the end of the liberal tunnel? Robert Reich, President Clinton's secretary of labor, is one liberal who understands the distinction between *party* and *movement*. In an early 2004 op-ed for the *New York Times*, he warned against the assumption "that recapturing the presidency depends on who triumphs in the battle between liberals and moderates within the party. Such thinking . . . is inherently flawed. The real fight is between those who want only to win back the White House and those who also want to build a new political movement— one that rivals the conservative movement that has given Republicans their dominant position in American politics."

Bingo! Reich's got five across the card!

Reich continues by advising Democrats to "pay close attention to what Republicans have learned about winning elections. First, it is crucial to build a political movement that will endure after particular electoral contests. Second, in order for a presidency to be effective, it needs a movement that mobilizes Americans behind it. Finally, any political movement derives its durability from the clarity of its convictions. And there's no better way to clarify convictions than to hone them in political combat."

Bingo! Now he's got five *down* the card!

Are the liberals up to the task? The only area in which we've seen some real potential is in the Dean campaign's use of the Internet (Chapter 14).

If "the Left's real problem [is] a lack of new and coherent ideas," as *Time* magazine put it in 2003, then the early Dean campaign at least gave us *clear-cut* ideas. His positions on gay rights and against the war in Iraq earned him the two audiences that propelled his early rise over the Internet. Later, though, as he shifted emphasis to economic issues, he was caught in a classic Democratic bind: He had governed Vermont as a fiscal moderate (the libertarian Cato Institute gave him a grade of "C" in 2000, better than seven Republican governors that year), yet now he had to cater to the party's leftists on economics too, not just the war. The result was anything *but* clear and coherent ideas, and even fewer ideas that resonated with the American public. Instead of pledging a return to fiscal sanity, he promised to raise taxes for everyone!

Then there's the matter of a long-term business plan. As we saw in Chapter 8, conservative direct mail was self-funding advertising—that is, it spread the word across America about the conservative position on a host of issues, and it paid for its own advertising with the responses from the people who received that mail.

A second decisive factor in the success of conservative direct mail, as we saw in Chapter 7, was the nature of the business relationship between The Viguerie Company and its clients. Viguerie financed the mailings for the client, but then *both* Viguerie and the client had access to the list of respondents. This list access was critical in expanding the base of the conservative movement. It had the effect politically that free trade has economically—it made for easy market access across borders (in this instance, organizational borders), since Viguerie was, in effect, the NAFTA framework governing conservative lists. If the donors to group A were likely to contribute to group B, group B had easier access to a "ready made" prospect file of conservative activists. Group B obviously would benefit from the additional donors, but this helped group A as well, since it would be just a matter of time before group A would get access to the expanded group B list, not to mention the lists of countless new organizations. Essentially, Viguerie's "house list" was a conglomerate of the names of contributors to many right-of-center causes. Just as free trade dramatically grew the world economy in the second half of the 20th century, so this "common market" of conservative names led to constant expansion of the conservative universe.

By centralizing access to many conservative supporters, conservative organizations were able to prospect at less expense, not to mention faster and with greater precision. It made the "movement"—which consisted of multiple leaders and organizations—more efficient as well, because it was easier to target supporters who were shown to be predisposed to conservative issues.

So far, we don't see anything representing such a long-term business plan when it comes to the Internet, from either the Left or the Right. What we *have* seen with the Dean campaign and with MoveOn is a lesson in how to raise large amounts of money from a large pool of potential donors utilizing compelling issues, and that's a start.

Perhaps it's even more than a start. Roger Hickey, co-director of the Campaign for America's Future, wrote on TomPaine.com that "the new progressive movement has already pioneered new methods of organizing and networking—the Internet-era equivalent of the direct mail techniques that Richard Viguerie pioneered for conservative politicians and causes starting just before [*sic*] the Goldwater run for the White House. A new progressive vision combined with these new community-building and empowerment techniques is bound to continue to shake up politics in the same way the conservatives did over the last 40 years."

We'll see. We'll see whether the Deaniacs make the transition to long-term movement-building, or whether they lose heart. We'll see what happens with that list of 600,000 Dean supporters—indeed, who *has* use of that list? And we'll see what clear and compelling ideas the Left can run with once the November 2004 election is history, and especially if they no longer have George W. Bush to kick around. This is a work in progress.

Alternative media and the future of conservatism

Conservatives face an opposite set of problems than the Left faces—conservatives have the problems of success. We don't exist in a static universe, yet too many conservatives think the alternative media are *their* realm and always will be.

We see two key issues confronting conservatives: (1) The liberals' head start in utilizing the Internet as a fundraising and movement-building tool. And (2) the surrender of the conservative movement to the Republican Party, resulting in the corruption of the conservative message into a merely GOP message.

Conservatives must not downplay the significance of the Dean campaign's success and MoveOn's success on the Internet (Chapter 14). They have clearly demonstrated that the Internet has potential equal to direct mail for raising money and organizing troops. We saw how conservatives had a decade's head start in using direct mail (Chapter 8), and how crucial that decade was for the emergence and success of the conservative movement The wake-up call for liberals was the election of Ronald Reagan as president on November 4, 1980. If conservatives allow liberals to have a few years' head start on the Internet, much less a decade's head start, they may face a similar wake-up call— say, the election of President Hillary Rodham Clinton on November 4, 2008. How's *that* for a nightmare scenario to motivate the conservatives into action!

Nothing in politics seems to be a 100-percent blessing. Even direct mail has been both a blessing and a curse to the conservative movement. We've elaborated on the blessing throughout this book. The curse is that it has allowed a lot of conservative leaders to reign as armchair generals, rather than head for the front and organize the troops. It's so much easier to sit behind a desk and say, "Give me some more direct mail copy to approve" or "Let's send out a press release about that." And at the grassroots level, direct mail makes it so easy to just make a donation and say you've done your part, no need to get involved in actually trying to convince people as a precinct worker or by organizing a rally.

With enough armchair commandeering and enough armchair "activism," the battle can be lost.

As for the second issue confronting conservatives—their relationship to the Republican Party—we will limit ourselves to a few observations here, hoping to expand on them after the 2004 election. Our first observation is that the Republicans, controlling the presidency and both houses of Congress for the first time since any of us has been alive, have given us the biggest jump in federal spending since FDR and the New

Deal. That's *conservative?* And with Social Security and Medicare already heading into insolvency, they've given us the biggest entitlement increase—the Medicare drug bill—since LBJ. That's *conservative?*

And what are conservatives doing about it? They're talking about what a "big spender" John F. Kerry is! The conservative message of limited, constitutional government has been virtually silenced, co-opted by my-party-right-or-wrong partisanship.

For decades conservatives have been lecturing blacks about the dangers of putting all your eggs in one basket: "You're taken for granted by the Democrats, and all you get is symbolism and tokenism." Perhaps it's time for blacks to return the favor and point out that most of what the conservatives are getting with their subservience to the GOP is symbolism and tokenism.

Liberals on the Internet have organized themselves as a movement independent of the Democratic National Committee, no matter who they'll vote for in November. The Dean campaign, MoveOn, and the others can and do act independently of the DNC agenda. Conservatives, meanwhile, have ceded virtually all Web political organizing to the Republican National Committee, defending the biggest increase in federal spending since FDR as "compassionate conservatism." That way lies ruin, for the country and for the movement.

It's time to take another look at how the conservatives handled themselves when they were *growing* so successfully. During this period, as we noted in Chapter 8, the New Right leaders thought of *themselves*—not the Republican Party—as the alternative to the Left and the Democrats. And thanks to the independence provided by direct mail fundraising, none of the New Right's organizations depended upon the Republican Party for their existence. The great majority of these leaders did not hold public office, and had never held public office. Conservatives did not look to elected officials for their leadership. The politicians were necessary to organize votes for or against something, of course, but generally they did not provide the leadership on key issues. That came from the New Right leaders, utilizing alternative media.

Reverse the ideological references and that sounds more like a description of the Internet liberals today.

Stirrings on the Right

Toward the end of 2003 and the beginning of 2004, we started hearing a number of conservative leaders saying something that had been unthinkable a couple of years ago: that perhaps conservatives would be better off if George W. Bush went down to defeat.

If Bush wins, the reasoning goes, we'll have even more big-government programs since the second term of a GOP administration *always* is more liberal than the first. That, in turn, will lead to a massive Republican defeat in the 2006 congressional elections, since historically an incumbent administration does poorly in its sixth-year campaigns, and this time the conservatives would have no incentive to vote.

If, on the other hand, John Kerry were to sit in the White House, we could once again expect some backbone on the part of the Republicans in Congress, leading to the kind of stalemate we saw with President Clinton's programs. And that, in turn, could lead to a revitalized conservative movement starting in 2005.

Unhappy conservatives should be taken seriously. When conservatives are unhappy, there are real-life consequences for the Republican Party.

In 1948, conservatives were unhappy with Tom Dewey's "me-too" campaign, and the result was Dewey's unexpected loss to Harry Truman.

In 1960, conservatives were unhappy with Richard Nixon's "Fifth Avenue sellout" to Nelson Rockefeller, and the result was Nixon's razor-thin loss to John F. Kennedy.

In 1976, conservatives were unhappy with President Gerald Ford's selection of Nelson Rockefeller as his vice president and adoption of Rockefeller's platform. The result was Ford's narrow defeat by a peanut farmer from Georgia.

In 1992, conservatives were so unhappy with President George

Bush's open disdain for them and their beliefs that they staged an open rebellion with the candidacies of Pat Buchanan and Ross Perot. The result was an incumbent president who got a paltry 37 percent of the vote, and Bill Clinton's election with only 41 percent of the vote.

And in 1998, conservatives were unhappy because the Republican leaders in Congress had abandoned conservative principles to go along with Clinton's big-government initiatives. The result was a failure to make the major gains suggested historically in the sixth year of the

---

Give Us <u>Your</u> Views

Access our questionnaire at www.rightturn.us and let us know your thoughts about the November 2004 elections. We will send the results to the national media.

- Conservatives: Will you vote to reelect President Bush—or stay at home? What grade do you give the Republican Congress and its policies? What grade do you give President Bush and his policies?
- Liberals: Will you vote for John Kerry—or Ralph Nader? Who should be Kerry's vice presidential candidate? Do you wish you had a different nominee—Hillary, Dean, Edwards?
- Moderates and independents: Will it be Bush or Kerry for you—or "none of the above"?
- Everyone: Will Bill and Hillary Clinton do all they can to elect Kerry, or will they hold back so the field will be clear for Hillary in 2008?

Come to our Web site, www.rightturn.us, to grade Bush, Kerry, and Hillary on major domestic and foreign policy issues. If you do not have access to the Internet, you can write us at *America's Right Turn*, PO Box 4450, Manassas, VA 20108, and we will mail you a printed questionnaire.

Clinton administration. Instead, Republicans lost House seats, and Newt Gingrich was replaced as Speaker of the House.

Warning to the Republican Party: Conservatives are unhappy again.

Conservatives *will* find their voice and their heritage once again. We've got the tools—the alternative media that we built. And we will find the will to use these tools, not as blind follow-the-leader partisans, but as principled and independent *conservatives*.

BIBLIOGRAPHY AND SOURCES

Introduction

Center for Media and Public Affairs (www.cmpa.com): *Media Monitor* (November 1992 and November/December 1996); Feb. 24, 1998 press release, "Scandal News Not So Bad for Bill."

Chapter 1

Dickens, Arthur Geoffrey. *Reformation and Society in Sixteenth Century Europe* (New York: Harcourt, 1968).

Edwards, Jr., Mark U. *Printing, Propaganda, and Martin Luther* (Berkeley: University of California Press, 1994).

Eisenstein, Elizabeth L. *The Printing Press as an Agent of Change*, 2 vols. (Cambridge: Cambridge University Press, 1979).

Chapter 2

Bailyn, Bernard. *The Ideological Origins of the American Revolution* (Cambridge, Mass.: The Belknap Press of Harvard University Press, 1967).

———. *Pamphlets of the American Revolution, 1750–1776* (Cambridge, Mass.: The Belknap Press of Harvard University Press, 1965).

Brown, Richard D. *Knowledge Is Power: The Diffusion of Information in Early America, 1700–1865* (New York: Oxford University Press, 1989).

Copeland, David A. *Debating the Issues in Colonial Newspapers* (Westport, Conn.: Greenwood Press, 2000).

Davidson, Philip. *Propaganda and the American Revolution, 1763–1783* (Chapel Hill, N.C.: University of North Carolina Press, 1941).

Encyclopedia Britannica. *The Annals of America, Volume 2, 1755–1783: Resistance and Revolution* (Chicago: Encyclopedia Britannica, 1976).

Fischer, David Hackett. *Paul Revere's Ride* (New York: Oxford University Press, 1994).

Foner, Eric. *Tom Paine and the American Revolution* (New York: Oxford University Press, 1977).

Frichtman, Jr., Jack. *Thomas Paine: Apostle of Freedom* (New York: Four Walls Eight Windows, 1994).

Gipson, Lawrence Henry. *The Coming of the Revolution, 1763–1775* (New York: Harper & Row, 1954).

Hawke, David Freeman. *Paine* (New York: Harper & Row, 1974).

Holifield, E. Brooks. *Era of Persuasion: American Thought and Culture, 1521–1680* (Boston: Twayne Publishers, 1989).

Johnson, Paul. *A History of the American People* (New York: HarperCollins, 1997).

Joyce, William L., ed. *Printing and Society in Early America* (Worcester, Mass.: Oak Knoll Press, 1983).

Landsman, Ned C. *From Colonials to Provincials* (London: Twayne Publishers, 1997).

Langguth, A. J. *Patriots: The Men Who Started the American Revolution* (New York: Simon & Schuster, 1988).

Levy, Leonard W. *Emergence of a Free Press* (New York: Oxford University Press, 1985).

Maier, Pauline. *From Resistance to Revolution* (New York: Vintage Books, 1972).

Paine, Tom. *Common Sense,* edited and with an Introduction by Isaac Kramnick (London: Penguin Books, 1976).

Schouler, James. *Americans of 1776: Daily Life in Revolutionary America* (Williamstown, Mass.: Corner House Publisher, 1984).

Shalhope, Robert E. *The Roots of Democracy: American Thought and Culture, 1760–1800* (Boston: Twayne Publishers, 1990).

Wahlke, John C., ed. *The Causes of the American Revolution* (Lexington, Mass.: D.C. Heath and Company, 1973).

Wood, Gordon S. *The Radicalism of the American Revolution* (New York: Knopf, 1992).

Zinn, Howard. *A People's History of the United States, 1492–Present* (New York: HarperCollins, 1999).

Zobel, Hiller B. *The Boston Massacre* (New York: W. W. Norton & Co., 1996).

Chapter 5

Andrew, John A., III. *The Other Side of the Sixties* (New Brunswick, N.J.: Rutgers University Press, 1997).

Edwards, Lee. *The Conservative Revolution* (New York: Free Press, 1999).

McManus, John F. *William F. Buckley, Jr.: Pied Piper for the Establishment* (Appleton, Wisc.: John Birch Society, 2002).

Regnery, Henry. *Memoirs of a Dissident Publisher* (Chicago: Regnery Publishing, 1979).

Chapter 6

Edwards, Lee. *The Conservative Revolution* (New York: Free Press, 1999).
Perlstein, Rick. *Before the Storm* (New York: Hill and Wang, 2002).
Rusher, William A. *The Rise of the Right* (New York: William Morrow and Co., 1984).

Chapter 7

Weintz, Walter H. *The Solid Gold Mailbox* (New York: Wiley & Sons, 1987).

Chapter 8

Devine, Donald J. *Reagan Electionomics: How Reagan Ambushed the Pollsters* (Ottawa, Ill.: Green Hill Publishers, 1983).
Edwards, Lee. *The Conservative Revolution* (New York: Free Press, 1999).
Viguerie, Richard A. *The Establishment vs. the People* (Chicago: Regnery Gateway, 1983).
———. *The New Right: We're Ready to Lead* (Falls Church, Va.: The Viguerie Company, 1981).

Stop ERA

Dial, Karla. "Founding Mother." In *Citizen Magazine* (published by Focus on the Family), November 2002, pp. 18–21.
Eagle Forum Web site: www.eagleforum.org.
Felsenthal, Carol. *Phyllis Schlafly: The Sweetheart of the Silent Majority* (Chicago: Regnery Gateway, 1981).

Chapter 9

Dees, Morris, with Steve Fiffer. *A Lawyer's Journey: The Morris Dees Story* (Chicago: American Bar Association Publishing, 2001).
Hart, Gary. *Right from the Start: A Chronicle of the McGovern Campaign* (New York: Quadrangle, 1973).
Malchow, Hal. *The New Political Targeting* (Washington, D.C.: Campaigns and Elections Magazine, 2003).

Chapter 10

Barker, David C. *Rushed to Judgment: Talk Radio, Persuasion, and American Political Behavior* (New York: Columbia University Press, 2002).

Brown, Robert J. *Manipulating the Ether: The Power of Broadcast Radio in Thirties America* (Jefferson, N.C.: McFarland & Co., 1998).

Colford, Paul D. *The Rush Limbaugh Story: Talent on Loan from God* (New York: St. Martin's Press, 1993).

Craig, Douglas B. *Fireside Politics: Radio and Political Culture in the United States, 1920–1940* (Baltimore: Johns Hopkins University Press, 2000).

Kurtz, Howard. *Hot Air: All Talk, All the Time* (New York: Times Books, 1996).

Laufer, Peter. *Inside Talk Radio: America's Voice or Just Hot Air?* (New York: Times Books, 1996).

Talkers Magazine (www.talkers.com)

Boortz, Neal. "Why Liberals Fail in the Talk Business." May 2001.

Byrne, Ted. "The Move to Reinstate the Fairness Doctrine." October 1993.

Harrison, Michael. "The Nineties: Talk Radio's Golden Era." December 1999/January 2000.

Hartmann, Thom. "Liberal Talk Radio—An Awakening Giant?" July/August 2003.

Jon Sinton interview. March 2003.

Dr. Laura Schlessinger interview. July/August 2003.

Linder, Alan. "Small Business Loves Talk Radio." July/August 2002.

Linder, Alan, and The Lone Liberal™. "What about Liberals?" April 2001.

The Lone Liberal™. "Busy December." December 2002/January 2003.

Ratner, Ellen. "The Ongoing Battle against Dr. Laura Schlessinger." May 2000.

_____. "Why Al Gore Didn't Win the Election by 10 Points: A Talk Radio Perspective." November 2000.

"The Talk Radio Research Project." www.talkers.com.

"Vintage Rush." August 1990 interview, reprinted August 2000.

Chapter 11

Hirsch, Alan. *Talking Heads: Political Talk Shows and Their Star Pundits* (New York: St. Martin's Press, 1991).

Kurtz, Howard. *Hot Air: All Talk, All the Time* (New York: Times Books, 1996).

Chapter 13

Poe, Richard. *Hillary's Secret War: The Clinton Conspiracy to Muzzle Internet Journalists* (Nashville: Thomas Nelson/WND Books, 2004).

Sources Cited Throughout

Pew Reports

To contact the Pew Research Center for the People & the Press, write to: 1150 18th Street N.W., Suite 975, Washington, D.C. 20036; call (202) 293-3126; or visit http://www.people-press.org.

Pew Internet and American Life Project, Pew Research Center for the People & the Press. *The Internet and the Iraq War* (Washington, D.C.: Pew Center, April 1, 2003).

_____. *Counting on the Internet* (Washington, D.C.: Pew Center, December 29, 2002).

Pew Research Center for the People & the Press. *The Tough Job of Communicating with Voters: Sources for Campaign News* (Washington, D.C.: Pew Center, February 5, 2000).

_____. *Public's News Habits Little Changed by Sept. 11* (Washington, D.C.: Pew Center, June 9, 2002).

_____. *Political Sites Gain, but Major News Sites Still Dominant* (Washington, D.C.: Pew Center, January 5, 2003).

The State of the News Media 2004

Project for Excellence in Journalism, an institute affiliated with Columbia University Graduate School of Journalism. *The State of the News Media 2004.* http://www.stateofthemedia.org.

ACKNOWLEDGMENTS

Richard A. Viguerie

You're fortunate indeed if you have one strong professional mentor or teacher. I was blessed with three giants that I was also honored to call my friends: Marvin Liebman, Edward Mayer, Jr., and Dick Benson. They are now deceased, yet during their lives they not only opened my eyes and ears to the world of marketing, but Ed and Dick did the same for tens of thousands of others through consulting, teaching, and books.

When I started in direct mail, I didn't have to play Lewis and Clark because these and other giants had come before me and paved the way. All I did was apply successful commercial marketing ideas to the non-profit and political arenas. All who want to market via the Internet, however, will either have to be 21st century Lewis and Clarks or wait for others to be the pioneers. Today there is no successful business model usable by others to change history as the conservatives did with direct mail.

And of all the people I'm indebted to in my professional life, none has been more important than my assistant of over 20 years, Nancy Bakersmith. Nancy has made my trains run on time and she daily performs small and large miracles, most of which I'm unaware of—as she periodically reminds me.

Richard A. Viguerie and David Franke

This book could not have been completed without the gracious help of many people. With our fingers crossed in the hope that we haven't forgotten anyone, we proceed to thank them by name.

First, our appreciation to the world's best book agent, Robert B. Barnett, and his assistant, Ana C. Reyes, for their invaluable help in securing the right publisher and for gently reminding us, when necessary during contract negotiations, that we are not lawyers—and they are.

Next, it has been a pleasure working with Jeff Stern, president of Bonus Books, and his team in Los Angeles, including our editor Caralyn Bialo and publicity director Stephanie Adams. Caralyn in particular had to bear the brunt of rushing this book through the production process in record time, despite the authors' predilection for last-minute copy changes, and she maintained her good humor at all times.

Craig Shirley and Diana Banister, the principals of Shirley & Banister, have a well-deserved reputation as an outstanding public relations firm working the Right side of the fence. They and their team will now have another opportunity to demonstrate their value to authors in particular.

Many people gave generously of their time and knowledge by granting us interviews. We express our appreciation, in alphabetical order, to Jeff Butzky, Roger Craver, Dave Cullen, Morris Dees, Joseph Dougherty, Pam Fielding, Ron Godwin, Marty Gross, David Keene, Wayne LaPierre (and his associates Millie Hallow and Rob Seidman), Hal Malchow, Bill Meehan, Bill Rusher, Phyllis Schlafly, John Stormer, and Mal Warwick.

Many people at American Target Advertising, the current incarnation of The Viguerie Company, have also given generously of their time and talents. Special thanks are due Viguerie assistants Nancy Bakersmith, Donna Rhudy, and Jill Walker. Joe Martin was our erudite research assistant, providing us with enough raw material for at least another three books. Mark Fitzgibbons gave us expert legal advice, and Stephen Theriault, Mike Krempasky, and Joy Potter helped us in countless ways.

Paul Weyrich and Morton Blackwell critiqued the manuscript, which was especially helpful considering their key roles and lengthy experience in the conservative movement. Ron Burr, Jameson Campaigne Jr., and Tim Wheeler, as well as Eric Olsen and others at the Leadership Institute, also provided helpful assistance during the course of writing this book.

Finally, our thanks to the resources and helpful staff at George Mason University's Fenwick Library in Fairfax, Virginia, and the library of the Institute for Humane Studies in Arlington, Virginia.

ABOUT THE AUTHORS

RICHARD A. VIGUERIE transformed American politics in the 1960s and '70s by pioneering the use of direct mail in the political and ideological spheres. He used computerized direct mail fundraising to build the conservative movement, which then elected Ronald Reagan as the first conservative president of the modern era. As the "Funding Father of the Conservative Movement," Viguerie motivated millions of Americans to participate in politics for the first time, greatly expanding the base of active citizenship. He is our era's equivalent of Tom Paine, using a direct mail letter rather than a pamphlet to deliver his call to arms. *George* magazine credited this as one of the defining political moments of the 20th century.

Viguerie's advertising firm has mailed more than 2 billion letters over the past 40 years, and will mail over 100 million pieces of direct mail in the 2004 election year. The *AFL-CIO News* said Viguerie "made it all possible" for conservatives, and the *Washington Post* has called him "the conservatives' Voice of America." Mr. Viguerie and his wife, Elaine, are natives of Houston, Texas, and have been married for 42 years. They have three children and five grandchildren and live in the Virginia countryside on 230 acres of conservative-friendly environment.

DAVID FRANKE was one of the founders of the conservative movement, having started the first nationwide activist group on the Right in 1959. In the movement's formative years he served on the editorial staffs of *Human Events* and *National Review*, and was a senior editor at Arlington House Publishers and the Conservative Book Club. Later he was the founding director of the Liberty*Press* and Liberty*Classics* book imprints, conceived and edited newsletters dealing with investments and alternative health, and for several years wrote the *John Naisbitt Trend Letter*. He also has started two Internet sites.

Franke's articles have appeared in the *New York Times, National Enquirer, Esquire,* and other leading publications, and he is the author of nine previous books, including *Safe Places* and *The Torture Doctor*.

THE AUTHORS may be contacted at *America's Right Turn*, PO Box 4450, Manassas, VA 20108, or at www.rightturn.us.

INDEX